Once Upon a Family

✧

Also by Jean Grasso Fitzpatrick

✦

SMALL WONDER

SOMETHING MORE

THE SUPERBABY SYNDROME

Once Upon a Family

Read-Aloud Stories and Activities

That Nurture Healthy Kids

JEAN GRASSO FITZPATRICK

VIKING

VIKING
Published by the Penguin Group
Penguin Putnam Inc., 375 Hudson Street,
New York, New York 10014, U.S.A.
Penguin Books Ltd, 27 Wrights Lane,
London W8 5TZ, England
Penguin Books Australia Ltd, Ringwood,
Victoria, Australia
Penguin Books Canada Ltd, 10 Alcorn Avenue,
Toronto, Ontario, Canada M4V 3B2
Penguin Books (N.Z.) Ltd, 182–190 Wairau Road,
Auckland 10, New Zealand

Penguin Books Ltd, Registered Offices:
Harmondsworth, Middlesex, England

First published in 1998 by Viking Penguin,
a member of Penguin Putnam Inc.

1 3 5 7 9 10 8 6 4 2

LIBRARY OF CONGRESS CATALOGING-IN-PUBLICATION DATA
Fitzpatrick, Jean Grasso.
Once upon a family : read-aloud stories and activities that
nurture healthy kids / Jean Grasso Fitzpatrick.
p.   cm.
ISBN 0-670-86202-9 (alk. paper)
1. Emotions in children.   2. Emotions in infants.   3. Emotions in
adolescence.   4. Child rearing.   I. Title.
BF723.E6F57   1998   97-23325
649'.58—dc21

This book is printed on acid-free paper.

Printed in the United States of America
Set in Goudy
Designed by Kathryn Parise

for Des

Lovers and madmen have such seething brains,
Such shaping fantasies, that apprehend
More than cool reason ever comprehends.
. . . And, as imagination bodies forth
The forms of things unknown, the poet's pen
Turns them to shapes, and gives to airy nothing
A local habitation and a name.

—*A Midsummer Night's Dream*

Acknowledgments

✧

For collegiality and fresh perspective, I'd like to thank the candidates and members of the Westchester Institute for Training in Psychoanalysis and Psychotherapy. The children's storytelling project at Brookside School in Ossining, New York, has been an ongoing inspiration. I thank Beth Morrison and Jane Rechtman for their help. For sharing stories and much more, I am grateful to Renee Fogarty, Abbie Galvin, Alice Joselow, Nancy Maloy, Mary Schneidman, and Julie Stuckey. For advice and encouragement, many thanks to my agent, Heide Lange. For our fruitful collaboration, I am grateful to my editor, Mindy Werner. And as always, Laura, Matthew, and Des have shared their honesty, love, and laughter.

Contents

✦

xii

CONTENTS

Once Upon a Family

✧

One

Opening a Hole
in the Wall

✧

Parenting books usually aim to teach you techniques or to offer advice. In this one, instead, I hold out an invitation. As you read the stories and do the activities in these pages, I hope to help you discover *within yourself* all that you need to nurture your child's emotional growth. You'll learn how to do so through attentive listening, honest talk, and old-fashioned play. You'll discover how to draw on your own life experiences—your victories, mistakes, and hard-won lessons—to help your child grow. As you follow the path presented in these pages, you'll get to know your child and yourself better, and share some new experiences with each other; you'll begin to build an intimate, nurturing connection no assortment of advice from a traditional parenting manual could possibly replace. After all, since most of us don't have a book in hand at those moments when our kids really challenge us, what could make more sense than learning to recognize and use your *own* resources—your own instincts and life experiences? In the process, if you're like most of the parents I work with, you'll come to find that family life grows less stressful and more rewarding for both you and your kids.

Since family storytelling is at the heart of this book, a good way to begin is with a story. Here is an old Yiddish tale that, with characteristic humor, speaks to seekers and givers of advice, like you and me.

A YIDDISH TALE

One rabbi said to another, "Why don't you watch your followers to make sure they obey the precepts of the law and pray the way they should?"

"Let me tell you a story," answered the second rabbi, and here is the one he told.

Once, three men were locked inside a dark prison. The first man was a fool who didn't know how to do anything. He couldn't dress himself or even hold a spoon in his hand. The second man spent all his time trying to teach the first man how to do things. But the third man just sat there in the dark, doing nothing.

"Why are you just sitting there, instead of helping me teach this fool?" the second man asked the third.

"It's so dark in here that no matter how hard you try, you're not going to teach him anything," replied the third man. "I'm sitting here thinking of ways to make a hole in the wall. Once I let in the light, he'll learn for himself everything he needs to know."

Many parents tell me they turn to childrearing books when they feel as though they're groping in the dark—when they feel a little bit like the fool in the story. What they often find is what the second man offers, plentiful advice and techniques on "handling" kids effectively. Reading those can be reassuring. But I call it "virtual parenting." In the long run, when we approach childrearing by applying other people's advice, we miss out on some of the richest rewards family life has to offer. We deprive ourselves and our kids of the pleasure and growth that come from being spontaneous and human. We lose faith in the instinctual knowledge of our children and in our daily experiences with them, which are our most trustworthy guide as parents. We turn our kids into problems instead of people. No wonder they sulk, rebel, talk back, and feel picked on!

When we are willing to wait and discover, like the third man in the story, wonderful things can happen. You already know that. Remember those early days with your child, when you were first getting to know him? You probably didn't have much experience with kids; you doubted you should really be parenting without a license; you wondered occasionally if your baby would ever make it to his first birthday. Yet somehow along the way, the two of you learned to communicate. You came to know when he was overwhelmed by sound or touch and needed soothing. You listened for his different cries—the ones for hunger and sleep and fear. You learned that you could trust in *your own awareness*, go with your gut instincts. And by sharing your feelings in ways your infant could understand—smiles and coos and hugs—you discovered the importance to him of your *presence*.

In these pages I will encourage you to stay on that path. As kids move into the toddler, preschool, and school years, sharing feelings and being present gets more complicated. Too often we get stuck in a pattern: our preaching and their back talk. Judging from the statistics, this state of affairs isn't too satisfying for anybody. Sadly, there are indications that today family members are spending less time together than ever. One study found that U.S. mothers devote as little as *eleven minutes a day* to conversation with children—not counting time spent on giving advice and criticism—and fathers as little as eight minutes on a weekday. We're losing touch with our kids.

In this book, you'll learn to connect in ways that will mean more to you and your children. As I hope you'll discover, when we're willing to trust our awareness, the way we did when our children were infants, we notice a shift in our family relationships. When we try to "train" our kids, we then let them know we're willing to listen to and care about their struggles, and really share ourselves with them. Now we're having more fun. Life with kids is more rewarding for them and us. We are creating a safe space in our family life for the true intimacy—the richness of feeling, honest communication, and mutual respect—that is at the heart of a child's healthy growth. We are "opening a hole in the wall."

How to Use This Book

Getting started. Think of each of the chapters that follow as a workshop on paper. I want to help you recognize how much you have to offer your kids. You'll find a variety of resources to help you along the way. In chapter 2, I'll discuss why emotional "coaching" isn't what helps your child grow into a whole, caring adult.

In chapter 3, we'll explore some of the ways your child's growth is intertwined with your own. Here you'll find a synopsis of development from birth to adolescence, along with advice and suggestions on how to recognize your child's particular struggles, listen responsively, and encourage dialogue. You'll learn to recognize some of the patterns in your own emotional life—your particular way of approaching challenges, your style, strengths, and the ways you get "stuck" or "hooked"—and begin to understand how to use this awareness to help your child grow.

In chapter 4, I'll show how sharing stories—folktales, fairy tales, sacred and family lore—can support and enrich your child's growing awareness of his or her emotional life, ability to communicate feelings, and caring connection with others.

Focusing on particular challenges all kids face. Each of the remaining chapters is devoted to a particular aspect of a child's growth, of your child's emotional wisdom, including motivation, fear, aggression, loss, competition, and love. Because the development of a healthy self is founded on what Rollo May once called "the courage to *be*," the first two chapters focus on nurturing your child's *motivation* and *courage*. You'll find developmental guidelines on how you can foster your child's natural motivation from the earliest days of life to learn and to work toward goals. You'll find out how to help him cope with common childhood fears, recognize fear as a healthy warning sign of danger, and avoid being overwhelmed by it.

The last three chapters focus on helping your child with some of the *social* challenges that come with his increasing capacity to engage in relationships with others. In chapter 7, you'll learn how to help him use his *aggression* appropriately and productively, to resolve conflict appropriately, and to express his needs clearly.

Chapter 8 shows you how to help your child deal with *sadness, loss,* and *grief*, and understand how accepting these "shadow" feelings enriches his or her humanity.

In chapter 9, you'll find age-appropriate guidelines on how to help your child handle *competition* at home, in school, and on the playing field, as well as how to encourage teamwork.

Finally, chapter 10 is devoted to nurturing your child's potential to *love*. Love happens naturally, if you believe what you see at the movies, right? Actually, poets and theorists alike seem to recognize love as an achievement, even as the pinnacle of emotional development; here we'll focus on the ways kids move beyond need-based connection and toward empathy and compassion. You'll find out how to help your child begin to recognize the delicate balance between expressing his own needs and reaching out to others.

The stories. At the heart of each of these chapters you'll find wonderful folk and fairy tales from cultures around the world, ancient and modern, that offer a fresh look at the topic through imagination's window.

Parents tend to be very focused on the demands of the "real world" in raising kids. Naturally, we want to prepare them for success and achievement in adult life. We hope they can realize their potential. But their *dreams* are important, too. Much of our humanity depends on a kind of reality that can't be seen or touched, and on our openness to feeling and imagination. Children instinctively know this. "My first and last philosophy, that which I believe in with unbroken certainty, I learnt in the nursery. . . . The things I believed most then, the things I believe most now, are the things called fairy tales," wrote G. K. Chesterton in his delightful "The Ethics of Elfland." "A certain way of looking at life, which was created in me by the fairy tales . . . has since been meekly ratified by the mere facts."

Stories ground us in the traditional, most ancient ways of nurturing emotional wisdom: family, culture, spiritual roots. They provide parents and children with a shared language whose words—words like *fee, fi, fo, fum* and *Excalibur* and *Jacob have I loved*—have a touch of magic, words that give expression to feelings that otherwise too often remain unspoken. When we hear the words *Once upon a time*, we are invited into a way of experiencing life that is out of the ordinary, and yet uncannily like our own.

Nothing is truer than a story. Grown-ups don't always remember how it feels to be a short person in a six-foot world, but storytellers do. Stories offer an understanding of human nature far subtler than any clever catch-phrase or "emotional literacy" lesson can capture, and one that means far more to children. Chances are you've already discovered this if your child has been taught about "stranger danger." An important safeguard concept, and a phrase that's certainly easy to remember, isn't it? But I recognized its limitations one day when I brought my own son, who was nine years old at the time, to a clothing store to try on jeans. "You're too big to come into the women's dressing room now," I told him. "Go into the men's, and come out and show me how the pants fit."

He'd always been an outgoing, confident kid, and I expected him to be proud to make this new, grown-up move, but I was wrong. "I'm not going in there by myself and taking off my pants," he protested. "How can you expect me to? It's full of *strangers!*" We spent some time talking about the word *stranger*, "unpacking" the slogan he had learned as a preschooler, but I couldn't help thinking it had only given me a false confidence about his ability to stay safe.

Obviously, we don't really want to teach our children that everyone they don't know is dangerous. Nor would we want to suggest to a child that—contrary to all statistics about child abuse—he is perfectly safe with all the people he *does* know. And just who *is* a stranger, anyway? How about the ice cream man? Or a pleasant passerby who says hi to the dog you're walking? Or an elderly person who needs help with groceries? Finally—and this is a question we need to face as we raise kids in a world torn by ethnic and racial division—how does a child raised hearing about "stranger danger" come to understand that love of neighbor includes people who look or speak in ways that may be different or even rather strange?

Slogans don't teach kids lessons like these; loving adults do.

And stories help because instead of presenting advice tied up in a neatly wrapped package, they *open* up discussion. As the psychoanalyst Bruno Bettelheim pointed out in his landmark book *The Uses of Enchantment*, scary stories help a child explore the dangers in the world on a *symbolic* level, not by offering simplistic or puzzling "rules," but by encouraging children to trust and hone their "natural protection system"—their own *instincts*. In a fairy tale, when the protagonist fails to pay attention to what his eyes, ears, and heart are telling him, houses get blown in and grandmothers are gobbled up by wolves. By the story's end our hero (usually with some help from a friendly hunter or wise woman) emerges unscathed and much the wiser. A child who hears stories is not only warned to be cautious but also is reassured that with time and cleverness—and help from the grown-ups who care for him—he will one day learn to keep himself safe from harm.

Stories teach not through precepts but through *word-pictures*. In these pages, I'll show you how to use them to help your child learn about feelings and relationships by engaging his imagination. By transforming a child's inner struggles into colorful characters and lively adventures, stories provide the mental playthings he needs to explore emotional reality—much the way he learns spatial relationships by arranging wooden blocks. Just as an X ray picks up images we can't discern with the naked eye or an ultrasound shows us a living fetus before we can even feel it kick, a fairy tale puts flesh and blood on emotions that are just beginning to take shape in a child's heart and mind. And as human beings have known for millennia, stories make lessons in human nature *fun*.

For easy and pleasurable reading, the tales included in each chapter are set off from the rest of the text. I've drawn these stories from a wide range of sources and retold them in my own words—adapting them to be read aloud to children without, I hope, sacrificing their distinctive cultural "flavor." Most are suitable for children three and up, who will understand and enjoy them at different levels. They have been "child-tested" in my own family and by parent participants in my storytelling group and workshops, who have read them aloud at home and told me which ones their kids were eager to talk about, and to hear again.

Family Time. After each story, you'll find a section with activities for parents and kids. These are simple projects, games, and ideas that will help you both extend the tale into your home life and connect soul to soul with your child, no matter how busy you are. Don't worry; these aren't the dull "discussion questions" you may remember from English class in junior high. Instead, they're an assortment of imaginative games, role-plays, projects, outings, and conversation starters designed to help you and your child engage with each tale and have a good time doing it. Some are designed to be tried immediately after sharing a story; others can naturally become a part of your mealtime conversation or driving time. These activities offer a chance to let the tale sink in and work its magic on both of you.

The Parent's Path. Finally, because we have the most to offer our kids when we nurture our *own* emotional wisdom, there are exploration sections following each tale designed for you alone. These include questions and exercises to help you hold up a mirror to yourself—with all your strengths and weaknesses—make sense of your own experience and struggles from childhood to the present day, and maybe consider some new ways to approach old problems. By enhancing your insight, these exercises will help you develop a personal approach to nurturing emotional wisdom that grows out of your particular life experience, values, and relationships with your child. *These sections will be most valuable to you if you keep a notebook or journal and record your answers in it.* Writing down and holding onto your responses are important, because in some of the exercises you will be invited to turn back to your answers in a previous section for further exploration. This book will mean more to you if you keep track of your own comments and questions and set aside a space for your own observations.

You'll also find a list of resources—storytelling tips, children's literature, films, Internet addresses, and music—to bring additional pleasure and support to your journey with your child.

Now that you've come this far, maybe you're beginning to worry that you're in for more work than you expected. What's so bad about traditional advice manuals, anyway? Aren't they a lot simpler and more straightforward? Does childrearing really require all this soul-searching?

I'd like to answer those questions with another story, this one from my own life. Once upon a time when I first began writing books and articles for parents, I thought that the widespread dissemination of child development information—guidelines on kids' physical, social, and cognitive development—would change the face of family life. In those days

I naively believed that by educating parents about kids' growth and needs, authors like me could help transform the world into a safe place for children.

In the years since, I've worked with a discouragingly large number of parents who can recite the dates of their kids' developmental milestones and can speak expertly about a wide spectrum of childhood challenges, from toilet training to sibling rivalry to eye-hand coordination. Yet all this information does them or their children little good, because they have not learned to *be present* in their children's lives. They approach childrearing as though it were a task to be accomplished.

In my work as a psychoanalyst, I've discovered that we all can be so easily caught up in abstract theories that we forget the magic that can happen between two human beings. The best therapists I know have a great deal in common with the most effective parents. Both are the ones who cultivate an awareness of their own feelings, and who recognize that growth comes out of the authenticity of the *relationship* that unfolds between them and the child (or the patient). My life as a mother brings daily reminders that developmental information and advice are only a beginning. Now that my own two children are growing toward adolescence, they challenge me more than ever to really *listen* to them. As you might expect, they've never been particularly impressed by my familiarity with theories and research studies. What they do seem to appreciate is my willingness to *engage* with them—to make myself available when they need to talk, to respect and appreciate them as individuals, to tell the truth about what I'm thinking and feeling, to enjoy a story, a book, a trip to the theater. More than ever these days, the problems we talk about—at the dinner table, at bedtime, in the car on the way to soccer practice—can't be resolved with slogans or moral precepts or lessons. My children, like their peers everywhere, are struggling with the paradoxes, challenges, and disappointments of life in the real world, and they need a real parent—not some "parenting expert"—to help them sort things out and gain perspective.

For the past dozen years I've been exploring the connections between children's development and contemporary approaches to spiritual growth, and I believe we need to help our kids develop the soulful qualities—a rich inner life, the ability to care about and get along with others, and the capacity to bring creativity to seemingly hopeless situations in their own lives and around the globe—on which their future depends.

I won't lie to you. Approaching family life this way takes time and energy. It can be emotionally challenging. Happily, as I and the parents I work with have discovered, a story-centered family life nurtures adults and children alike. In the next chapter, I'll show you how and why the stories and activities in these pages can bring more fun and growth into your home than any emotional "coaching" method.

Two

Why Emotional "Coaching" Is Not Enough

✧

You may or may not think of yourself as the "creative type," but on the day you became a parent you put your foot on the oldest and most transformational creative path known to humankind. Your child is on the way to discovering the world and, in the process, to *becoming himself*, and you are sharing the journey, with all its ups and downs, delights and detours. This is your sacred trust.

We've been fortunate, over the last two decades, to have had access to an enormous body of child-development research documenting how kids grow. For me, the important question is: How do we *use* all this knowledge? Since the early eighties—when the economy was booming, opportunities seemed endless, and many parenting books were telling readers how to raise an "early learner"—I have found myself drawn to a different way of writing about children and family life: one that focused on childrearing not as a method of pushing kids along, but as a creative endeavor that deeply engages both parent and child—one that acknowledged the wonder of day-to-day living with kids, and the power of parenting to prepare kids for life in society and to teach them to *transform* it. Today, with horizons lowered for many of our nation's children, self-interest dominating our public discourse, and violence in our streets, I hear more and more parents recognizing that the rising generation will need more than material ambition and high self-esteem to find satisfaction in life. Our children's future depends not only on their capacity to *compete*, but on their ability to make a *contribution* to the world around them.

"Sounds ambitious," I can hear you saying. "But in my family we're still working on the small stuff, like remembering lunch money, cleaning their rooms, and not bickering at the dinner table. Maybe we'll be ready for creativity and transformation next year. Or the year after."

You won't. The daily details of childrearing don't go away. Day care, diapers, and car pools only give way to dating, designer jeans, and car keys. But as I see it, the minutiae that litter your family life—the table manners, the temper tantrums, the TV time negotiations—aren't distractions. They can be stepping-stones along the path. I'm not interested in offering you an emotional skill-building program to do with your child, as though you were helping him with the ABCs—or the SATs. Programs like that only get in the way of the real treasures that await you and your child when you cultivate the two keys to a child's healthy growth: awareness and intimacy. In this book you'll share stories. You'll learn to keep your eyes and ears open for "teachable moments" as they present themselves in the course of a typical busy day. You'll get to know yourself better, learn to recognize how much you have to offer your child, and see how your own struggles and limitations may be getting in the way. You'll learn to be more honest and, I hope, more playful. And you'll learn creative ways to cultivate that rich, fertile soil from which wholeness grows—the relationship between you and your child that is often puzzling, always changing, never quite what you're expecting.

In these pages, you will learn how to help your child develop the capacities that you've probably heard discussed by Daniel Goleman and others as "emotional intelligence": the ability to tolerate and identify feelings, manage and express them; to respond to others appropriately; and to delay gratification in order to meet a goal. We all need to be able to do these things. The process of learning to recognize and manage our feelings develops the "front office" part of the psyche, metaphorically known to mental-health professionals as the "executive ego." This self-observational capacity is believed to originate as early as the fourth to eighth month of a baby's life, when caregivers respond in appropriate, attuned ways to cries, movements, and facial expressions—feeding, holding, diapering, or soothing when needed. Once you've laid that foundation, you can build on it through all the years of childhood. As you encourage him to reach out to others, point out what he's doing wrong and why it matters, and help him learn to resolve conflicts and face challenges, you're doing "emotional coaching," not as a school-based social skills program, but the way parents have always done it—on the fly: reminding kids about table manners, helping settle spats, encouraging them to try new activities, talking about the stories you come across in your family life and in books like this.

Not surprisingly, children raised in homes where these emotional capacities are fostered at an early age reap rich rewards, both socially and in other areas of their lives. By school age, kids who are emotionally competent have been found to have fewer behavior problems than others, and to score higher in math and reading. Emotional literacy training programs can and do teach valuable skills, and—particularly for children whose households are deficient in role models—they meet an urgent need for our children and our future.

But although it's tempting to think kids could grow emotionally and socially by exposure to a standard lesson plan, the results are much like trying to microwave a Thanksgiving turkey; some things take time and care. A child grows up capable of responsible, loving relationships not through lessons—no matter how enlightened or well-intentioned—but through *experiencing* a responsible, loving relationship with an adult. Right from the start so much happens between us and our kids that doesn't ever get put into words, but it lays the groundwork for everything we tell them about life. Otherwise, teaching amounts to little more than mouthing slogans. I'm thinking of an episode of the T.V. show *Rug Rats* where Lillian tells the bickering Angelica and Susie not to fight and offers a classic slogan from emotional literacy training: "Use your words," she says.

"What's that s'posed to mean?" asked Philip, Lillian's bewildered twin. Lillian looks blank. "I don't know," she answers.

Emotional growth is an everyday process that starts at birth. Long before a child is capable of thinking or talking about his emotions, he needs to experience the world of feelings and relationships on a level that doesn't involve explicit training. From the earliest days of life, your child is soaking in myriad *unspoken* lessons about his feeling self, communicated through the touch, voices, and faces of those who care for him. Coaching is no substitute for daily contact with caregivers who are both sensitive and strong enough to cope with a small child's emotional ups and downs—and who can manage their own.

What exactly *are* emotions, anyway? In talking about the psyche, many theorists draw distinctions among *affect, feeling,* and *emotion.* How they're precisely defined, and how they connect with one another, are hot debate topics in some academic circles. For our purposes it's helpful to think about them this way:

Affect is a visceral response, like your baby's startle when she hears a loud voice. Affects are *body-based.* The wide-eyed look on your face when you've had a fright, or the chills up and down your spine, are known as "affect." Young children, who naturally express emotion from head to toe, are very much in touch with their affect, although not always in ways that make logical sense; that's why we remark on their spontaneity and aliveness. On the other hand, you've probably met a few grown-ups with "flat" affect, people who, like the comic-strip character Dilbert, express just about anything—anger, joy, frustration—in a monotone. They're the world's affective "Johnny one-notes."

For now, just keep in mind that even though affect might sound less sophisticated than feeling or emotion, it's just as important. Now and then most of us (especially when we're nervous or frightened) tend to "go numb" or "blank out" or "not know what we're feeling," and those are ways of saying that we've temporarily lost touch with our affect. Our affects are the seat of visceral awareness, our link between body and soul; if you're not in the habit of paying attention to yours, you're "living in your head."

Feeling is the *mental awareness of affect.* It's the capacity to think about what you're feeling in words; that is, not only noticing the chills up and down your spine but also expressing the fright as "I'm scared." A child who can "feel a feeling" is owning her own response internally. Now she can stop seeing her affects as having a life of their own in the world around her, or in other people. Instead of saying, "That stupid

Lego!" when her building collapses, she can (on good days) think, "I'm mad I can't build a Lego building," and decide to set the bricks aside or try again. Instead of just acting on impulse, she can put affect into a symbolic form—into words—that can be shared with other people.

Since Paleolithic times, human beings have found many ways to express feelings symbolically—through images, carvings, and special garments reserved for particular occasions. The most common way to communicate feelings is, of course, speech, and in the chapters that follow, you'll find words, phrases, and expressions to help your child grow more articulate and foster communication in your home.

Emotion is more complex. Rather than a direct response or expression of human feeling, an emotion is actually a process, an inner experience. One way to understand emotion is to think of it as the *layers of meaning* we bring to feeling, by weaving together our own personal tapestry of memories, experiences, and cultural associations. You might think of emotion as a story, or collection of stories, that you tell yourself about a particular feeling.

You and I can both feel the same feeling and have very different emotional responses to it, reflecting differences in *temperament* (our sensitivity to affect and our ability to tolerate it, something that's often evident in kids as early as infancy) as well as our particular *life experience*. When you're frightened, for example, what's that experience like for you? If you're thinking about riding the roller coaster at an amusement park, maybe you consider the fear part of the excitement. On the other hand, your apprehension might send you off into hiding in the direction of the cotton candy booth. Or maybe in your mind you hear a parent's voice from your childhood saying, "There's nothing to be scared of," and you end up feeling embarrassed about your fear (after all, don't all the other people in line look like they're looking forward to the ride?). Emotions are subjective by definition.

And because emotions are subjective, we can't know what other people are experiencing, or vice versa, unless we *communicate*. In our late-twentieth-century culture, we tend to use language to convey *information*, not feelings. We speak in emotional shorthand. Too often we ignore feelings, both our own and our kids'. Unfortunately, by doing so we don't equip our children to respond to their own feelings or express them, or to appreciate others' experiences—all lessons they desperately need to learn as they come of age on a planet where people with dramatically different histories and beliefs need to live together. This diverse, nuanced world of emotion is opened up to children through stories. Sadly, too many of our children are learning their "emotional vocabulary" from television, popular music, and Internet chat rooms. What they see there are often the cultural icons we make of those who *don't* express their feelings: the composed Jackie Kennedy at her husband's funeral or the determined U.S. gymnast who vaulted with an injured foot in the 1996 Olympics, or the action movie heroes who act out rage.

Instead of trying to fill the gap with coaching, we need to rediscover and revalue the simple joys of sharing experiences with those closest to us. When the BBC production of *Pride and Prejudice* aired in this country, as I was writing this book, many of my clients wistfully remarked on how articulate Elizabeth and Darcy were in talking about their emotions, and how respectful in listening to each other. What my clients were describing was true *intimacy*, and that's something kids begin to learn through everyday life at home and through sharing stories and other literature. Consider the difference between a three-year-old child who is afraid of the dark and refuses to go to sleep—or lies in the dark, alone and wide-eyed—and the one who knows he can remind a parent to leave a light on, or say, "I'm afraid of the dark, just like the kid in that poem you read me last week. Can you sing me a song the way you always do?"

The way a child moves from an infant's intense but not very organized affective life to a rich capacity for true emotion is through intimate relationships. There are no shortcuts. As you listen responsively and help your child express and shape her observations, you teach her to listen to an inner voice that grows stronger through the years. Through everyday conversation with you, your child hones her emotional wisdom by developing her capacity to grasp emotional nuance and grow more articulate in expressing it.

For younger kids, affects and feelings aren't really experienced internally. They're tagged onto other people, like labels. Just as the stove is hot, another child is "mean," a dark room is "scary," and a book is "good" or "bad." Your conversations offer an opportunity to help your child learn to recognize his *inner* states, and eventually to go beyond labeling. In order for a child to experience a feeling as his or her own, rather than as a physical response or something that is somehow connected to other people, he needs a word to represent that feeling. Even three-year-olds can begin to learn simple vocabulary to describe their emotions and experiences: *fun, scary, surprising, disappointing, hard to understand.* You help when you listen and supply words as needed. ("Was that story exciting? scary? suspenseful?") Invite younger kids to describe the facial expressions of people on cereal boxes, in magazine advertisements, in artwork, in picture-books.

Older kids tend to use the same five slang words for everything they like and don't like. You encourage their expressiveness when you ask them to tell you in detail what they appreciate about a friend, a movie, the latest clothing fad. And with a child of any age, expressing your own feelings precisely is one of the most effective ways to teach him or her to do the same, and to relate to someone who sees things from a *different* point of view.

At any age, sharing the arts with your child is one of the richest ways to experience and express emotion. A child who dances a "sad" dance or writes a poem when a friend moves away, or who can appreciate stories, theater, film, poetry, or music that treats themes of sadness and loss, has a richer capacity to express his feelings and cope with them and has a frame of reference to share with others. Kids are often more willing to speak openly about characters they meet in a story or on stage than they are to talk about themselves—just like most adults.

A soulful path. A child needs to discover that his feelings are respected by those he loves as a *source* of knowledge about his world, that he can trust what he knows on the level of his being, that he has an inner compass. When you help a child learn to pay attention to the promptings of his soul, he learns to be responsible in the original sense of the word— to *respond* to what his heart tells him and to his connection with others. In conversation with you about the stories in these pages, your child can learn to speak from the heart: to recognize different feelings and name them, to trust his perceptions, to make meaning of the events in his world. When conflicts arise and you respond authentically, without being overly harsh with him or giving in, he can learn how to face up to feelings that are hard to talk about and also listen to others' points of view. How much more a process like this means than slogans! He is learning not only how to "fit in" or be "well-adjusted," but how to approach life creatively.

Creating a story-centered family life is a path that I call *spiritual*, but in using that word I don't want to suggest something otherworldly or abstract, nor do I have in mind the kind of shortcut to serenity, harmony, and transcendence of feeling that is so often associated with the word *spirituality* these days. Instead, this is a path through everyday family life in all its daily joy, stress, and heartbreak. It leads, over the years, from the delicious, exuberant connection parents enjoy with a young child who is learning to recognize and express affect, all the way to the complex struggle to find meaning in the shades of gray that characterize mature relationships.

To foster the growth of a child's soul is to recognize a child's *aliveness*, his natural impulse toward growth and relationship. The method you'll find in these pages has very little to do with offering noble-sounding precepts. It grows out of having your feet on the ground.

Maybe you've read some of the "wisdom literature" of the Bible—Proverbs, Job, Ecclesiastes—where we find a wealth of teachings about human wholeness and virtue drawn not from abstract values or otherworldly pronouncements but from *life experience*. Wisdom, personified as Sophia in the Gnostic gospels, from the Greek, is a divine, feminine being who is not the "thought" of God but a compassionate being with a yearning to relate and to create. Sophia can move between the heavens and earth, and in nurturing our children's emotional wholeness through stories, we do exactly that. We need to struggle to make connections between soulful values and everyday experience.

Children tend to have more immediate access to their feelings than adults do, and they struggle to reconcile their feelings with their developing awareness of life in all its complexity. Stories help a child live in a "real world" of paradoxes. They teach him to dance along the precarious line between individuality and caring, between being a team player and standing up for what he believes in, between finding serenity and summoning courage.

Describing the process is one thing, but I'd rather let you see it in story-pictures. The most memorable tale I know about how parents help children grow is this traditional Eastern European story about a tiny doll handed to a little girl by her dying mother.

As you read, sit close enough to be able to touch your child or put your arm around him, or invite him to cuddle up, but not so near that you can't make eye contact. If he gets "antsy," try encouraging him to bring his energy *to* the story instead of running interference. Some children engage with a tale if they can sketch the characters in action as you talk. Offer paper and crayons or markers. When the story's over, invite your child to talk to you about his drawing. What was the character doing or feeling? Why did your child choose that part of the story to draw? If drawing proves too distracting but your child still seems to need a visual connection to the tale, try sketching simple stick-figure scenes as you're telling; this is a traditional practice in many cultures of the world, where stories are often traced out in sand or snow, or illustrated on elaborate storycloths. In many cultures, tellers or listeners pass around a handicraft during a story—a ceremonial doll or figure, for example—which seems especially appropriate to do for the tale of Vasalisa.

✧   ✧   ✧

VASALISA THE WISE

Once a man, a woman, and their daughter, Vasalisa, all lived together in a little hut. They were very happy until one day the mother got very sick. As she lay on her deathbed she called to Vasalisa and handed her a tiny doll. "Keep this doll and take very good care of her," said Vasalisa's mother. "Don't tell anyone about her. If you are ever lost, or if you need help, feed this doll and listen to her. She will help you all your life." Then Vasalisa's mother touched the top of her little girl's head, blessed her, and died.

Vasalisa and her father were very sad. But after a long time had gone by, Vasalisa's father found a new wife. She was nice to him, but not to Vasalisa, and she had two daughters of her own who were very unkind. Vasalisa's new stepsisters hated her, because her skin glowed and her eyes shone and she had a lovely bright smile. Whenever Vasalisa's father went out, they gave her chores to do, hoping she would get tired and ugly. "Sweep the kitchen, chop wood for the fire, milk the cow, and weed the vegetable garden," they ordered Vasalisa.

But the stepsisters' plan didn't work. With her tiny doll to help her, Vasalisa always got the sweeping and chopping and milking and weeding done with time left over for a good nap. Every day she grew stronger and healthier looking.

One day Vasalisa's father left home to journey to the farmers' market in a neighboring village. Vasalisa was left all by herself in the hut with her stepmother and her two stepsisters. As night fell, Vasalisa started to feel sleepy, and she tucked herself into bed. Her stepmother and stepsisters stayed up late, gossiping by the fire and saying mean things about everyone they knew. The three of them were so busy gossiping that they forgot to put logs on the fire, and after a while the flame went out. "Now what shall we do?" they whined to one another. "The hut will get cold. One of us will have to go to Baba Yaga's house to get a light."

"I'm not going," said the first stepsister, who knew that Baba Yaga was a horrible witch who liked to eat children and drink their blood.

"Neither am I," said the second sister. "Let's send Vasalisa." So they shook her awake and pushed her out the door and into the cold, dark night.

Vasalisa stood there all alone under the stars, so cold and scared that she was shivering from head to toe. She reached into her bag and found her tiny doll and felt better just touching her. Vasalisa whispered to her doll and told her how afraid she was of the wicked Baba Yaga, and how lonely she felt in the cold, dark forest. The doll told her not to worry and guided her along the winding path through the forest and over the hills.

Vasalisa walked all night and all day, until she reached the strangest-looking hut she had ever seen. The hut was made of wood, and all around it was a fence made of human bones and topped with human skulls. And instead of being built on solid ground, the hut was high in the air, on giant chicken legs.

Vasalisa's eyes grew wider and wider as she stared at the hut, but then she was startled by a loud, cackling voice. "I smell *flesh!*" said an old woman, who had just come out of the forest in a witch's flying cauldron. "Who's that standing in front of my house?"

Vasalisa knew right away that the old woman was Baba Yaga. "It is I, Vasalisa," she answered in a small voice. "The fire in our hut has gone out, and my stepmother sent me to you for a light."

Baba Yaga cackled again. "Oh, *I* know your stepmother," she sneered. "So, you need a light, do you? Well, we'll see about that. First, come inside and sweep the floor. Then, chop wood for the fire and milk the cow and weed the vegetable garden." She pushed Vasalisa through the bony gate and into her yard. "And if you're not finished by the time I get back tonight," warned Baba Yaga, "*you'll* be my dinner!"

Off went Baba Yaga in her flying cauldron. Vasalisa stood in the yard with tears on her cheeks, wondering how she could ever get so many chores done by nightfall. Then she took out her tiny doll and talked to her. "Don't worry, Vasalisa," said the doll. "You'll get all the chores done. I'll help you." Vasalisa fed the doll just as her mother had told her to do, and then the two of them swept the floor and chopped wood for the fire and milked the cow and weeded the vegetable garden. Then, Vasalisa lay down to take a nap.

When Baba Yaga got home, Vasalisa woke up with a start. "Worn out, are you?" cackled the witch, smacking her lips as she imagined how delicious Vasalisa would taste for dinner. Then Baba Yaga looked around and saw that all the chores had been done. "What's this?" she shrieked. "You've swept the floor and chopped wood for the fire and milked the cow and weeded the vegetable garden?" Her cackling ended in a scream of rage as she realized she wasn't going to be able to eat Vasalisa after all.

But then Baba Yaga remembered another chore. She shoved Vasalisa back out into the yard and pointed to a big mound of dirt. "That mound is full of poppy seeds, thousands and thousands of them," she told Vasalisa. "I want you to go through the mound and pick out every single poppy seed. By tomorrow morning, I want to find two piles out here, one pile of poppy seeds and one of soil. If you don't get this chore done by the time I wake up, *you'll* be my breakfast." And off Baba Yaga went to bed.

Vasalisa stared at the mound of dirt, and tears began to roll down her cheeks in two big streams. "How will I *ever* sort out all of the poppy seeds?" she sobbed. Then she reached into her pocket to touch her tiny doll. "Don't worry," the doll whispered. "I'll help you." Vasalisa sat down on the ground and began to pick out poppy seeds, one by one, from the mound of dirt. First she picked out one poppy seed and put it on the ground. Then she picked out another and put it beside the first. She picked out another, then another, and another. Finally, Vasalisa fell fast asleep on the ground.

The next morning Vasalisa awoke with a gasp. "The poppy seeds!" she cried. "I didn't finish! Now Baba Yaga is going to eat me for breakfast!" Vasalisa began to sob, and just then Baba Yaga stomped out to the yard.

"I see you did your chore," said Baba Yaga with a very loud sneer. She pointed to the two piles, one of dirt and one of poppy seeds, that Vasalisa's tiny doll had made during the night. This time Baba Yaga decided that even though the chore was done she would eat Vasalisa for breakfast anyway. She invited Vasalisa to come inside the house, lit the woodstove to boil water, and chatted away, trying to distract the little girl. "You know, Vasalisa," said Baba Yaga slyly, "you are very clever for such a young child. Tell me, how did you grow to be so wise?"

"By my mother's blessing," said Vasalisa with a smile.

Baba Yaga's eyes grew so wide they bulged out of her head. *"Blessing?"* she shrieked. *"Blessing?* We want no blessings in *this* house. Get out! Take your light and go!" And with those words Baba Yaga took a stick from the ground, put a skull from her bony fence on the tip of it, held the stick over the woodstove until the skull's eyes were glowing with flame, and handed it to Vasalisa. "Get out!" Baba Yaga shouted, and Vasalisa took the stick and ran over the hills and along the winding path through the forest, all day and all night, with the tiny doll guiding her home to her family's hut.

When Vasalisa arrived, her stepmother and stepsisters were waiting in the doorway, frowning and tapping their toes. "What took you so long?" they snapped. Vasalisa was just about to tell them the whole story when all of a sudden the stick she had brought from Baba Yaga's house jerked in her hand, and the skull on its tip spun around until its eyes blazed on her stepmother and stepsisters and burned them down to three piles of ash. Vasalisa buried the skull in the garden, and a beautiful red rosebush grew out of the ground on that very spot. That same day Vasalisa's father came home from the farmers' market. She told him everything that had happened, and he was very proud of her. And ever since that day, Vasalisa and her father and the tiny doll have lived together in peace and happiness.

Whenever I tell this story, my voice always catches in my throat at the moment when Vasalisa's dying mother hands her little girl the tiny doll. For most of us parents, it's hard to imagine wishing for anything more valuable than the chance to offer our child something that will last, something that will keep him safe in the face of danger, something that will never leave him feeling alone. As long as Vasalisa follows her mother's instructions—as long as she cares for the doll and listens to it—she is sure to have comfort and help whenever she needs them. The doll is a soul gift.

Your child's growth toward health and wholeness in adulthood depends in large measure on that "something," which I think of as his ever-increasing capacity to be aware of his thoughts and feelings and to use these to make meaning out of the world around him—an internal capacity that will serve, like Vasalisa's doll, as an inner guide to his own behavior. In our action-oriented media culture, inwardness is a tough sell, especially with kids. After all, on television, feelings are behaviors that can be *seen*; anger is yelling or shooting, and love is kissing or having sex. To teach a child to experience feelings as *internal states* is to open up opportunities for him to become more reflective. Instead of merely reacting to the events around him, like a ball bouncing back and forth in a pinball machine, he needs to develop the capacity to stop and think and try to understand before acting. Psychologists call this reflective function "self talk." Religious people call it prayer. You may find it helpful to picture it as the "inner feminine" that is part of both men's and women's psyches: the interior space that holds our thoughts and feelings—much the same way that a mother's arms hold a baby, smiling and soothing and responding—where we experience the *being* out of which authentic *doing* grows.

Family Time
"VASALISA THE WISE"

Make time to connect. I know you're busy, but this is the only family life you and your kids have together. You won't get a second chance. If you have the uneasy feeling that you and your kids don't spend enough time together, trust it; pay attention. You can find a way to turn that around. Maybe one problem is that the traditional gathering times—dinner, for example—are impractical. Even if all of you can't get together as regularly as you'd like, make it a point to plan times for the whole family to share as well as ways to connect with one child at a time. Instead of family dinner, set the alarm half an hour earlier to make time for a real family breakfast. Instead of carpooling for every activity, plan to make at least one "run" yourself, when you and your child can chat in the car. Take your child along to the grocery story and stop for bagels and a one-on-one talk along the way.

When you're overworked and exhausted much of the time, family meals can feel more like obligations than opportunities. Could you be avoiding them because, frankly, after a long day they're not all that much fun? Too often we turn our attention to nagging our older kids about their bad table manners, reminding them of chores left undone, and quizzing them about how well they're doing at school and in sports. Or we use dinner as a strategy session, catching up on all the things we need to get done. Trouble is, the less we talk, the less we have to say to one another.

Make mealtime fun.

1. **Try shifting the focus to connection,** with no advice, no criticism, and no planning of errands, bill paying, or driving. Your goal is none other than to enjoy one another's company, *to get to know one another better as people.* If your kids are small, try to keep in mind that just sharing one another's presence over a meal—mopping up spilled apple juice, stirring soup to cool it down, cutting a sandwich the "right" way, listening when they tell you a silly riddle—is the glue that bonds you together. Out of the unspoken connection you're making now, more sophisticated conversation will eventually begin to grow.

2. **Set some ground rules:**
   The answering machine gets the phone.
   No one's excused from the table until everyone is finished.
   No put-downs.
   Take turns talking.
   Listen to and look at the person who's talking.
   No advice, no criticism.

3. **With kids three and over, try some open-ended questions** that get kids thinking and let them know you're interested in how they're doing: What's the best thing that happened today? What's the worst? What did they learn this week that surprised them?

   With kids over six, try eliciting ideas and opinions about family activities: Where would they like to go on vacation this year? Is there an outing they've enjoyed in the past that they'd like to go on again?

   As children grow toward adolescence, their interests begin to diverge, often dramatically, from yours. Help keep your worlds connected by letting them educate you: What was the best movie or theater performance they've ever seen? The most amazing play in a baseball game? What can they teach you about hockey or music or butterflies that you don't know?

4. **With older kids, help them to connect the day's news reports with their own experiences, and to talk about their feelings on issues** such as hunger, homelessness, war, racism, and sexism. A child with a rich emotional life is not only sensitive to his own feelings but also caring about the wider world. I know one father who comes to the table armed with a topic, usually some news or a feature he's read in the paper that he knows will interest a variety of family members and start some discussion. To avoid having the whole discussion go over your kids' heads or frighten them, be sure to use words they can understand, elicit their feelings about the topic, and share your own.

Talking about world hunger, for example, a sensitive child can be easily overwhelmed; she needs to know that you can connect with her sadness and her fear that she could go hungry, too. She will appreciate learning about people in your community or in the newspaper who are working hard to create change.

Help a school-age child learning about a civil war in Africa find the country on a map or a CD-ROM encyclopedia, and learn something about its culture and customs. Help him develop a personal connection by engaging his ability to imagine. "Can you imagine what it would be like to live in a war zone?" you might ask. Reading Zlata's Diary or Anne Frank's diary helps a child connect with such experiences in a personal way.

By the time a child reaches adolescence, encourage her to imagine how to handle a problem differently, and to share her feelings about how adults are doing with it. Offer opportunities to see films and read novels that will help her respond emotionally to the issue and develop a social conscience. (See Appendix on page 246.)

5. **If you're feeling tongue-tied, be patient.** As you work through this book, your family will begin to share a variety of common experiences—stories, games, conversations, and reminiscing—that will give you plenty to say to one another. Don't expect

your kitchen table to resemble the Algonquin Round Table overnight. But in time, you'll start to discover that instead of feeling like a burden, these meals turn into a time for everyone to reconnect, a time everyone looks forward to.

Share yourself with your child. Just as kids love seeing the grown-up world of work with Mom and Dad on Take Our Daughters to Work Day, they're often interested to hear about parents' emotional challenges and experiences. Kids are eager to get to know what's going on in *your* life— what you're doing at work, with volunteering, or what you think about the day's news. When you talk about your own joys, struggles, and sadness in appropriate ways, you show your child that yours is a family where feelings can be talked about. You let her know that she isn't alone in her frustrations or happiness. And you provide vocabulary that will help her learn to talk about her own feelings.

1. **Share childhood memories.** When opportunities come up, tell your child what you remember doing and feeling when you were her age—making the team (or not making it), getting a first bra, going to a sleepover party.
2. **Instead of venting or hiding your feelings, explain yourself.** Make an effort to express yourself as thoughtfully as you can when you're talking about your own day. On a bad day, for example, you might be tempted to call your boss a "jerk" and leave it at that. That might help *you* blow off steam, but it's upsetting to many kids (especially the sensitive ones) and does little to help a child learn to express herself. (Clamming up doesn't help, either.) Putting feelings into precise language, rather than flying off the handle, is an important part of learning to manage them. Being *specific* about your feelings helps your child learn to express hers: "He's so out of touch he left a pile of papers on my desk and he seriously thinks I'm going to get done with them by Friday. I'm exhausted and frustrated." Or "I haven't talked to Mary Lynn for a long time. I really miss her since she moved to Seattle. Tonight I'm going to give her a call."

The Parent's Path
"VASALISA THE WISE"

Write a letter to your child. Here's an opportunity to articulate your own experience of your child, and your own values. It's the writing itself that matters. You may decide to give him this letter on an important occasion in the future—a graduation, for example—or choose to keep it tucked away in your journal. Either way, you'll bring the letter to your relationship with your child.

Be as honest as you can. What are your hopes and dreams for him? What do you most wish to pass along about what really matters in life?

What kind of person do you imagine him growing up to be? Are there particular qualities you've already noticed in his personality that you appreciate and value—a sense of humor, an ability to focus on goals, a willingness to reach out to others who need help? Be as specific as you can; include that funny or touching anecdote, that telling detail, that conveys so much more than a list of adjectives. ("I remember when you used your allowance money to buy the neighbor's dog a cone from the ice cream man.")

What do you like most about yourself? Spend a few moments thinking about the special qualities you bring to your relationship with other people. If you have a hard time seeing yourself this way, try to remember comments and compliments you've heard from others.

Are you particularly thoughtful? funny? sympathetic?

Do others appreciate your common sense? your insight? your sensitivity?

Are you especially good under stress?

Are you a caring listener?

This week, why not start paying attention to the things you do and say that your *child* seems to respond to. Are you one of his favorite playmates? A source of comfort? Someone who offers challenges that help him grow? By focusing on your own strong points, you'll begin to notice how much you have to pass on to your child.

What do you struggle with? Let's face it: we're *all* struggling with something. Recognizing your particular emotional pitfalls is important, because it helps you feel more empathy with your child's difficulties and understand that some aspects of his behavior may remind you of parts of yourself you'd rather ignore.

Do you have a hard time handling your anger appropriately? Do you hold it in, or lose your temper easily?

Do you dislike your own or your child's weaknesses? Are you impatient with fear or uncertainty?

Do you consider yourself a problem solver who'd rather find a way to make things better than sit and offer empathy to someone who's feeling discouraged, sad, or worried?

Be honest. What do others tend to tell you you need to work on? If your partner could change one thing about your personality, what would it be?

If you still haven't come up with anything, try this approach: what is it that annoys you most about your child? your partner? your friends? Chances are if you do some real soul-searching, you'll recognize that it connects with something you'd rather not acknowledge in yourself. As you'll see, that's no cause to feel inadequate. Think of it as an opportunity to grow along with your child. Let's take a closer look at the ways that can happen in your everyday life together.

Three

Your Path and Your Child's Growth

✧

Long before your child can use words to converse with you about her feelings, you are helping her develop the capacity to relate to herself and to others. As you know, over time, what you *do* is likely to mean more than what you preach. In my own family, for example, I talk to my kids a lot about ways to reduce stress. "Plan your homework assignments ahead," I tell them. "Get to bed on time. Make sure you have some playtime every day." I tell them these things as I rush up and down the stairs between the washing machine, my computer, and my consulting room. And with the honest eyes of children, they see the irony. One Sunday morning my nine-year-old read me a comic strip. "It's about a mother who's joking that she can't ever get a break from work and chores," she said evenly. "I agree with that." I realized that my tightly scheduled life—and my tendency to put "having fun" at the very bottom of my to-do list—was speaking much louder on the subject of stress management than the little lessons I was so fond of giving.

We're all growing. Sometimes we need to stop worrying about what to *tell* our kids and instead seek to deepen our awareness of how our child's struggles are locked up with our own. There are times we get "stuck" behaving a certain way because our own grief or anger or lack of understanding is lodged so deep inside, or feels so overwhelming, that we need to spend some time nurturing ourselves. Children, and especially very young ones, have an uncanny way of picking up on the things that trouble their parents—depression or anger or discomfort with sexuality—even when these aren't discussed in so many words.

For many of the parents I talk to, that's not necessarily good news. "How can I know what to do with my child when *I* grew up in a family where nothing felt normal?" one daughter of alcoholic parents asked me tearfully. "I'm still struggling myself." Even if you might not describe your own family of origin in such painful terms, maybe you're worried that you didn't grow up in a household where emotional wholeness was a priority; maybe doing the right thing, or measuring up to a family ideal, was more important than intimacy. In my practice and workshops, I'm often touched by parents whose own upbringing was marked by neglect or abuse, and who nonetheless bring a conscious awareness to their relationships with their kids that dramatically alters a pattern that has gone on for generations.

As we raise our kids, we re-parent ourselves. Sometimes, especially when we find ourselves often feeling depleted or angry, we need to be willing to turn inward, to live closer to the bone, to release our own untapped reserves of wisdom, strength, and love. We need not instruction but *insight*. Those times when we're caught up short by our children—as I was when my daughter read me the comic about the busy mother—they challenge us to face more truth than we ever thought we could, and to give more than we ever knew we had.

"I'm glad you don't like to give advice," a woman told me in one of my workshops. "I don't think you can give your child anything unless you already have it for yourself." I appreciated her kind words, but I don't entirely agree. The woman's assumption was not far removed from that of many traditional child-care manuals—that parenting means filling up our children with something we have and they don't. If that were true, what flesh-and-blood human could ever raise a child? We grow and learn, each of us, all through life. Even if you *could* perfect all the parenting techniques you read about, you'd be doing your child a disservice. He needs to connect with a parent who is *real*. Try as we may to be sensitive and supportive, we all disappoint our kids at times. That's part of being human. A nurturing home is not one where conflict, disappointment, and pain are absent. It is one where a child is safe to express these feelings, and to know someone cares, someone is listening. When you share stories and your responses to them, you connect as the people you really are.

Accepting your child instead of "fixing" him. The story that follows, "The Happy Man's Shirt," is an Italian tale about a king who tries to cheer up his unhappy son. It's not easy to deal with a child's problems. We like to think of kids as happy, especially when we're stressed out ourselves. Often it's tempting to try to solve everything, or to find solutions offered by someone else, just as the king searches for a stranger's shirt to put on his son. We think we're supposed to have all the answers. And yet, paradoxically, when we can accept our kids as they *are*—when we can listen and help them hold onto their feelings, rather than smooth them over or cover them up—we let them know they have the support they need to heal and grow. *That's* a happy childhood.

✧   ✧   ✧

THE HAPPY MAN'S SHIRT

Once there was a prince who was never happy. His father tried hard to cheer him up. He invited all sorts of performers to come and entertain him—actors, musicians, dancers, jesters—but nothing made any difference. The prince was still not happy. Day after day he sat staring out the window without a word.

The king decided to get help. He asked learned people from many lands to come and visit and offer advice. Soon the castle was filled with doctors, professors, and philosophers. "How can I help my son?" the king asked them.

The learned people spoke among themselves and they looked at the stars and they thought and thought for a long time. At last they came to the king with an answer. "Your Highness," they said, "there is only one thing to do. Find a truly happy man, and exchange your son's shirt for his."

The king sent word around the world that he wanted to meet a man who was truly happy. The first person to come to the castle was a priest. "Are you happy?" the king asked him.

"Oh yes, your Majesty," said the priest with a big smile.

"Would you like to be my bishop?" asked the king.

"If only I could!" said the priest quickly.

"Away with you!" said the king. "I'm looking for a man who is truly happy as he is, not one who says, 'If only.' "

Before long, the king heard about a ruler from another country. This man was supposed to be very happy. His lands were peaceful, and he had a wonderful wife and five beautiful children. The king sent his messengers to ask the ruler for his shirt, but when they arrived they found him pacing back and forth. "I have everything anyone could ever want," he was wailing, "but I can't sleep nights, because I know one day I'm going to die and leave it all behind!" The messengers decided that this ruler wasn't a happy man after all, and they went home without his shirt.

The king was beginning to lose hope of curing his son. Would he ever find a truly happy man? To take his mind off his troubles, he went out hunting in the meadow. As he was chasing a hare, the king heard a man singing at the top of his lungs. "Anyone who sings like that must be happy!" the king said to himself. He followed the sound of the music until he came to a garden, where a young man was pruning fruit trees and filling the air with his voice.

"Good morning, your Majesty," said the young man.

"Good morning," said the king. "Would you like to come live at court with me and be my friend?"

"Thank you, your Majesty, but I like it right here."

"At last!" thought the king. "A truly happy man! My son is saved!" And the king reached out toward the young man. "I'll give anything you want, if you'll just give me . . ." and he grabbed the young man's jacket and began unbuttoning it.

"What, your Majesty?" asked the young man, startled.

"Only you can save my son," said the king, but then he stopped and stared.

The happy man wore no shirt.

✧   ✧   ✧

Why isn't the happy man wearing a shirt? In the concrete world of everyday, we'd assume it's for practical reasons—because he's too poor to own one, or maybe because he'd feel too warm working in a garden under the hot sun. But in the realm of story, where every detail is rich with symbolic meaning, we understand that the man's wearing no shirt tells us something about the state of his soul. The happy man wears no shirt, and yet he is filled with joy, because joy is mostly found in shedding things, in getting back to our original nakedness, the nakedness of the joyful baby. Unlike the prince, who sits passively (a little like a child who mopes around whining he has "nothing to do"), the happy man in the story is fully engaged in the present moment, filling the garden with song.

Notice that the king does not summon the happy man into his presence, as he does his first two "prospects." This time he follows the sound of music until he finds the one who is singing. When our children come to us with their unhappiness, how much more helpful we are by resisting the urge to rush in to "solve" the problem and instead follow their lead, guided by our own instincts and experience. If we know how to listen, our kids very often tell us exactly what they need. If we let our instincts guide us along the path, we can learn to help them.

Family Time
"THE HAPPY MAN'S SHIRT"

Ask your child to draw an imaginary shirt for a happy man. Whatever your child draws, ask him to tell you about it. Don't judge, comment on its shallow values, or try to make a point about its connection to the story. The shirt might be covered with stars or fire trucks or hearts or dollar signs. It might be satin and jewel-encrusted, fit for a king, or metallic and meant for a person of the future. It might be a Superman shirt.

Use the drawing as an opportunity to open up a dialogue with your child. Have some fun with it. What does he like about the images he's put on the shirt? How did he choose the colors? What does the shirt tell you about the man who wears it? As you listen, you are getting a glimpse of the world from your child's point of view. In the process, you are giving your loving validation, letting your child know you value his creativity and his dreams.

Invite your child to decorate a happy man's shirt to wear himself. Give him a plain, white T-shirt and some paint pens, and invite him to decorate the shirt with all the things that give him joy. Be sure to suggest he include not only objects, such as toys, sports equipment, and clothes, but the people who live with him, the natural world, and the imaginary creatures from books and stories who add richness to his life. Let him know you're interested in hearing him tell you about his decorated shirt.

Role-play a conversation between the king and his son. Have the king ask his son why he is so sad, and what he wishes the king would do or say to help. Many children find it easier to express feelings this way, through fantasy play, than directly. If your child is one of these, don't spoil the pretend play by asking questions about his or her own sadness or happiness. As you and your child play at talking about feelings, you lay the foundation for sharing them in "real life" when the time is ripe and he needs your help or willing ear.

Make a "treat box," a variation on the traditional cookie jar. Do some brainstorming with your child and come up with as many of the joys of life as the two of you can think of: love, baking cookies, being under the covers on a cold morning, origami, birdwatching, hiking, you name it. Write them down on small slips of paper. Give your child odds and ends to decorate a small box or container, and put the treat slips in the box.

Next time your child has "nothing to do," invite him or her to reach into the box, eyes closed, and take out a treat slip. Help him to treat himself for real if you can—fill the bird feeder, go for a walk, exchange hugs and kisses—or to enjoy the treat in his imagination by reminiscing together about a time you remember.

Compare notes with your child about the times when each of you is really happy. Is it at the beach? in the backyard hammock? finger-painting? Thanksgiving dinner? Don't lecture him or her on how "the best things in life are free" or get upset if your preadolescent mentions watching *Beverly Hills 90210*. Just accept what he brings up, and tell him some of your own experiences of happiness. (For help recalling these, see Parent's Path below.)

Set aside a few minutes each day for you and your child to talk about what made you happy. Talking about happy times is a good way to keep communication lines open. It lets your child know that you enjoy hearing what he's enthusiastic about, what's really important to him. Otherwise it's all too easy to get caught up in nagging and arranging the day's details.

The Parent's Path
"THE HAPPY MAN'S SHIRT"

If you could borrow the shirt of one happy person, whose would you choose? Is it a friend who has more money, time, or freedom? A leader in your community or on the national or world scene? Your spouse? Try to pinpoint what it is that you think makes that person happy. Now ask yourself: Are there ways you could find more in your own life of whatever that is? How? What's getting in the way now? a hectic schedule? an overdeveloped sense of responsibility to others? a belief that your happiness doesn't matter all that much? How can you start to change the pattern today?

Get out your crayons and draw a picture of a happy time from your childhood. Was it summer vacation? Sledding? A visit to Grandma's? Running through the sprinkler? Is there a time now when you feel just as happy, from head to toe, as you did then?

One of the lessons of "The Happy Man's Shirt" is that joy does not depend on putting on something extra, but often on being willing to strip away that which is unnecessary. So often we chase after joys—from cookie-binging to cars—that do very little to satisfy our real needs and yearnings. We'd be better off getting naked and singing at the top of our lungs.

Take some time to see what's getting in the way of satisfaction and joy in your life. Find a quiet place and sit comfortably, either in a straight-backed chair or on the floor. Breathe in and out slowly and deeply. Let your body relax.

What comes into your awareness?

Is it your weekly calendar?

Is your schedule so busy that you have left no time for simple pleasures?

Maybe you're thinking of all the things you have failed to accomplish this week.

Are unrealistic expectations of yourself wearing you down? Feel their heaviness in the tightness in your chest or the knot in your stomach.

Or you may have in mind a friend or family member who needs help. Do other people's needs loom so large that you feel guilty when you're not taking care of them?

Is there a sadness or worry or fear that has covered up all your other feelings?

You may need to share your burden with a friend, or resolve to deal with it over time. But just for now, let yourself experience this moment. Try to imagine taking off that heavy garment—whether it's busyness, guilt, sadness, or worry—just long enough to bring yourself into the present moment. Come to your senses.

Feel your breath moving in and out of your body, from deep in your belly all the way up to your mouth.

Is the air warm, fragrant, cool, refreshing?

Wriggle your toes and fingers. Listen to the sounds you hear—birds, cars, kids.

What do you wish your parents had given you as a child? Since you've become a parent yourself, you may have a better appreciation for how much your own mother and father gave you. Every child grows up with disappointments and resentments, a sense that something he or she yearned for was missing or not understood. Throughout this book you will find questions to help you recognize how your childhood experiences influence the way you respond to and manage certain feelings today, and what you are teaching your child about them.

For now, here is an exercise to help bring you back in touch with the earliest times of your life, and with the "feeling quality"—the moods, the level of expressiveness, even the noise level—of your childhood home. At first you are likely to have difficulty with it. Some people have trouble remembering; others may be overwhelmed by emotion. You may wish to take turns reading it aloud with a friend or partner, and then do the written part in privacy.

Set aside a pencil and paper or have your journal handy. *Now find a quiet, uncluttered place, and sit on a straight-backed chair or cross-legged on the floor.*

Close your eyes, and slowly inhale and exhale while you relax your body— head, neck, chest, fingers and toes.

Now picture yourself as a child of school age, somewhere between seven and twelve, somewhere at home.

Are you in your room, the kitchen, the attic, or somewhere else where you spend a lot of time?

Are you alone or with others?

Are you playing, doing a chore, reading?

Where are the grown-ups?

What sounds do you hear? Is there laughter and talking? Is there arguing or shouting? Is the house very silent?

Now imagine one of your parents coming into the room. Do you see your mother or your father? What is it that seems most familiar about him or her— face, eyes, hands, smell, walk?

Notice what you're feeling in your body; pay attention to any tightening in your chest or knot in your belly.

Do you expect a hug, or do you long for one?

Are you told to get up and do something constructive? Are you ignored altogether because he or she is too busy? Do you feel intruded on, interrupted?

Try to stay with the feelings as long as you can, then slowly open your eyes. Now take the sheet of paper and let yourself freely respond to these questions:

- *What did you most want from your parents that you didn't get?*
- *How did your family express affection? Can you remember what made you really feel loved?*
- *How were disagreements handled? How did you know when your parents were angry? How did they feel to you? How did they respond to your anger or frustration?*
- *Did you work hard to earn their approval and feel that, instead, a sibling was always "the good one"? Or were you the good one? What happened when you did things your own way?*
- *Was there a particular period or aspect of your childhood that your parents seemed to have trouble coping with? your exuberance? your shyness? your teen years? What happened in your relationship?*

- *Was there something special about your mother or father that you really enjoyed—a wonderful laugh, a comforting warmth, a particular way of tucking you into bed or ruffling your hair—that you wish had happened more often? How is that "something special" a part of your life today?*

Remembering what you missed can be helpful because it helps you grow aware of how you deprive yourself of the things that would mean most to you today. In these pages I hope to help you to recognize the impact of those losses on your relationship with your child, to grieve, and to heal.

Learning to Listen

Let's take another look at "The Happy Man's Shirt." The king who wants to "make" his son happy is in the trap so many of us fall into when we focus on fixing our kids instead of understanding them. What if the king were to sit down with his son and really let him know he was willing to be present to his unhappiness? My own speculation is that the king's son has quit talking because he is so discouraged about communicating with his father, and so isolated. Often it's not the particular problems themselves that weigh our kids down, but the sense that we're all alone with them. On the other hand, when a child believes that help and support in coping can be found, he or she can face the challenges every childhood brings. Just learning to connect affects with words gives children the capacity to experience feelings consciously rather than be overwhelmed by them. And by internalizing the good aspects of the relationship with a parent or parents who can tolerate their own feelings as well as their child's, a child grows strong enough to feel feelings and cope with them. The process, as I've said, starts long before you can coach your child. Here are some ideas on how you help develop your child's emotional wisdom through everyday relating, with special attention to how to listen to kids at different ages.

Infants. In your baby's earliest months of life, as you come to recognize your infant's different cries for milk, sleep, and a clean diaper, she learns to trust that the world is responsive to her—that her feelings have meaning, that she can reach out and be heard, that she can find tenderness and comfort and play when she wants them.

In the first few months, your infant's affective life is connected to the development of her central nervous system. At this point, her growth centers on two basic "tasks." She is *engaging* with the world around her, using all her senses—eyes, mouth, skin, fingers, nose, ears—to explore her environment, and especially to recognize different stimuli, like the difference between your voice and a rattle. By three or four weeks, she already shows a preference for looking at live human faces; she is developing an intense bond with the people in her life. This is an active kind of learning; she isn't passively receiving sounds, like a radio transmitter, but actively participating in making sense of them. At the same time, your baby is learning to *regulate* her body in preparation for that engagement, developing the capacity to soothe herself.

As you listen your baby's cries and respond to her attempts to engage with you, and to her need for soothing and touch, you are nurturing in your baby an abiding sense of what Erik Erikson called "basic trust." This trust is the foundation for her sense of self, and for her later capacity to connect with others in an attuned way. (There is evidence to show that children with greater knowledge of and skill in understanding emotional situations tend to be considered popular with peers.) How different this attending, this responsiveness, is from the popular notion of *stimulating* a child. Baby reaches out for a toy or a necklace, or turns to us with a smile, and parents offer her the object to play with, or smile back. Yet we honor her rhythms: When baby frets or turns away, we offer soothing or some quiet time. Through this early listening we help her stay in touch with her feelings, tolerate them, and learn to share them.

Toddlers. A toddler pours sand and water, bangs on pots and pans, discovers that she can do things *herself*. What a joy it is to know that she can be on her own and still get a helping hand or hug from a caregiver when she's had enough exploring. "I'm *trying!*" a neighbor's child told me happily as she clutched the magnets on my refrigerator, one by one, and pulled them off.

It's not always easy to tolerate a toddler's joyful adventures, but if she is to grow up feeling secure and independent, she needs to know you accept her as a person with needs and wants and energy all her own. When a child learns that he can get angry or sad in the presence of an adult who will listen instead of turning away, criticizing, or letting him lose control, he learns to *contain* the particular emotion—to "feel the feeling" as his own and to experience it without losing control. With time and coaching he comes to *integrate* the emotion—to learn to express it appropriately, aware of the consequences of his behavior and of the needs of others. The two-year-old wants to explore, to reconcile opposites—good and bad, yes and no, empty and full. This is often a frustrating time for both parents and child, but your toddler is in a wonderful, transformative place. Through her struggles and tantrums, she is learning to *tolerate ambiguity* long enough to grapple with complex problems. This is an important step toward her eventual capacity to learn to resolve conflicts, rather than blaming or attacking herself or others. Not all growth toward emotional wisdom looks pretty.

Preschoolers. By the preschool years, your child is gaining a sense of your expectations and standards. By now because of the way you listen *actively*—recognizing, labeling, and supporting her expression of particular emotions, she comes to recognize the kinds of feelings *you* feel comfortable with—and the kinds you don't. Most three-year-olds know what it means to be in a situation that feels happy, sad, or mad, and sometimes scary. If certain feelings don't tend to be shared through facial expression or in words (if, for example, you're used to hiding your sadness and ignoring hers), your child will not learn to share these; in fact, she's likely to lose touch with the capacity to consciously feel them. On the other hand, if you teach her the vocabulary she needs to express her feelings in words, she can continue to feel them and learn to share them appropriately with others.

Not surprisingly, many of the gender differences in the way men and women express themselves and listen to each other pointed out in a variety of recent books and articles, most notably Deborah Tannen's *You Just Don't Understand*, may well have their origin in these early years. A variety of studies indicate that by the age of five, a child's ability to recognize particular feelings and label them varies according to family (and appears to be strongly related to the emotional style of the parent of the child's same sex), but also according to gender and culture. There is a great deal of research to show, for example, that mothers in the United States tend to spend less time responding to children's negative expressions of feeling than to positive ones. Five-year-olds are more likely to recognize happiness than sadness, and they confuse sadness and anger. Studies have found that mothers of infants smile more at their daughters than at sons, and mothers are more expressive with boys at playtime. In one creative 1981 study, researchers gave mothers and fathers a wordless storybook to share with their preschool sons and daughters. They found that fathers used more emotion words with their daughters than with their sons, as did mothers, and that mothers minimized discussing anger with girls. It's not clear whether these differences are the result of parents' socialization, or a response to innate gender differences in the children's behavior and the response it evokes. But the results are not surprising: Boys are more easily able to recognize anger than girls are. And girls tend to be better than boys at conveying emotions through facial expression.

At this stage, your child is not only learning to recognize and express her feelings, she is connecting them with her thoughts through her imagination. She is likely to often invite you to participate in fantasy play. She is beginning a pattern of expressing her observations, struggles, and hopes to you, and imagining what it would be like to turn her daydreams into reality. "Those giant monsters can't get me!" she says triumphantly. "I can fly!" A preschooler puts on grown-up shoes and scarves and sashays around in a world of her imagination. She creates whole universes with building blocks and small figures. She invites Mom or Dad to make the dolls talk or the knights battle. (If you have a hard time making the transition from grown-up reality, see the exercises on page 50 to help you loosen up.) These developments are important in the growth of emotional wisdom because they mark a tremendous surge in the child's social interest in others, her interest in genuinely reaching out; in her capacity to imagine new possibilities, which will equip her to face challenging situations with optimism and flexibility; and in the creative powers that will equip her to be an emotional "wizard" who can transform painful or intransigent situations into something different. In a discount department store, I saw an exhausted-looking mother with a boy, about three years old, sitting in a shopping cart. "Give me a quarter to call myself on the phone," he asked several times, and she ignored him.

"You don't need to call yourself on the phone," she finally said, irritably. "You're right here."

The child looked up, eyes wide. "I was *pretending*," he said simply, apparently realizing he had to explain the obvious to a grown-up. That capacity to hold onto an inner vision, in the face of a world that is often uncomprehending or even hostile, is essential to the development of emotional wisdom. It is what gives us the confidence to know there *can* be a better way, even when all looks bleak.

School-age children. During the school years your child can, with your help, really blossom emotionally into a little person with a capacity for emotional richness and nuance that may surprise you. Your child's understanding will grow more sophisticated as her cognitive capacity grows, and she will gain valuable communication skills through games and talks with peers. Unlike the preschooler, when she's unhappy or angry, she doesn't only think in terms of changing the situation she's in; she can begin to try to understand what's going on, control her feelings, and even have multiple feelings at the same time, or blends of feelings. She may appear to be chattering and needs your patience. But if you listen attentively, you will notice that she has become a storyteller of sorts. A fourth-grader might tell you she is "scared, excited, and happy" before her appearance in the school play, for example, while her brother in kindergarten is more likely to focus on his costume. If she is upset about a teacher's decision—say, to put her desk beside a child she dislikes in class—she is capable of containing her sadness and anger while also talking with you about strategies to work toward a change, or even to realize that she can make the best of it until desks get moved again.

The school-age child can also begin to understand that different people might not always feel the same way about different situations— that she enjoys crowds but a friend is shy. And she is recognizing that people aren't always honest or direct about what they're feeling. "He's acting like he's in love with her but he just wants to marry her because she's rich," she'll say knowingly about a movie villain.

As your school-age child grows emotionally in so many ways, she needs time to talk with parents, to "bounce" her ideas off the people she loves. You can let her know you're available by being an open, receptive listener. Too often we communicate to our kids that their worries aren't really important ("One day you'll look back on this and laugh"). Or, by reacting too intensely or inappropriately, we persuade them that we're incapable of being a sounding board.

For example, let's say your child comes home and reports, "Two kids were talking in class today, so the teacher said we *all* had to stay in for recess." Your child is upset, you agree it's unfair. What can you do? Here are some pitfalls to avoid: *Don't short-circuit your child's feelings by discounting them in advance* ("Well, she's the teacher. It's only for one day. You'll get over it"), or by *rushing in with your own responses* ("That's terrible! I'm calling the principal right away!"). Instead, *give children room to express themselves.* They came to talk to you, and before anything else, they want you to *listen.* "I see," you might begin. "I know you usually look forward to recess." With some kids, a neutral comment serves as a sign of your interest and an invitation to express their disappointment. Others need a direct invitation. "How are you feeling about this? Is there anything you'd like me to say or do to help?" Still others need space and time to mull over their thoughts or collect themselves. These are the children who tell you at bedtime or later in the day. And with all kids, when in doubt, ask: "How would you like me to help you with this?" "Do you want me to just listen or help you solve the problem or tell you how I felt about this when I was a kid?" (There's more about listening after the next story.)

By school age, play is the serious business of trying new things and learning to be good at them—shooting hoops, running a race, playing a musical instrument, reading chapter books. A child with healthy self-esteem enjoys such challenges. But what may be a joyous experience for one child can be overwhelmingly stressful for another. Pay attention to warning signs. If your child is often lonely, very competitive, or if he or she frequently suffers symptoms (abdominal pains, diarrhea, constipation, skin rashes, or a change in appetite) not explained by a physical examination, ask yourself if she or he is under too much pressure. Would it help to pare down on after-school activities? Does your child need more time to talk with you about the challenges he faces—schoolwork, the teacher, the class, sports—or just to shoot the breeze?

Adolescents. Although adolescents are often characterized as "very intense" and more "emotional" than the rest of us, there's actually a great deal of research to indicate that during these years kids' range of feelings *overall* is becoming more stable and consistent.

Adolescents do experience turmoil about the changes in their bodies as well as their social status. What could be better than being more independent, feeling popular, having a more grown-up body, having the future at your feet? And yet what could be more painful than having an "off" day, when "nobody likes me" and "I never get to do anything" and "I have a zit on my nose"?

At this age your child may tell you clearly that she'd much rather talk to friends than Mom and Dad, but don't be fooled into thinking you're history. As your child rides this roller coaster, he may sound as though he wants you nowhere near him, but that's not exactly the case. He still needs to know you are willing to listen, without rushing to criticize or judge him. (That doesn't mean, of course, that you won't point out the error of his ways on a regular basis—leaving homework till the last minute, not coming in on time, talking on the phone too long—but when he wants to share a problem with you, try to honor that experience and respect his need to be listened to.) Sometimes, all your child needs is an audience.

Keep in mind that kids this age tend to express concerns in dramatic terms. Teen talk tends to sound very intense and to include the expression of strong feeling: "Wow! That's amaaaaazing!" you'll hear, along with a wide range of the latest slang words. Sometimes parents get turned off—or scared off—by adolescent expressiveness. It may help to remember that your teen isn't necessarily looking for you to take drastic action, but just practicing getting her feelings across. Don't be too hard on your teen for blowing a problem way out of proportion, either; a hug or verbal show of support ("Sounds like you're really worried") is usually welcome.

Another important change that comes during adolescence is a cognitive leap. Your child is no longer limited to thinking about concrete objects and situations but is capable of "formal operational," or abstract thinking. She can wonder about the future and about events that might be. She's interested in the realm of possibility. And to this new ability to think, the adolescent brings her emotions. Her feelings no longer are tied to what's happening right now but are integrated into belief systems (religious, political, and philosophical) and artistic expression. The adolescent's challenging and arguing are her way of struggling toward a stronger, independent sense of values and beliefs about the kind of person she wants to be; she is struggling to use her passion and her capacity for abstract thinking to forge the inner meaning that will become her "rudder," the guide for her behavior in the face of enormous pressures from peers and the media.

When your child doesn't want to talk . . . Developmental guidelines can be helpful, but there's no substitute for paying attention to your own child. Each child is different, and each child goes through different stages, depending on reactions to challenges related to age, gender, and surroundings. *Expect* periodically to hear, "Oh, Mom!" and to see a glare that loudly tells you, "I don't want to talk about it right now!" Through the years kids go through periods of wanting to talk and not wanting to talk. When they need to feel more separate from you, more independent—during the toddler years, for example, around the age of seven, and in adolescence—they may withdraw or push you away. *That doesn't mean they don't need you. What they need is a relationship in which they can feel more like their own person.* They need you there so that they can push you away. Through the years, by making your presence and interest known, even when they want or need to reject you, you let them know you're still available, and you still love them.

Avoid labeling. One child smiles and whistles half the day, bringing sunshine into the house. Another quietly writes poetry in his room. One offers to help cook dinner and clean up afterward; another forgets her lunch money every other day. It's easy to see patterns in kids, to think of one as happy and one as shy, to say, "He's our cooperative one, and his brother tends to be hard to get along with."

Not surprisingly, though, when you label kids this way you often end up with a self-fulfilling prophecy. Keep in mind that although kids are born with different temperaments—some more expressive than others or more easygoing or more sensitive or more likely to feel blue—by categorizing them you only cause resentment. "You always think *she's* the good one!" one younger brother exploded at his parents, who realized they needed to let him know that they appreciated his playfulness, even though it seemed to get him into more trouble than his sister.

When you label your child—good or bad—you hold him back. Even a timid child experiences happiness in his own way. In time, and with frequent reminders, the forgetful child can grow more responsible. And both the helpful child *and* the mischievous one need your approval.

I'm including the following Afghan tale, "What Music Is the Sweetest?" because of the way it uses a riddle to point out how inadequate our generalizations and theories tend to be. The fourth minister offers a memorable lesson to everyone about being present in the here and now, and about paying attention to what we learn from our senses.

WHAT MUSIC IS THE SWEETEST?

One day the prince of Persia was talking with his government officials. "What instrument plays the sweetest music in the whole world?" he asked them.

"The flute," one official answered.

"No," said another." "I think it's the harp."

"I don't think it's either one," said a third official. "The violin makes the sweetest sound."

The three officials argued and argued all evening about the answer to the prince's question. All that time a fourth official, who was very wise, sat and listened without saying a single word.

That night the fourth official invited the prince and the other officials to a magnificent banquet in his courtyard. There were musicians strolling among the guests, playing every instrument you can think of—guitars, trumpets, flutes, harps, violins, oboes, and more. But something was missing. Even though the tables were set with shining gold and silver bowls and crystal goblets, there was nothing to eat or drink.

After a while the guests were very hungry, and they wondered when the food would be served. But they were all too embarrassed to ask. So they sat and sat with their stomachs rumbling until it was very late.

When the clock struck twelve the fourth official called to a waiter, who walked into the kitchen and came back carrying a steaming casserole with a lid on it. As the waiter walked toward the tables, he tapped the lid with a serving spoon: Clink! Clink!

As soon as the guests heard that sound, they sighed with

relief. "The clink of plates of food in the ears of hungry people," said the prince. "That is the sweetest music in the world."

I like this story because it speaks to parents and kids on at least two different levels. For parents, it's a reminder of the limitations of theory and techniques, and of the importance of listening. Think of the sweet music in this tale as representing the soulful, nurturing connection between parent and child. Each of the three officials in the story has a point about the beauty of his favorite instrument (just as most of the caring parents I know can talk theory and name techniques with considerable skill). But the fourth official shows them all that the sound that touches the guests at the banquet is the one they hear when they are operating at a "gut" level. Likewise, we and our children really communicate not when we use any particular "right" techniques, but when we are willing to *really listen*, to open up to our natural awareness in the moment, when we're present to our kids, body and soul.

Trusting your gut. When your child talks to you, he wants to hear from a parent, a grown-up who can be vulnerable enough to respond with honesty and feeling. The more authentic your listening—the more truthful and the more in touch with and expressive of your own feelings you can be—the more fully you offer him the opportunity to experience a real connection.

That's where this story's next layer of meaning comes in. A child's emotional wisdom, like an ear for music, grows not out of learning someone else's precepts but out of a willingness to recognize one's own feelings and perceptions, and to honor them. As you've seen, much of this awareness begins to grow in the earliest days of life, as he comes to trust that his needs for touch, holding, nurture, and rest will receive a reasonably attuned response. Once a child can talk, he develops a *voice* by being listened to with similar attunement. When he can trust that he has the time, space, and attention to struggle to express his perceptions and ask questions, he can learn to communicate on an emotional level.

Let your child lead. That's important to remember when you're tempted to coach your kids instead of relating to them. If you rush in with advice, or even with well-meant slogans, you miss out on the opportunity to listen to what you're really supposed to hear. Even with the best of intentions, you shame your child into believing that whatever is on his mind is less important than what you're busy telling him. When that pattern happens regularly, you've got yourself a communication breakdown. I overheard one in the making in a restaurant—actually, a converted firehouse—during a busy lunch hour when I sat close to a man and his son at the next table. Apparently this was the end of a father-son outing; the two of them had just gone on an "educational trip" to a construction site, and the father was asking the boy (about seven years old) a litany of questions: "Wasn't that interesting? What do you think holds the wood together? What do you think our house is made of? Would you like to build a car like Tommy who won the Scout derby?"

The boy shrugged and grunted, his eyes roaming over all the antique firehats, hose, and axes decorating the walls. Finally he interrupted his father's questions: "Dad, are you taller than Uncle David?" he asked.

The father looked startled. "I think so," he answered quickly, then resumed his interrogation. In his effort to turn the day into a field trip, he had completely missed his son's interest in him as a human being. Instead of nurturing the bond between them, he was a bossy, distant "adviser."

Family Time
"WHAT MUSIC IS THE SWEETEST?"

In the following sections, you'll find ways to extend "What Music Is the Sweetest?" into playful experiences to share with your child. Comparing "notes" about musical sounds, and experimenting with making your own, might seem like a silly way to nurture emotional growth. It *is* silly; that's why it's fun. In the process, it helps you and your child develop your own awareness and learn to talk with each other about what you experience— and both of these qualities are at the heart of intimate relationship.

One of the best ways to get kids involved with "What Music Is the Sweetest?" is to encourage them to make music. After all, there's hardly anything kids enjoy more than making spontaneous sounds. With a young child, encourage him or her to find homemade instruments around the house. A wooden spoon on a pot lid is a time-honored favorite, but a wire whisk makes a feathery scrape along a rough floor, a bowl of cereal crunches loudly under the press of a wooden spoon, the teeth of a comb make a *plink!* against a fingernail. How could you describe the sound of each one? What do you like about them?

How many different sounds can you and your child produce with your voices? Don't worry about how well you sing; it's how much variation you can produce that counts. Who can make the highest-pitched sound? the lowest? the happiest? scariest? Animal sounds, transportation sounds, weather sounds—use your imagination. Or get your whole body into the act; try your own version of "slap dancing," the African American tradition of clapping the hands rhythmically all over the body, chest to arms to thighs and back again.

Invite your child to pay attention to sounds at home or on a walk. A blue jay at the bird feeder, the beep of a misplaced digital watch, the drip of a faucet, the crack of a baseball against a bat—what does each sound tell him? Invite him to describe what might be happening when he hears the sound.

Name the sounds you consider the sweetest in the world. A favorite recording of Chopin, the cry of a loon, a baby's chuckle, the ice cream man. This is an imagination game you can also play with your other senses: What's the sweetest scent in the world? What's the most beautiful sight? What's the most wonderful thing to touch?

The Parent's Path
"WHAT MUSIC IS THE SWEETEST?"

When you were a child, how did your parents and other caregivers listen to you? Return to your quiet place, sit down for a few minutes, and inhale and exhale regularly, letting your body relax.

Now go back to the days when you arrived home from school with a lot to say, or any time you needed to talk to your parents about something that mattered to you.

Were they interested in your news?

Did they offer more advice than you wanted to hear?

If you were upset about something, did you hear, "You don't know how lucky you are"?

Do you remember a lot of put-downs ("How can you possibly enjoy that? No one else in this family does")?

Did your worrying seem to get a parent so upset or angry that talking only made matters worse?

Did they "turn off" when you expressed particular feelings—anger or fear or excitement?

Did you give up talking about things that were really important to you because you didn't expect anyone to help?

Maybe you can recall some really supportive experiences. Was there a certain person you knew you could always talk to?

What made that person special or different?

How could you offer some of that same quality to your child today?

How well do you listen to yourself now? Think back over the past week or month, to a time when something was worrying you—a problem at work or with your child—or when you wanted to try a new activity, maybe a sport or a new routine.

How did you respond to your own feeling? When you're upset about something or eager to try something new or curious, do you cut off your own inner voice with replays of the same childhood messages you recall from the questions above?

Do you try to drown out unpleasant feelings by keeping too busy, eating and drinking too much, or other escape tactics?

Conversation Stoppers

When your child comes to you with a problem, offering one of the answers on the list below is a guaranteed way to cut off communication. It also tells your child to be ashamed of his or her needs and feelings. A child does not learn to let things "roll off her back" or "get over it" by sheer willpower. That only teaches her to ignore her feelings, to develop a false veneer of toughness. It is *shaming*, the surefire antidote to family closeness. Likewise, if your responses are so strong or so overprotective that talking to you gets her more upset than she was in the first place, she will learn to keep her distance.

> You'll get over it.
> What's the big deal?
> None of the other kids minded.
> Don't worry.
> Don't cry.
> Don't be afraid.
> You're too sensitive.
> You're never happy.
> Just let it roll off your back.
> Stop crying. I'll buy you an ice cream.
> Stop being such a baby.
> Stop being such a sissy.
> Your brother never acted this way.
> Who cares what other kids think, anyway?
> That's awful! I'm calling his mother!
> That settles it! You're never playing with her again!

Communication Builders

You're not responsible for soothing away all her hurt or for meeting all her needs, but for helping her cope with her feelings. With the reassurance that you care—that you are a safe, responsive person to talk with—when she is sad or hurt, she can sort out her feelings with you and listen to advice on how to get along with others. In time, she will grow more resilient. Next time your child is upset about something, one of the gentle responses below may serve as an expression of your interest and caring:

> Hmmmm.
> Ohhh.
> Sounds like you had a rough day.
> Do you want to tell me more about this?
> How could I help you work on this problem?

Do you need a hug?
Let's sit down together.
Do you want to explain the problem so I can understand it?

These may be helpful especially for school-age kids or adolescents:

What a bummer.
That's rotten!
I'm sorry to hear that.
I'm proud you're working on this problem.
It sounds like a struggle.
I'm glad you're talking to me about this.

Now that we've set the stage for family storytelling as part of a rich, authentic relationship between parents and kids who are both growing, let's bring on the drama of the tales themselves and how you can make them a meaningful part of your home life.

Four

Filling Your Home with Stories

✦

You probably already love reading bedtime stories to your child. By now I hope you've shared a few of the tales you've come across in these pages, and begun trying some of the suggestions in the "Family Time" and "Parent's Path" sections. Now let's focus on ways to deepen that experience—to enjoy that familiar closeness, those delightful journeys to the world of imagination—by developing your own family storytelling tradition. In addition to the tales in this and other books, telling anecdotes about your day, family lore, or sacred stories from your religious tradition is one of the most satisfying kinds of nourishment you can give your child. The key to keeping kids enthusiastic is to keep your stories as down-to-earth as you can. Don't clean them up too much.

I've seen some professional storytellers who have, over the years, grown pretty slick, and the result is a deadness that gets in the way of enjoying the story and caring about it. I want to connect with the tale—and with my listeners—on a gut level.

As I hope you've already noticed, the stories I've retold in this book aren't a group of morality tales collected to turn your child into a better person. They're not the polite allegories from the Victorian era that have recently become popular with parents. These are stories that mirror the human experience, in all its diversity, misfortune, and wonder. Some of them are funny. Others, as traditional tales do, contain scenes that may strike you as too scary or disgusting for your adult idea of what ought to be good for kids. They *engage* us and our kids, challenge us, let us know we're not alone in our struggles.

I love hearing from parents who tell me they've shared a particular story they worried was "inappropriate" and then discovered how much their kids enjoyed it, and what interesting conversations it provoked. In a culture where larger-than-life media images bombard our kids from an early age, we need to share stories that are full of action, intensity, and drama; if we only offer our children polite, Victorian-sounding tales, we lose their attention and we deny the real truth about human nature, in all its richness, conflict, and ambiguity. Fortunately, tellers of tales in cultures around the world have always known this, and it's not difficult to find stories that speak to the secret places in our hearts.

The story that follows, from southern India, is a perfect example of a tale adults find slightly unsuitable and kids love. It's a surprising account of how much can happen when a person, no matter how skeptical, lets himself get caught up in a story.

✧   ✧   ✧

WHAT HAPPENS WHEN YOU REALLY LISTEN

Once there was a man who didn't like storytelling. His wife loved stories, but no matter how hard she tried to get him to enjoy them, he had no interest.

One day a singing storyteller came to their village to recite the most famous epic poem in all India, the *Ramayana*. Everyone knew the storyteller was wonderful to listen to, and they all packed into the tent to see him—all except the man who didn't like storytelling. But his wife insisted until he finally decided to go. As soon as he got into the tent and sat down on the ground, he fell fast asleep, and he snored for hours with his mouth wide open. When the teller got to the very last verses, candies were passed around the audience, according to custom. Someone dropped a piece of candy into the man's mouth, and he was so startled he woke up.

When the man got home, the wife was thrilled that he had stayed for the whole performance. "Did you like it?" she asked.

"It was very sweet," answered the man, and his wife smiled.

The next evening the storyteller was reciting more verses of the *Ramayana*, and the wife once again insisted her husband go and listen. As soon as he sat down and leaned against a wall, he fell fast asleep. A child in the crowd climbed onto his shoulder to get a better view of the storyteller, and when the performance was over the child jumped down and went home. The man woke up with a very sore shoulder.

When the man got home, the wife was again thrilled that he had stayed for the whole performance. "Did you like it?" she asked.

"It was very painful," said the village man, and his wife smiled, thinking he had understood the tragic aspects of the poem.

The third night of storytelling, the husband went to the tent, lay down on the ground, and fell fast asleep. As he snored, a dog came by and peed in his mouth.

At the end the man woke up and walked home, and his wife asked, "Did you like it?"

"It was awful," said the man who didn't like stories. "Too salty!"

Now the wife realized something was wrong. " 'Salty'! " she cried. " 'Awful'! Something's certainly awful about the stories *you've* been telling *me!*" And she insisted her husband explain himself until he finally admitted that he had been fast asleep through every performance.

"Tomorrow night is the last performance," she said, "and this time I'm going with you." They sat together in the front row, and the man promised to stay wide awake and pay attention. Soon the storyteller was telling his listeners about the adventures of Hanuman the monkey. He told them how Hanuman leaped across the sea to rob the great god Rama's signet ring for Sita, Rama's wife, who was being held captive in the kingdom of the demon. The man who didn't like stories was listening closely now, and his eyes were growing wider and wider. The characters in the poem were starting to come alive in his mind. Next came the most exciting part of the story: the breathtaking moment when Hanuman, holding the signet ring in his paw, took a daring leap back across the sea and the ring slipped from his paw and dropped into the water. Hanuman needed to bring the ring to Sita. What was he going to do?

"Don't worry, Hanuman!" the man who didn't like stories shouted from the front row. "I'll get the ring for you!" And he jumped up from the ground, dived into the sea, got the ring, and carried it back to Hanuman.

All the villagers who were in the tent that night were amazed. "This man must be someone very wise," they all said. And ever since that day, the man who didn't like stories has been respected for his great wisdom. That's what happens when you really listen to a story.

Stories yank us out of ordinary time and space, and into a realm where human feelings have the power to transform reality, just as the village man did. In the world of stories, feelings can make ordinary people powerful enough to kill witches, trick giants, slay dragons, and win a prince or princess. Stories hold out the hope that even though the world may be puzzling and scary, monsters deserve to be slain and true love can triumph in the end. Stories help us and our children recognize possibilities. In the face of the hurt, disappointment, and conflict that so often characterize the human condition, stories tell us we can bring our intelligence, perspective, and imagination to bear.

You probably already enjoy reading aloud to your child, but I'd like to encourage you to try something a little different: *telling* stories to your child. I'm not suggesting you put away your books (certainly not this one) and suddenly become a performer. Storytelling that nurtures emotional literacy is best understood as a *communication*, not a performance. The telling of a tale is a ritual moment in the lives of teller and listeners. You meet face to face. You make eye contact. "Tell us a story from your mouth, Mommy," one woman tells me her children often ask.

Try an experiment. Think of the stories you find written down not only as written texts, but as oral *springboards* to a shared exchange with your child. No story is complete as written on a page. It takes two people to tell a story. (Maybe you've seen some of the tales collected in Africa, which are written down in dialogue form just as they're told, with traditional responses and questions to help the teller and listeners connect and to build suspense and drama.)

Remember the story "Stone Soup" most of us heard in kindergarten, the one about the strangers who came to a village with a magical stone that made delicious soup? Naturally, the soup tasted much better when the townspeople added their own "extra" ingredients—carrots, celery, potatoes, and so on. Stories are like that stone soup. Like the townspeople, we bring our own particular ingredients, the richness of our own life experience, to the telling of a story. Without us, like the broth with nothing added to it but stones, the stories are missing something. They lack the flavor that keeps children coming back for more. They lack the richness of personal connection that nurtures hungry hearts.

If your child interrupts the telling to let you know that something is familiar in the story—a meadow you walked through last year on vacation or the winter night you stood together under the full moon—welcome the interruption. You've got his attention. He's involved. Together you will make the story your own.

On my desk I keep a Russian icon engraved with images of the saints. The figures have no faces; instead, according to tradition, the artist cut holes in the silver, through which the devotee is taught to look and see God. The idea is to develop the inner eye, to help us bring ourselves and our experience and our *imagination* to our spiritual lives. No two people do this in exactly the same fashion. And so a ready-made face on the silver icon would only get in the way. Likewise, when we and our children really connect with stories, we bring ourselves to them. We see the characters in our mind's eye, we watch them triumph over villains, rise from poverty, and fall in love, and we recognize that they are deeply familiar. We see in them our own experience, and the people we know. The stories open our eyes to the sacred dimension in our everyday struggles, and to all that is most truly human. That's why each time we tell a tale, it's never quite the same. "The tale is not beautiful if nothing is added to it," says the Italian author Italo Calvino, citing a Tuscan proverb.

Don't take your storytelling too seriously. Let the story come alive in the space between you and your listeners. Watch the knights and ladies kiss. See boys shiver and girls spin flax. The sound of your voice, your turns of phrase, your laugh, and the way your eyes shine when you're deeply touched, these are all vital parts of the storytelling experience for your child. They let her know that courage and honor and love are not only the stuff of story but of *your* heart and mind. Keep in mind that for the most part, these are not morality tales designed to drive home a simple point. Stories teach by touching. If you worry about trying to explain what they "mean," you only get in the way of your child's direct experience of the tales. A story isn't really "about" anything; it just *is*. Great stories have a way of sneaking up on you. They catch you off guard. They unsettle you. They open your eyes to new ways of seeing, show you the demons and tricksters and lovers who inhabit your inner world, and help you to befriend them. (For further suggestions on how to develop your own storytelling, turn to the Appendix on page 243.)

Family Time
"WHAT HAPPENS WHEN YOU REALLY LISTEN"

Create a story space in your home. You and your child will both find it easier to settle in together for a tale and a talk if you set aside a special place. Choose a quiet, comfortable spot away from toys, clutter, and television. A young child's room is often not the best spot, because it may offer too many distractions; an overstuffed armchair in the living room may be a better choice. For some kids, the sound of a parent's voice and the closeness of storytime are a wonderful prelude to sleep. But if scary or exciting stories keep your child awake nights or bring on bad dreams, try setting aside twenty minutes or so after dinner or at some other time that works for you. Personally, I like to keep storytime spontaneous; when I'm in the mood and the moment feels right, I'll suggest we share a tale, and if the kids say yes, we sit down together for the telling. (On the other hand, if a child comes to me with a problem that reminds me of a story—

a traditional tale, an anecdote from our family life, a childhood memory of my own—I'll ask, "Would you like to hear a story this problem reminds me of?" If I get the green light, I tell it then and there.) But if you're relatively new to storytelling, and if your household is as tightly scheduled as most are these days, you'll need to deliberately *plan* storytime as part of your weekly routine or you'll probably never get to it.

Some families find that having a simple ritual helps everyone relax and connect. It might be nothing more than announcing, "It's storytime!" You can turn the lights low or light a special "story candle." (One father told me his family uses a 1960s lava lamp he picked up at a church auction.) If your child is young, wear a special shawl or necklace to announce that it's storytime. Not only does this begin to convey that something special is happening, but it gives him or her something to play with during the telling.

Start a story-collecting habit in your family. Each fairy tale and folk-tale you share is inextricably linked with who you are and with *all* the stories you tell your child—the ones about how your town was founded, how your ancestors came to America, how your grandfather made things with his hands, how you got your first job.

When parents and kids exchange stories, we carry on a custom beloved by families around the world for many generations. We adults hear anecdotes every day from friends. Waiting for the bus, standing at the supermarket checkout, sitting in the doctor's office—people everywhere are sharing their troubles, triumphs, and surprises. Your child hears stories on the school bus, at the playground, in the classroom. When we consciously start to *pay attention* to the stories we hear (and overhear), and when we make a point of *listening* to the stories our kids come home telling us, our lives are greatly enriched. Keep your ears open and you can probably collect a story a day without even trying, and you never know when they'll come in handy.

The Parent's Path
"WHAT HAPPENS WHEN YOU REALLY LISTEN"

Choosing stories. The best stories to share with your child are the ones you love. No one except you and your child knows which stories will mean the most to the two of you. As you look at the ones in this book, you're likely to find some that feel right for now. As time goes by, others may seem more appealing or relevant. Most of the stories in this book, in the best folktale tradition, can be enjoyed by a wide variety of age groups. That's why I have, for the most part, avoided the guidelines for "age appropriateness" you're probably used to finding in parenting books.

You've undoubtedly noticed differences in temperament between one child and another. Each child's particular style is important to keep in mind as you select stories. A child who is squeamish or easily startled is probably not eager to hear about monsters or murders. A very active youngster, on the other hand, may not sit still for anything else.

In some cases, however, I've indicated that it's probably not a good idea to share a particular story with a young child because it is too scary. Since children under five have difficulty distinguishing fantasy from reality, very graphic scenes can be overwhelming. Preschoolers are more likely to appreciate simple tales with animal protagonists. Older school-age kids, on the other hand, need the opportunity to face strong feelings, including fear and anger, in the world of the imagination. They want powerful stories with brave heroes who stand up to terrifying odds.

In the following traditional Irish story, about a reluctant hero named Brian O'Brannigan, we learn something about the connection between stories and relationship.

THE MAN WHO HAD NO STORY

Once there was a basketmaker called Brian O'Brannigan. Brian traveled the bogs, looked for reeds, cut them, made baskets out of them, and sold them.

One day, after Brian O'Brannigan had cut all the reeds for miles around, he saw that there were none left to cut. Brian had made all his baskets, sold them, and spent the money. He didn't know what to do. So he decided he would walk up to a little glen called Alt an Torr, where there were some very fine reeds growing, and cut some there. No one ever cut any reeds in Alt an Torr, because it was a fairy glen.

Brian O'Brannigan took along a lunch and a hook and a rope and walked all the way to Alt an Torr. By the time he had cut two fine bundles of reeds, a thick fog had set in, and he decided to sit down and eat until the fog lifted.

But when he finished eating it was dark, and Brian O'Brannigan felt very frightened. He looked all around, first to the east, and then to the west, and in the distance he saw a light. If there's a light there must be people, Brian said to himself, and he headed toward it through the fog, stumbling and bumping into things along the way. When Brian got to the light, he saw a big house. The front door was open, so Brian put his head in, and he saw an old woman and an old man sitting by the fire. "Welcome, Brian O'Brannigan," they said, and invited him to come and sit between them.

The three of them chatted for a while. "Now, Brian O'Brannigan," said the old man, "can you tell us a story?"

"I never told a story in all my life," answered Brian. "I'll do anything except tell a story."

"Well, then, do something for your keep," said the old woman. "Take the bucket down to the well and fetch some water."

Brian O'Brannigan took the bucket and headed for the door. "I'll do anything," he said, "except tell a story."

Brian went down to the well. He was filling the bucket with water, when out of nowhere came a huge gust of wind and swept him up into the sky and blew him this way and that way until all of a sudden he fell to the ground. He looked around, first to the east, and then to the west, and in the distance he saw a light. If there's a light, there must be people, Brian said to himself, and he headed toward it through the dark, tripping and falling along the way. When he got to the light, he saw a big house, even bigger than the one where he'd seen the old woman and the old man. The front door was open, so Brian put his head in, and he saw that there was a wake going on.

"Welcome, Brian O'Brannigan," said a young girl with curly black hair who was sitting by the fire. She invited him to come and sit beside her.

The two of them chatted for a while, and then a big man stood up and said, "We need a fiddler at this wake so we can have dancing."

"Well, we have the best fiddler in Ireland among us tonight," said the girl with the curly black hair, "and his name is Brian O'Brannigan."

"I've never played the fiddle in my life," said Brian. "I'll do anything except play the fiddle."

"Don't make me a liar," said the girl with the curly black hair. "Pick up that fiddle and bow, and play us a tune."

And before he knew it, Brian O'Brannigan was playing away and they were dancing away, and everybody said they had never heard a better fiddler in Ireland than Brian O'Brannigan.

Then the big man stood up and said, "We need a priest at this wake so we can say Mass for this corpse."

"Well, we have the best priest in Ireland among us tonight," said the girl with the curly black hair, "and his name is Brian O'Brannigan."

"I've never been a priest in my life," said Brian O'Brannigan. "I'll do anything except say Mass."

"Don't make me a liar," said the girl with the curly black hair. "Put on those vestments and say Mass for us."

And before he knew it, Brian O'Brannigan was saying Mass, and everyone said they had never heard a better priest in Ireland than Brian O'Brannigan.

Then they put the corpse in a coffin, and four men lifted up the coffin on their shoulders. But one of the men was big and tall, and the other three were short, so when they started to walk they couldn't keep the coffin level.

Then the first big man stood up and said, "We need a doctor to shorten the legs of the big tall man, so they can all carry the coffin without it tipping."

"Well, we have the best doctor in Ireland among us tonight," said the girl with the curly black hair, "and his name is Brian O'Brannigan.

"I've never been a doctor in my life," said Brian O'Brannigan, "and I'll do anything except shorten the big, tall man's legs."

"You certainly will," said the girl, and before Brian O'Brannigan knew what was happening he was cutting a piece off the big man's legs and sticking the feet back on so he was just as short as the other three.

All four of the men carried the coffin to the graveyard. There was a big stone wall all around it, and one by one they climbed up over it and down into the graveyard. Brian O'Brannigan was the last man to start climbing up the wall. But just as he put his foot on a stone, a huge gust of wind came and swept him up into the sky and blew him this way and that way until all of a sudden he fell to the ground. And there he found himself sitting beside the well near the first big house he had visited at the beginning of the night. Brian took the bucket and went up to the house. The front door was open, and the old woman and the old man were sitting by the fire, and Brian walked over and sat between them.

"Now, Brian O'Brannigan," said the old man, "can you tell a story?"

"I can," said Brian O'Brannigan. "I am the man who has got a story to tell."

And Brian O'Brannigan told the old woman and the old man everything that had happened to him since he had gone to fill the bucket at the well. He told them about going to the wake and playing the fiddle and saying Mass and cutting the big, tall man's legs.

"Well, Brian O'Brannigan," said the old man, when Brian had finished, "wherever you go from now on, anytime anybody asks you to tell a story, tell them that one. You are the man who has got a story to tell."

The old woman got up and cooked supper and the three of them ate together. Then Brian O'Brannigan went to bed and fell fast asleep. And when he woke up the next morning, he was lying in Alt an Torr with his head resting on the two fine bundles of reeds. Brian O'Brannigan got up and went home, and he never cut another reed again.

How does Brian O'Brannigan discover how wonderful he really is? Through relationships with people who believe in him. (A little magic from the fairies helps the process along.) Emotional growth in our children works pretty much the same way. Much of childrearing happens by accident, like Brian O'Brannigan's adventures. Through the variety of daily interactions you have with your child—the hugs, the fantasy play, the time-outs, the walks—your child begins to "take you in," just as she takes in milk and food. You are not only the Mom or Dad who eats at the same dinner table and has a bedroom down the hall, but an "inner parent" she will carry around in her heart for a lifetime, just as Brian O'Brannigan's encounters turn him into a "man who has got a story to tell."

Family Time
"THE MAN WHO HAD NO STORY"

Take inventory and reclaim "connecting time" for your family. It's getting together with others that changes Brian O'Brannigan's life, and that's true for the rest of us, too. So often we spend more time with the television set and our to-do list than with the people in our lives. What does that teach our kids about how much they, or their souls, mean to us?

The stories in this book provide one new opportunity to bring family members together in a more satisfying way, but please don't stop there.

Sit down and go through your weekly routine, from Monday to Friday, and add up how much time you spend really *connecting* with your family. What do I mean by that? You know it when it happens. Setting rules, like "no electronic entertainment," doesn't really fit with the natural fluidity of life in a real family. Connecting time doesn't include aimlessly sitting in front of the TV together for hours on end, as though it were moving wallpaper; on the other hand, it *does* include making popcorn and gathering to watch a terrific film you know will touch everyone and start a conversation.

Connecting time might mean having a wonderful heart-to-heart talk with your child, but it can also be sharing something utterly ordinary, like watering the garden or choosing new kitchen wallpaper. It might mean coaching your child's soccer team, but it could also mean making room for an unstructured activity just the two of you enjoy, like reading aloud to each other from the newspaper.

Can you "reclaim" some time by eliminating a task or commitment that isn't essential?

Can you make time in unexpected ways, like waking up fifteen minutes earlier for a quiet breakfast with an early riser?

Can you clear away some space without planning anything, and leave room in the day for some spontaneous fun to develop?

Play "The Best Fiddler in Ireland," a cooperative game, for players age four and up, that helps players imagine themselves in new experiences. Players sit in a circle. One player stands in the middle and imagines a talent or an achievement or a challenge: for example, climbing Mount Everest, hitting a home run at Yankee Stadium, dancing with the American Ballet Theatre, eliminating world hunger, bringing home a great report card, winning a gold medal in the Olympics, learning to talk to the birds. (A player who chooses a situation that those in the circle consider inappropriate or nasty is automatically disqualified.) The player in the middle closes his eyes, points, and spins around three times until he points to a player in the circle. With the help of everybody else in the circle, that player acts out the middle player's imaginary achievement. If he is successful, he moves to the middle of the circle, and the next round starts. If he isn't, he's out of the game. If you make it all the way around the circle without losing any players, everybody wins.

Try a storytelling "duet" with your child. Ask your child to respond to a story you tell by sharing a story of his own, one he knows from a book or one he makes up himself. Or invite one child to choose a favorite story and tell it to the others. Share the telling in a way that suits your personal styles and the story itself. One of you can be the narrator, the other playing characters with funny voices. Or divide up the characters. Or just alternate the telling by switching off after each turn of the plot.

By encouraging your child to be your storytelling "partner," you help him learn to communicate thoughts and ideas in a coherent way, convey his feelings with expression and nuance, and know the joy of participating in a creative experience.

The Parent's Path
"THE MAN WHO HAD NO STORY"

Share stories with other families. Reading a book to yourself is a very different experience from sharing a story. A tale can better work its magic on you if you tell it to or hear it from another person, and something special happens between you in the sharing. Choose a story you and your child have enjoyed; tell it to a friend so that she can share it with her child. Ask her to return the favor with a story of her own. If your child enjoys a particular tale, encourage him to tell it to a friend. Maybe he'll come home with a story to tell.

Invite another family or two to your home for an evening of snacks and stories. People are welcome to share family lore, fairy tales, folktales, sacred stories, ballads, even jokes if they like. Keep it simple and fun.

Name the people who helped you become the person you are today. Spend some quiet time thinking of the family members, neighbors, teachers, and other mentors in your life.

What did they do or say that seemed to mean a great deal to you?

How did they help you discover something important about yourself?

Are there certain remarks that stand out because they helped you see your talents or personality in a new light? "You remind me of your grandmother, who was such a strong person," an aunt or uncle might have told you. Maybe a camp buddy observed, "You write a terrific letter."

Try to remember how you felt when you were in their presence. Write down the remark that meant so much (or draw it as a comic strip) and hang it on the bathroom mirror, the refrigerator, or your computer monitor.

This is an exercise that helps put you in touch with just how powerful words can be—an important reminder when you consider how easy it is to spend the day nagging (or thinking your child never hears a thing you say).

Think of the "little people" who have touched your life. Leprechauns and fairies are so hard to see that you might not believe they're really there. Sometimes the people who have helped us most are like that, too; we hardly realize how much they've meant to us. In our mobile age, we may only have known them briefly.

You can probably recall some people who have passed through your life but made a difference through a small act of kindness—an arm around your shoulder, a wink when you were under pressure, a casserole after a loss. It may be helpful to leaf through your family albums or old yearbooks to remember some of these "angels" in your life.

What are the wordless gifts you and the members of your family exchange today with one another and with others in your community?

Here's a list of "gifts" you can post on the refrigerator; encouraging everyone in the family to exchange these on a regular basis will help them learn to communicate appreciation and connection:

> kisses
> hugs
> smiles
> back rubs
> love notes
> a helping hand without asking
> breakfast in bed
> a cup of tea
> a comic on the bathroom mirror

Who were the "You'll never do it" people? This is an exercise to do when you have some quiet time. *Sit down in an uncluttered place, inhale and exhale for a few minutes, and let yourself hear from the people in your past who always seemed to have a critical word to offer, or a worry to express when what you needed was encouragement.*

"You'll never get an A."

"You're no good at math."

"No one in our family can sing."

Sometimes the negative statement was left unspoken, but you got the message loud and clear: You were the "bad" kid and your brother or sister was the "good" one (or the other way around). You made too much noise. You were a burden.

Looking back now, what do you wish you could say to your childhood self? How would you like to have comforted that younger part of who you are today? Be compassionate with yourself. Don't decide that by now you ought to have outgrown your childish feelings. Honor the child in you who recognizes that you deserved support and guidance. Doing so is important, because it will open your heart to what your own children need today.

Collect—and recollect—family stories. Family stories are central to our children's growth *not* because they recount the heroic deeds of the paragons of virtue on our family trees. Family lore lets a child know that life is not only about the "success stories" and violence they hear on the media. Rather it is about simple, enduring things, everyday surprises and struggles, disappointments, moments of love and grace.

Telling family stories helps children feel grounded in the human community past and present; they remind us that those who came before us faced struggles of their own, and that we are responsible to those who will follow us.

We don't really remember a family story; we *create* one. A story is something we construct, piece by piece, out of fragments of memory to which we give meaning. Because family stories are often retold by different people on different occasions (accompanied by the traditional sighs and rolled eyes and groans of "I heard that one already"), each retelling is an opportunity for teller and listeners to embroider the tale, make it more colorful, notice something new.

Get out the family album, and let the faces in the pictures talk to you. Don't limit yourself to stories with a moral "point"; you'll end up sounding preachy and you'll be eliminating a lot of good tales that will help your kids get to know you and yours as human beings. Start with a simple anecdote about the day your brother chased you with a flapping fish he'd caught in the lake near your house or the morning Rover followed your mother into church. Try to imagine the color of the sky that day and what you were wearing and how you felt.

Family stories aren't only about the distant past, of course. We add new ones every day. They grow with the help of memory jogged by ordinary household objects, special holidays, heirlooms, and children's questions. The story starters below can help you discover the tales in your life so that you can share them with your child.

Story Starters

I remember on the day you were born . . .
I remember when you used to be scared of the vacuum cleaner and one
    time . . .
When my grandmother was on the boat to America . . .
My aunt crocheted this afghan and gave it to me when . . .
One time I was in my grandfather's vegetable garden and . . .
One holiday your grandma brought out the turkey and your uncle
    said . . .
When I was a child my favorite story was . . .
On my first day of kindergarten . . .
My favorite game when I was growing up was . . .
When I was a child if you had a dollar you could buy . . .
The weirdest kid in my high school was . . .
I remember the day I met your father . . .
My first boss told me I'd never amount to anything, but . . .
When I was in London I met an old woman who . . .

You're becoming a storyteller. Your time with your child means more to you and him or her these days, because you're more honest with each other. You're not working so hard at child rearing. You're having more fun. Now let's turn to some of the particularly challenging aspects of growing up and see how shared storytelling can work its magic on them. The first of these areas is your child's motivation.

Five

Raising a Motivated Child

✦

A newborn, held for the first time to his mother's breast, hungrily sucks his first meal. A few weeks later he is lifting his heavy head to look around. Sometime around his first birthday he will take his first steps forward with no one to hold him steady. Kids start out knowing what they want and are determined to go for it. How can parents help them hold onto that early eagerness and turn it into a lifetime of enthusiasm, persistence in the face of setbacks, and confidence? Perhaps most important, how can we teach them to focus their energies on constructive, life-giving goals, instead of getting sidetracked by things—drinking, drugs, empty relationships—that we know will only hurt them? In this chapter you'll find three stories to help you nurture your child's motivation: "Making Everybody Happy" (Yiddish), "The Tale of the Three Wishes" (found in many traditions), and "Sir Gawain and the Lady" (English).

First let's talk about what goes wrong with kids' motivation. Too often parents and dispensers of parenting advice tackle these questions by talking in terms of *what a child wants, and whether those wants are good or bad.* They seek to point a child in the right direction by directing the *content* of his wants, as though keeping him motivated means filling him up with the right stuff. I'm talking about overly indulgent parents who see a child's wants as "basically good" and let kids stay up until all hours, for example, or who shower them with material things out of proportion to the household's finances. This often produces a child who feels so "special" that he not only has little respect for the wishes of others but also fails to develop the *perseverance* to work toward challenging goals. I'm talking about parents who value academic achievement trying to motivate a child to love learning by enrolling him in a nonstop round of educational programs. And I'm talking about parents who advocate "traditional family values" by sheltering kids and inculcating them (sometimes with moralistic stories) with abstract "higher" ideals—honesty, unselfishness, loyalty—in the hope of balancing out the values implicit in the popular media, where money, sex, and violence equal excitement and success.

All these approaches grow out of a mistaken belief that children's motivation is all about *what* they think and want. In building motivation, though, more important than the *content* of a child's wants, especially at early ages, is the *process* of recognizing his deepest wants and learning to steer by them. Once upon a time this was called "strength of character."

Delaying gratification. Real motivation comes not when parents habitually fulfill a child's wants, as overly indulgent parents do. When everything comes to a child with unrealistic ease, he has little to work toward. He lacks the experience of coping with the creative tension between what *he* wants and what *parents* want and expect.

In a famous study begun in the 1960s by psychologist Walter Mischel at a preschool on the Stanford University campus, an experimenter showed four-year-olds a marshmallow and offered them a choice. They could have the marshmallow right now, or wait until the experimenter ran an errand and then have *two* marshmallows as a treat. The study found that those four-year-olds who managed to wait (by covering their eyes so they wouldn't see the marshmallow, by trying to go to sleep, by playing games with their hands and feet) turned out dramatically different as adolescents from their peers who grabbed the marshmallow right away. The group who waited for the two marshmallows, researchers found, turned out more eager to take the initiative and plunge into projects, better able to cope with frustration, and less likely to fall apart under stress. It's important to keep in mind that these kids weren't pint-size ascetics who quietly gave up on the first marshmallow, or deprived themselves in order to get a pat on the head from an adult. They held out for what they wanted *most*.

In this chapter I'll show you how to focus less on the content of your child's wants and more on helping him work on the *process* of using his heart and mind to set goals, order his priorities, and stick to what he believes even in tough situations. Kids need to develop the decision-making skills, the moral-reasoning ability, and the connection with their inborn moral emotions, which can guide them all through life.

Real motivation develops from inside the child. It's the *motor* that powers all his actions. When we fuel the child's inner motor, and teach him to steer himself safe on the road, we help him grow up strong, motivated, and goal oriented. To adopt this approach takes a willingness to listen to a child, to be sensitive to his needs, and to help him learn to work toward them. It also means recognizing that parents play an important role by teaching him to respect *our* wants; with us he learns how to deal with real-life relationships with other people who have wants of their own.

Learning to focus. The story I've included here is one of the best illustrations I've ever come across of what goes wrong when we offer too much advice about the content of our own and our children's wants, instead of attending to the challenging, creative process that happens between parent and child, which fosters the development of real motivation. This Yiddish tale, "Making Everybody Happy," is a comic picture of how things can go wrong.

MAKING EVERYBODY HAPPY

A father and son were leading a camel through the desert. The sun was hot, and they walked slowly across the sand until they met a traveler. "Why are you both walking when you have a camel to carry you?" he asked.

And so the old man got up on the camel, and the son followed along behind on foot. The two of them traveled this way under the hot sun for many more miles, until they met another man. "How can a father treat his son this way?" asked the man. "Look at the boy's feet! They're covered with cuts and blisters. How can you force your son to walk?"

The father felt very ashamed. He got down off the camel and helped his son mount. The two of them continued along under the blazing sun, until they met another man, who exclaimed, "What a disgrace! Here's an old man walking under the hot sun, while his healthy young boy rides along comfortably sitting on a camel's back."

When the old man heard that, he got back up on the camel behind his son, and together they rode along under the blazing sun. But soon they met a fourth man. "How cruel!" the man cried. "Forcing that poor camel to carry two people on such a hot day! What a heartless way to treat an animal."

The father and son quickly dismounted and lifted the camel up onto their shoulders. "Someone will probably come along now and tell us carrying our camel is stupid," said the father with a sigh. "But there's nothing else to do. No matter how we try, we can't make everybody happy."

Each traveler the father and son meet in this story has an opinion about what they ought to be doing. Notice that the father and son themselves don't ever express a personal preference; we never learn whether they'd rather walk or ride. They only react to what others desire. In the end they choose to carry their camel on their shoulders, the hardest way, without a doubt, to cross the desert. Of course, we don't hear that they're hurrying to get anywhere in particular. This father and son have no destination, no goal. They're a perfect picture of lost motivation, and so they are easily led by everyone else's wants.

As the man says, we can't make everybody happy. But many of us grow up believing that that's what we were put on earth to do. We work so hard at pleasing everybody else that we lose track of our real wants, and with them go the courage and determination to achieve our goals. We don't keep kids motivated by telling kids what's good for them. (When was the last time *you* got excited about doing something because somebody else told you you ought to?) Just as physical exercise builds a child's fitness, learning to focus on what she *wants* develops a child's motivation. A child who learns to pursue her wants appropriately is a child who develops the strength to grow, to learn, to strive. Wanting goes along with growing. I don't think our children want too much. Too often we learn to want too *little*. We set aside the hunger for connection, the love of exploration, and the eagerness to grow that we all start out with, and we make do with shallow relationships and passive entertainment.

How Do Kids Lose Their Motivation?

How does family life so often teach us to carry our camel instead of riding it where we want to go? How do so many children grow up out of touch with their real wants? Let's take a look at how wanting develops through the earliest years of your child's life, and what you can do to help her stay motivated.

Infants. Even in the earliest days of life, when mother and child are so close it's hard to tell where each of you begins and ends, your baby is learning how the world around her responds to her wants. When a parent is attuned to a baby's signals, meeting her needs for food, sleep, and affection without being intrusive or overly depriving, an infant learns that she can "make things happen." Think of that wondrous moment when your infant latches onto the nipple and you see her suddenly relax, blissful from head to toe. She has got just want she wants. But it is not only the getting of milk or even the sucking that matters in the development of motivation. The milk is nourishment. The baby's *seeking* the breast or bottle, the *wanting* itself—like the preschooler who stretches hands high overhead to "touch" the sky—is essential to the growth of motivation. If her stomach needs milk, her soul needs the chance to feel hunger and to know that she can create the opportunity to satisfy it. (That is the reason "on-*demand* feeding" is so named, and why it's not the same as what one mother described to me as "walking around with the baby on your boob"). The British pediatrician and psychoanalyst Donald Winnicott, who had a special gift for seeing the world through a baby's eyes, described the process in fairy-tale language: the baby feels hungry, pictures the feeding in her mind, and *as if by magic* the nipple appears.

What does an infant learn when this process goes awry, when she is fed even though she turns away, when her cries are signaling a wish for cuddling or for a rest and she is regularly offered milk, or when there is a lack of response from caregivers? When a pattern like this develops, the baby loses touch with the deeply empowering awareness that she can get her wants satisfied. She is too small to be able to think about this in words like, "Mom is giving me food that I don't want." Instead, in the lack of *attunement* between her wants and a parent's response, she feels overwhelmed, or deprived. She learns that her wants do not matter, that they have little importance in the world around her, that life in the world of grown-ups is beyond her control.

Toddlers. Toddlerhood is the golden age of wanting, although to parents it usually feels considerably less than golden. A one- or two-year-old's wants are expressed loud and clear—and often. "Me want!" is one of the first complete sentences many parents hear. "Mine!" proclaims the toddler. Or simply, "No!" At this stage, parents walk a fine line between "giving in" too often and crushing a child's spirit by being too harsh. You probably find that your child seems to want exactly the opposite of whatever you suggest. You're going out; she wants to stay in. You're making peanut butter and jelly sandwiches; she's in the mood for tuna. "There must be a better way," you say to yourself. "Am I too stubborn? Or is *she* a difficult child?" The truth is that neither is likely to be the case.

Through all these struggles, your child is working on an important discovery, one that is central to the development of motivation. She is learning for the first time that her wants can be different from yours. During infancy, you often seemed magically attuned to her wants, but now she is beginning to recognize that there is a "you" and a "me," and that you and she are not part of each other. She is growing aware that she is a separate person with wants of her own. When she needs to insist on her independence, she's hard to get along with; her whole world seems to depend on the cutting of a sandwich. On the other hand, sometimes being so separate feels lonely and scary to her. When she's frightened about that, she can get clingy, looking for reassurance that she is still "your baby." She needs to know that you encourage her independence (and can tolerate some hard-to-understand wants) and offer support *when she wants it*. How can you tell when that is? Children express themselves differently. Some kids ask for help. Others insist, "I want to do it myself!" Still others dissolve in tears and need encouragement to ask for a helping hand.

There is some evidence that girls in particular may be discouraged and even mildly depressed during this period of developing independence, especially as they approach the age of three. One mother, a successful, self-made businesswoman, told me how annoyed she felt when her two-and-a-half-year-old daughter continually asked for help with things she'd long known how to do—picking up a ball, opening a door, finding favorite toys in the toy bin. "I've struggled to get where I am today. I want my daughter to grow up to be a strong and independent woman, not some wimp," the mother told me. "So I told her, 'You can do these things yourself. You're a powerful girl.'

" 'No, I'm not,' she said, and burst into tears. Boy, was I surprised. I realized she was only going to grow up strong and independent with my *help*."

This mother recognized that her own personal struggles had been coloring her understanding of her daughter's needs. As your child slowly hammers out a sense of herself as an independent agent, it's not always easy to tell whether difficulties are growing out of the situation or out of the issues you bring to the situation. That's especially true if you find yourself involved in frequent power struggles. Parents often wonder, "How do I know if I'm setting appropriate limits or just being mean?" One way is to make a mental check of your own wants. "If I let her have her way, am I going to feel angry or put upon because I'm sacrificing something really important to me? Or am I just trying to teach her a lesson?" If you're too harsh, you're in danger of stifling her developing self, of trying to impose your wants on her. If, on the other hand, you go along against your better judgment, giving in too easily or too often, you delude her into believing that you are still a magical extension of her wishes without wants of your own; she has no opportunity to develop her capacity to *tolerate* frustration—which is one way to describe perseverance. Check whether you're erring on the side of indulgence by asking yourself, "Am I agreeing to something I don't feel good about, just so I won't have to listen to her whining? Am I making a real choice here, or just letting her have her way?"

Help your toddler recognize that you are interested in her wants, although you don't necessarily go along with them. You don't always give in, because you have wants of your own. Even the most good-natured child has wants that are often unrealistic. Wouldn't it be great to buy the whole toy store? Why can't I be with Mom when she's busy with the new baby? Unfortunately, parents often scold children just for wanting things.

"You're always at my heels," it's tempting to tell a clingy toddler when you're trying to get things done, instead of, "I know you want us to be together, but I have to finish the dishes now. Later, we'll sit down and read a story." I can't count how often I've heard parents in toy stores silence a child with, "What's the matter with you? You don't want that toy!" Actually, the child *does* want the toy. That doesn't mean he can have it. Maybe parents don't want to spend the money, or can't. Maybe as an adult, you know it's poorly made junk. But to the child, it's bright and shiny, or it has a picture of a cartoon character on it, and he wants it. Telling him that his wants are bad, or denying them altogether, is shaming. If your child is to hold onto inner motivation, he needs *education*, not shaming. After all, much of the time a child is in the same position as a grown-up who is short on cash and staring at the Hawaii posters in a travel agency window in January. Of course he's eager for that junky toy; it's the shiniest thing he's ever seen in his life. How is he to know why he can't have it unless you offer an explanation?

Instead of getting caught in a power struggle or labeling him greedy, teach your child some constructive ways to deal with his wants. One is to *delay gratification*. "I know you want that light-up doll, but we came to the store to buy Justin a birthday present. When it's your birthday, maybe if you still want the doll you can ask for it."

You can help him *redirect his wanting in a more realistic way*. "Remember the doll Grandma gave you? That has sparkly buttons, too. When we get home, let's take it out of the toy bin."

Of you can begin to teach him to *make choices*. "This plastic doesn't look very strong. I'd like to help you use this gift certificate you got from Aunt Jane to get something you'll really have fun with. How about one of these other dolls?"

The first time I came across the story "Making Everybody Happy," I thought of another, very different tale of a man crossing a desert and meeting a stranger, and it offers a vivid metaphor for parents of toddlers. I have in mind the Biblical story of Jacob wrestling with the angel. After struggling with the angel with all his might, Jacob is worn out and gravely wounded. Yet he refuses to give in. "I will not let you go," he tells the angel, "unless you bless me." Jacob knows what he wants. Wanting is at the heart of our capacity to struggle, to meet our goals, to fight against all odds. It's a paradox that in order to be strong enough to be truly generous and loving, a child needs to learn to focus on his *own* wants and needs first. That's what your toddler is busy doing.

Preschoolers. By three or four, your child has developed something remarkable—the capacity for fantasy play. She can invent a world or even a universe, and use costumes, blocks, art supplies, sand, and her imagination to decorate and people it however she wishes. You can help by suppling materials (dress-up clothes, lengths of fabric, small figures, crayons, and glitter), and most of all by your willingness to play along. It's tempting at this stage to allow her to watch a great deal of television, but keep in mind that the opportunity to create her own worlds of fantasy is one of the most important steps in the development of motivation. Even if you offer her a merchandising toy, she is likely to rename it and make up stories about it that have little to do with what you expect. Don't be surprised to find her borrowing bits and pieces from the stories in this book, mixing up characters and places from different tales to her heart's desire. If you "correct" her, you interfere with her capacity to spin her own enchanted web of fantasy. That doesn't mean she'll come up with an enthralling new realm each time she plays. Sometimes you'll be puzzled or frustrated. What adult could remember the exotic names she gives all her small figures (Esmerelda, Melda, Tilda, Beautilda)? She is learning to have faith in unseen possibilities, to realize that someone who believes in something can make it happen, to imagine new and wonderful worlds. If you give up, or try to distract her with television, a snack, or something more "educational," you only teach her to give up on her wants. Can you enjoy your small visionary?

That doesn't mean, of course, that you don't have responsibilities and needs of your own. It's not always easy to stay connected to her fantasies when bill-paying and errands are pressing, but try to respect what's important to her. To a preschooler, there's no such thing as "just" pretend. If you're rushing to bring her out of the house and she has to put Snoopie-pie to bed, don't tell her "he's just a toy." Instead, suggest she sing him a shorter lullaby today, and offer to give him a quick good night pat on the head before his nap. Play along if you can: "Snoopie-pie looks really tired to me. I think he's going to conk out pretty quickly."

School-age children. By first or second grade, your child is eager to move into the wider world. He's interested in learning about your community, competing with peers, and bringing his considerable industriousness to all sorts of endeavors—collecting cards and stamps, playing team sports, learning new facts (the parts of a plant or his favorite players' batting averages). Sometimes, in an effort to "fit in with the gang," your child may neglect some interests that you suspect are still important to him. At this stage in order to stay motivated, he needs support from outside your household. If he seems to be setting aside a passion for chess or a talent for art, encourage him to connect with like-minded peers in an after-school class or club with a mentor he can look up to. Learning to pursue interests that really matter to him, even if they're not "cool," is an important preparation for the increased freedom and peer pressure he will face as an adolescent.

Offer encouragement, not praise. "You sure are smart!" "You have the nicest eyes!" "You're a terrific athlete!" What could be wrong with complimenting kids this way? Not a thing, if you do it from time to time. By holding up a mirror to your child's gifts and talents, you let him know that you've noticed, and you help him recognize how much he has to offer. But praise isn't a motivation builder that sticks. Because it addresses *results* and *performance*—how well your child has done at something in *your* eyes—rather than *effort* or an appreciation of what he can learn from his process, it doesn't encourage your child to try new things or to risk possible failure.

To build motivation, focus on your child's own initiative. "You sure worked hard on that paper." "You braided your hair all by yourself this morning? And you only have two hands?" "You passed the ball a lot today. Looks like you're learning teamwork."

We'll look at motivation in adolescents later on in this chapter. For now, let's move onto some activities that will help you and your child engage with the story "Making Everybody Happy."

Family Time
"MAKING EVERYBODY HAPPY"

Invite your preschooler to bring his imagination to the tale. What other advice would he give to the father and son? Should they get a wagon? sit under the camel or avoid the sun? make a parasol for the camel? By encouraging him to play with the story, you give him an opportunity to be an active part of the story and to share his fantasy with you.

Ask your school-age child to role-play the story with you. If he's the son, what would he like to tell you, the father, each time he changes his mind about who rides where? How would the son like to cross the desert?

Play "Camel Across the Desert." This is an independence building game for school-age kids and adults. Set up a starting point at one end of your home and a finish line on the same floor. Blindfold the first player. Set a timer or stopwatch. Now let the blindfolded player make his way toward the finish line guided by advice from others: "A little to the left." "Back up." "Slow down, you're near a chair." (The game is more fun if players offer bogus "clues"; then the blindfolded player needs to rely on his own instincts.) Players take turns wearing the blindfold. The player who reaches the finish line in the shortest period of time wins.

Talk about goals in your own lives. Is there something your child is working hard to accomplish right now, maybe drawing comic book heroes or doing cartwheels or blowing bubbles with gum? Even if the goal itself doesn't seem especially important to you, keep in mind that your support of his *efforts* is a way of reinforcing motivation: "You're really working hard at that." "I see improvement every day." "It's great the way you keep trying." "You must feel good about the way you're getting better." "I'm proud you're working so hard to make your goal."

It's also helpful for your child to know that you, too, work toward goals. Sometimes to a child, grown-ups seems to have been born big, like Paul Bunyan, and able to do everything. Let your child know that you're trying a recipe for the first time or aiming for a promotion or struggling to double your morning sit-ups. Don't be surprised to hear him or her "egg you on" as you report each day's progress, or cheer you up about setbacks.

The Parent's Path
"MAKING EVERYBODY HAPPY"

One of the biggest problems many parents have in nurturing kids' motivation is that we deny or ignore our own wants. Connecting with your own neglected wants helps you find the tricky, motivation-building balance between being appropriately firm and empathic. Here's an exercise to help you do that.

Find a quiet place in your home where you can be alone. Bring along a pencil and paper. Begin by inhaling and exhaling slowly and deeply for a few minutes.

Pay attention to the sensations in your belly—a knot, an emptiness, any dullness. Now focus on that spot in your belly and let into your awareness a particular want you've been setting aside for some time.

Maybe you've been wanting something that seems insignificant, like getting around to planting herb seeds in pots for the kitchen windowsill. Maybe it's one of those things you always mean to get around to, like setting a regular workout schedule or having lunch with a friend.

Or a big move may come to mind. Is it a long-dreamed-of career change? a return to school? a business start-up?

Write it down.

Now read it out loud. Ask yourself: What keeps me from getting what I want?

You're likely to begin answering this question by naming practical problems, such a time or money. But spend a few moments thinking of obstacles you may be putting in your own way. Do you recognize yourself in any of the following statements? If many of the statements that follow sound like the inner voices in your head, you probably spend a lot of time ignoring your wants. You may not even be aware of it if you're in the habit of numbing yourself with food, drink, overwork, or sleep. (That's why this is an especially helpful exercise to try when you find yourself reaching for your third brownie, postponing a vacation, or canceling lunch with a friend.) If you're out of touch with your own wants or you're uncomfortable with them, you probably have a hard time dealing with your child's appropriately. (Later in this chapter, you'll find exercises to help you turn that around.)

- *Other people come first.* I put other people's priorities ahead of my own. They're more demanding, their wants are more urgent, and they need it yesterday. I can always get around to doing what I want when I have time—next week or next month or next year. If I don't keep up with my schedule I'll have to hear criticism from my boss, my spouse, or myself.

- *My wants are silly.* In the scheme of things they're really not that important. People in other parts of the world are starving. I'm basically happy. I have nothing to complain about.
- *My job is more important.* I rush out of the office at the end of the day to pick up my kids at the sitter's. I took four sick days last month when it was really my child who had the flu. I'm so stressed out from kids, home, and work that I'm lucky I still have a job. Why push it?
- *My kids are more important.* They're only going to be young for a few more years. If I don't give to them at every opportunity they'll feel unloved. I remember how much I hated it when I was growing up with self-involved parents.
- *It's not nice to want.* Nice girls don't. It's bad to be selfish. My mother-in-law wouldn't approve. Do unto others. To be an enlightened, spiritual person is to be selfless.
- *I'd probably never get what I want, anyway.* I hardly ever do. People in my family don't do this kind of thing. I'm lucky I've come this far; why jinx it now?

Learning to make choices. The story that follows, "The Tale of the Three Wishes," is one of the world's most familiar, with a motif found in cultures all over the world. It's a comical reminder of just what happens to people who don't take their wants seriously enough. As you'll see, the fairy in the story doesn't grant the husband and wife just anything they wish; she sets a limit. They can have only the first three things they ask for. Choose carefully, she warns them; even in fairyland, focusing on what you want most is a sign of health. But in the tradition of folktales the mortals in this story learn the hard way.

✧　✧　✧

THE TALE OF THE THREE WISHES

Once a husband and wife sat by the fire and talked about their rich neighbors, who seemed to be the happiest people in the whole world. "If I had the power to have everything I wished for," said the wife, "I would be happier than anybody."

"Me, too," said the husband. "I wish we had a fairy who would grant me anything I'd wish for."

The words were hardly out of his mouth when a beautiful woman in a glistening dress appeared in the room. "I am a fairy," said the woman. "I am here to grant you the first three things you wish for." She smiled a radiant smile. "But be careful," she said. "Once you make three wishes, I will not grant you anything more." And then the fairy vanished.

The husband and wife sat and scratched their heads, trying to think of three wishes. "Well, if it were up to me," said the wife, "I would wish to be pretty, rich, and famous."

"But even if you were all those things," said the husband, "you could be sick and worried and die young. It would be much wiser to wish for health, happiness, and a long life."

"But what good is a long life if you're as poor as a church mouse?" said the wife. "That would only mean being miserable longer." She sighed. "I think the fairy should have promised to grant us a dozen wishes, because I can think of at least a dozen things I want."

The husband agreed. "But we only have three wishes, so let's think it over from now until morning, and choose the three things we most need," he said. "Then we can make our wishes."

"I'll think all night," said the wife. "But for now, let's warm ourselves by the fire. And as she stoked the fire, she said without thinking, "How nice it is to sit by the fire. I do wish we had a nice sausage to eat." And the words were hardly out of her mouth when down through the chimney dropped a black sausage.

The husband stared. "You and your sausage!" he said angrily. "What a wish! I wish the sausage would stick to the tip of your nose!"

And now the husband knew he had been even sillier than his wife, because as soon as he made this second wish, the sausage jumped up and stuck to the tip of her nose. No matter how hard she shook her head, there was no way to get it off.

"Oh, my!" said the wife. "What a wicked man you are for making a wish that the sausage would stick to my nose!"

The husband put his arm around her. "I did not mean to, my love," he said sadly. "But what can we do about it? Let us wish for great riches, and then we can make a gold case to hide the sausage."

"Nonsense!" said the wife. "I am certainly not going to walk around with this sausage hanging from my nose! *I* want to make a wish. And if you don't let me, I'll throw myself out the window this very minute."

She ran toward the window, but her husband called out, "No, no, my dear wife! The third wish is yours. Make a wish, any wish you like."

And in the wink of an eye the wife said, "I wish that this sausage would drop off my nose." And the sausage dropped with a thump.

The husband and wife stared at each other. "Well," said the wife, "maybe the fairy did us a favor. Who knows? We might have been more unhappy with riches than we are now. Let's stop making wishes, and just sit down by the fire and eat our sausage." The husband agreed, they ate happily, and never again did they worry about the things they had planned to wish for.

What a waste of wishes! The husband and wife don't give much thought to what they really want. The wife blurts out the first thing that comes to her mind. The husband's wish is nothing more than an angry taunt. And the third wish is used up on nothing more than undoing the pointless results of the two misspent wishes. I love sharing this story with kids because, for all its silliness, it's so true: Think carefully about what you want or you might end up with a sausage stuck to your nose.

Often we think of kids as greedy, as wanting everything they can get their little hands on. As time goes by, we fear that everything they want is damaging; after all, don't we have long experience of *ourselves* and our own inglorious wants—doughnuts, Scotch, homes we can't really afford? I don't think that's the problem. I don't think we or our children want too much. Too often, like the husband and wife in the story, we learn to want too *little*. Think of the infant who struggles to grasp a toy, to flip over, to climb the stairs, to reach for the stars. Why is it that before long he no longer seems to be reaching for the stars, but instead for the latest toy he sees advertised on television? Why do we so often set aside the hunger for connection, the love of exploration, and the eagerness to grow that we all start out with, and make do with shallow relationships and passive entertainment? Thinking about "impossible" wishes like the ones in this story is important, because our lives are shaped less by what we have than by what we want, what we dream of having.

Decision-making with wisdom. Let's take a closer look at the story. The husband and wife are working on three important skills related to motivation. Through all their bickering they're trying to take three steps in making a decision:

1. Recognizing the options available to them;
2. Realistically weighing the relative merits of each one;
3. Making a choice compatible with their personal values.

The husband and wife fail at all three steps, of course, by falling into traps familiar to most of us. Instead of *recognizing the options available*, the wife sighs and complains that the fairy ought to have offered a dozen wishes, because three just aren't enough. Her husband doesn't show any greater capacity for decision-making than she does. A model procrastinator, he just suggests postponing the choice until morning. Instead of seeing the real possibilities before them, they get mired in fantasy and negative thinking. They're like the two-year-old who says no to every question.

For the child who gets stuck in negative thinking, as for the woman in the story, the idea that options are limited is so enraging that he is likely to forget altogether about what he wants. After all, it wasn't that long ago that he was an infant whose caregivers magically *did* seem to grant his every wish. (No wonder Freud called the infant "His Majesty the Baby.")

Now that he can stand up and walk around, he notices that he's a very short person in a world full of tall people. How can he ever get anything that's important to him?

You can help your child hold onto motivation even through disappointment by helping him recognize that although his options are limited he has the *power to make choices*. By providing a structure that affords opportunities for him to get a least *some* of what he wants, you help him learn to make decisions and pursue realistic goals. Let's say your toddler is at the stage when she says "No" every time you ask her what she'd like to do. You may be tempted to decide that she's so stubborn you're going to stop asking, and just decide *for* her. Unfortunately, by doing that you deprive her of the chance to tolerate her frustration long enough to learn that even in a world of tall grown-ups, her wants matter. Instead, try offering simple either-or choices: "Do you want to go outside before or after lunch?" "Do you want to hear a story or a tape?"

The husband and wife don't manage to take the second step of *realistically weighing the merits of each option*, because they get caught up in a power struggle over whose point of view makes more sense. You're likely to recognize this pattern if you're the parent of an adolescent. At this stage the problem isn't that adolescents are not motivated; it's that what motivates them often diverges widely from what their parents consider worthwhile. "What are you going to do today?" you ask, and the answer is, "Nothing." That "nothing" is likely to mean hanging around the house and talking on the phone all afternoon, of course (assuming you're not willing to drive him to the mall). Coming down too hard on him by threatening to cut the telephone line, or perhaps grounding him for minor infractions, is only likely to dampen his spirits and further diminish his motivation. On the other hand, letting him have everything he wants (like the parents in many suburban towns who have keg parties for high school kids) leaves him without goals. Instead, recognize that at this stage your child is likely to be motivated by his social life. Chances are he has outgrown stamp collecting.

It's time to work together and do some hard negotiating. First, limit his phone time on school nights, perhaps half an hour to forty-five minutes. Then sit down together and work out some ways to combine his social interests with activities that will help him grow in other areas. Is there a new sport, instrument, or hobby he's interested in? Is he ready for

an after-school job, like tutoring or babysitting? Help him explore programs, groups, and classes offered in your area at school, at local community and arts centers, at the library or the gym, at your community
college. Make it clear that *whether* he starts a new activity isn't optional.
As a parent, you want him to have the benefits of learning something
new and making a commitment to it, and you're willing to pay for classes
or supplies as your budget allows. Do make it clear that he has the
freedom to decide *which* activity he'd like to choose, and he is responsible
for sticking with it for a period of time the two of you agree on in
advance (one semester-long session, for example, or a season or a school
year).

What about the third step in decision making, *considering personal
values?* How does a child learn to connect values and everyday action? In
the story, the husband and wife never get that far, of course. They opt for
damage control, settling for nothing more than getting the sausage off
the wife's nose and having it for dinner. A child learns this step not by
hearing abstract values or virtues but through ongoing discussion with
parents, teachers, and other role models. Stories help because they provide a nonthreatening takeoff point for talking about everyday issues in
our real lives. Through the exercises that follow, you'll have the opportunity to help your child begin to articulate his ideas of what's really important to him. You'll learn how to share your own point of view on these
subjects in ways your child will listen to—not by delivering sermons but
by talking with him regularly about how you reach decisions at home, at
work, and in your community.

Family Time
"THE TALE OF THE THREE WISHES"

If you were the husband or wife, what would you wish for? Invite children older than three to imagine what could be more lasting or more satisfying—a castle, children, or a kingdom of their own? You might bring
out some art supplies; some kids do their best imagining with crayons and
paper. Without getting too heavy-handed about it, help the child older
than seven think about each choice and understand its consequences. If
the husband and wife wished for a castle, for example, would they have

needed to wish for guards? Would they have needed to wish for grain in the fields to feed the inhabitants of the castle?

Ask your child to close her eyes and imagine a fairy visiting your home (or, with an older child, walking out of the TV set) to grant her the first three wishes she makes. What would the three wishes be? What would be good about each one? How would her life be changed?

Give a make-believe check for $100 to a school-age child or a preadolescent. Now bring out the mail-order catalogs and sales circulars and invite her to "spend" the money on toys, sporting goods, clothing, hobby items, and snacks. Sit down together and ask her to explain her choices. How could she make the money go further?

Play "You're the Mayor" with a preadolescent or an adolescent. Open the local section of the newspaper and make a list of problems— sanitation, schools, recreation, housing. How do you imagine solving them? Which would you tackle first? Don't worry about coming up with practical solutions. The idea is to open an ongoing dialogue. If you like, focus on one particular issue and track it in the paper for several months at a time. Help your child get ideas by reading what the politicians propose.

Talk over a big decision. Let's say your family is planning a vacation or a weekend outing. Whether you're choosing a destination or planning your itinerary, sit down together and do some brainstorming. What are each person's goals for the trip: relaxation, time together, looking at scenery, hiking, water sports, visits to museums or historic sites? (Many younger children need help focusing on goals and expressing them; be patient, and if they have trouble coming up with ideas, supply some choices you know they've enjoyed, or expressed interest in, in the past.)

The Parent's Path
"THE TALE OF THE THREE WISHES"

What if a fairy granted you three wishes today? What would they be? Do you wish for an uninterrupted night's sleep, a weekend away with your partner, a stronger body, a puppy?

Now spend a few minutes thinking about your wishes. Have you wished for something for yourself? Your child? The wider world? Most of us feel more comfortable about some wants than others. Being aware of the wants you're willing to indulge, and the ones you frown on, can help you recognize patterns you may have in responding to your child. A parent who wants to go back to school may have a hard time with a child who wishes out loud every Monday morning that school would end. A parent who wishes for world peace may get upset when, after a sibling battle, a child says he wishes a brother or sister had never been born.

If you're having a hard time coming up with three wishes, you may have to notice how you're "disguising" them. Sometimes we get so used to ignoring our own wants that we can only find them by taking a round-about route. Pay attention to which of your child's wants really "set you off." If you regularly deprive yourself of something you really enjoy—time for a favorite hobby, for example—you may find yourself resenting your child's playtime. Although I really enjoy taking long walks in the woods around my home, I tend to get wrapped up in work and household chores and neglect my time outdoors. I often realize what's happening when I get in the car and notice I'm particularly resentful of driving my kids to soccer practice.

Take the checkbook test. Open your checkbook. Take a look at where the money goes. Is your money going to pay for things you really want, or are you spending money without thinking? Are there any surprises? Focus on one area where you're spending more money than you realized. How could you pare down and put those funds into something that means more to you? If you have a lot of fixed expenses, reordering your priorities isn't easy without a major change in your way of life. Try setting aside ten dollars each week for something that you really value or enjoy—a museum visit, a paperback book, a couple of hours of baby-sitting so that you can spend time with your partner or a friend. By practicing setting priorities for yourself, you can help your child do the same.

What were your biggest childhood wishes? One way to understand our children's wants is to remember what it felt like to be a child with wants of our own. (That doesn't mean we always give them what they want, but it does help us be more empathic, especially if you tend to be tough on yourself.) Here is an exercise to help you recall wishes you may have forgotten. Find a quiet place indoors or out. Sit down and close your eyes, and inhale and exhale slowly for a few minutes.

Now try to recall some of the things you wanted most in childhood.

Maybe you remember a certain letter to Santa, when you asked for a special doll or toy.

What did you ask for on your birthday, when you blew out the candles on your cake and silently made a wish?

What did you most want when you were alone in your room, maybe writing in your diary or, at younger ages, talking with an imaginary friend?

Did you yearn for something for playtime, like a bicycle or a sled?

Maybe you wished for a room of your own, where you could have some privacy.

Your wishes may have focused on trouble in your household. Did you wish for a healthier parent or a kinder one? If your parents were separated or divorced, did you wish for a reconciliation between them? If your parents argued a great deal, did you wish they would get divorced?

Think back to your young adult years, before you became a parent. This is a helpful exercise for those days when you feel that your kids' wants are incredibly immature. As a parent, you're probably heading toward middle age, coming to terms with some of your own life's disappointments, maybe saying to yourself, "If only I'd known then what I know now." It's tempting to try to make sure your child doesn't make the same mistakes. Sometimes you can. Unfortunately, kids can't stay motivated unless we give them opportunities to want shallow things and make mistakes of their own. Taking a trip down memory lane to your *own* immature self can be a real eye-opener—and a reminder that we can try to pass on the benefits of what we know, but some lessons are only learned by experience.

In those days what did you dream your life would be?

What did you think you most wanted in life: interesting work, love, a family of your own, a nice place to live?

How have things turned out as you wished? Are there wishes you've given up in favor of better things? What were you wrong about? Are there unfulfilled wishes you still regret?

The importance of desire. The following story, "Gawain and the Lady," is one of the most complex tales in this book, but nonetheless fascinating for ages four to adult. In playing with the difficult relationship between wanting and gender in our culture, the story reflects all the graciousness and ancient truth of its Arthurian origins.

At any age, but particularly as a child reaches adolescence, it's not easy to stay in touch with authentic motivation, the "fire in the belly" that comes from inside, from the soul. In the teen years particularly, it's easy for kids to give up on what they want in an effort to gain acceptance from peers by having the "right" hairstyle and clothes. Parents often conclude that "the problem" is hormones, that a child's emerging sexuality is mostly a threat to balance and wholeness.

This story suggests a different way of thinking, one that's crucial for parents and kids struggling to find a meaningful approach to sexuality in a media culture that simultaneously blows it out of proportion and degrades it. The tale helps kids see how very important our sense of ourselves as sexual beings is. It points out the *centrality* of sexuality to human motivation, something Freud noted centuries later. And, as we'll see, it zeroes in on the distinction between seeing human beings (and particularly women) as sex objects and as "sexual subjects."

Sir Gawain and the Lady

Long ago, in the days of King Arthur and Queen Guinevere, there lived Sir Gawain, who was the king's nephew and the kindest and bravest knight in all England.

One year at Christmas the king and queen held court at Carlisle, in the north, and Sir Gawain was with them. On the day after Christmas the king went out riding alone in the forest. Soon he came to an icy lake with a dark and gloomy castle beside it. As the king gazed at the lake's mirrored surface, a knight appeared at the castle gate, carrying a heavy club. The king galloped toward him, calling out a challenge. But as he drew close to the knight, King Arthur saw that the man was a giant. He was as tall as two brave horsemen. His face was fierce. The giant looked down at the king, grabbed his sword and lance, and laughed.

"You are my prisoner," he said. "But since you are the

king, I shall offer you one chance at freedom. If, in one year's time, you can solve my riddle, I shall let you go."

"Riddle?" asked the king. "Tell me the riddle."

"The riddle is this: *What is it that every woman most desires?*" answered the giant. "Meet me in this very spot, unarmed, one year from today. If you do not have the answer, you will be my prisoner." And with another hearty laugh he turned his horse and rode back inside his gloomy castle.

King Arthur rode back through the forest, puzzling over the riddle and worrying. When he arrived at court, he told his knights all that had happened. When they heard that the king would be taken prisoner unless he answered the riddle, the knights began to search from one end of the kingdom to the other, asking everyone to solve it. In their journeys they heard many answers. "Sparkling jewels," said one man. "A rich husband," said another. "Satin gowns," said others. And when the knights brought back these answers to the king, somehow he knew that none of them was the right one.

A year passed, and according to his pledge King Arthur was returning to the castle beside the icy lake. He rode slowly, his spirits low.

Suddenly a voice cried out: "Why so sad, my lord Arthur, the king?" He looked up and saw a woman ahead of him, seated on a log. She had a twisted nose, skin covered with ugly spots, and hair tangled and matted, and the king thought she was the ugliest woman he had ever seen. "Why so sad, my lord Arthur, the king?" the ugly lady repeated.

The lady knows my name, thought the king in surprise. He worried that she might see in his face how ugly he found her. He was careful to look away as he answered, "I am sad because I must answer a riddle," he said, "or become the prisoner of a giant knight."

"What is the riddle?" asked the ugly lady.

"*What is it that every woman most desires?*"

The ugly lady laughed. "That's an easy one," she said.

The king's heart began to pound. "Tell me, my lady," he said, "and I shall grant you whatever favor you ask."

"*Anything* I ask, my lord?" asked the lady, and she smiled an ugly smile.

Arthur carefully looked away again as he answered, "Anything, lady."

"Then let me whisper the answer in your ear," said the lady, and the king got off his horse, listened, and then, still not looking at her face, thanked her and rode away.

Soon the king reached the icy lake, where he saw the giant riding toward him out of the gloomy castle. "Well, my lord king," said the giant with a laugh, "have you brought me the answer to my riddle?"

And the king told him the answer the ugly lady had whispered.

The giant was furious. "You have the answer! There is only one person who knew! My sister! *She* must have told you." And he turned his horse and rode off, his angry roaring echoing through the forest.

Now it was Arthur's turn to laugh. Back he rode to the log where the ugly lady still sat. "Tell me, my lord king," she asked, with her ugly smile, "was my answer the right one?"

"It was, my lady," replied the king. "And now, according to my word, I shall grant you whatever favor you ask."

"I ask you this," she said. "I ask that Gawain, the kindest and bravest knight in all England, shall become my husband."

The king stared in horror. "Lady, even though I be king, I cannot force Gawain to wed against his will."

"You gave me your word," said the ugly lady. "Now fetch him for me."

Arthur rode off through the forest and back to court, again with spirits low. When he arrived the whole court rejoiced to see him safe, and they crowded around asking which answer to the riddle had been the right one.

But the king sighed. "None of your answers was the right one," he said. And then he told them about the ugly lady and her answer and the favor she had asked in return.

"I will marry this lady, Uncle," said Gawain quietly, because he was not only the kindest and bravest knight in all

England, but a devoted nephew. "I will do this thing for your sake."

And the king told him about the lady's twisted nose, and her skin covered with ugly spots, and her matted, tangled hair, but Gawain insisted. "I choose to marry her," he said, "out of love for you." He rode off into the forest, where he found the ugly lady sitting on her log. So startled was he by her face that he could not say a word. She seemed even more hideous than his uncle had said. But then he remembered that he had given his word to the king. And so, carefully looking away from the lady's face, he bowed before her and asked, "Lady, will you be my wife?" And she accepted.

Gawain and the lady were married in the abbey at Carlisle. Everyone feasted and danced, and then the guests led Sir Gawain and the ugly lady to the bridal chamber and closed the door on them. Now the two of them were alone. The lady smiled at her husband, and he smiled back with a sigh. Thinking that she still looked hideous, he took her in his arms, closed his eyes, and kissed her.

As soon as Gawain opened his eyes, he found in his arms the most beautiful lady he had ever seen. Her eyes shone like jewels, her skin glowed, and her hair curled around her face. Gawain stared in astonishment.

"Now you have broken half of the spell," said the lady. "My stepmother cast a spell on me so that I would be hideously ugly until I could find a good husband. Now I must offer you a choice. Which would you have me, Gawain, that I were the ugly lady by day and lovely at night? Or lovely to look at by day and hideous at night in our chamber?"

Gawain was silent. "I would have you ugly by day and—" he began. "No. Fair by day and—no!" And he thought and thought about the choice in his mind, until finally he sighed. "I cannot make this choice for you, my dear wife," he said at last. "You must choose for yourself."

And now the lady smiled a radiant smile, and she took his hands in hers. "You have broken the whole of the evil spell," she said with joy. "From this day forth I shall always be, by day and by night, as you see me now. You have freely given the answer to the riddle my brother put to the king: *What is it that a woman most desires?* The answer is: The power to choose what she wants."

And from that day forth, Sir Gawain and the lovely lady lived together in great happiness.

The power to choose what we want is what really counts, for women and men alike. Having the freedom to want, to strive toward goals of our own, is what keeps us going. This story invites us into a mythical world where attention to one's own wants, and respect for those of others, is the basis for authentic relationship. (Keep in mind that in using the word *want* here, I'm speaking on the emotional level discussed in chapter 2, not about affective urges, like fright or surprise, but of wants as conscious goal-seeking, or motivation.) The tale turns the traditional fairy-tale kingdom on its head. Here is a realm founded not on the king's might but on the inhabitants' love for and responsibility toward one another. This king is not a despot, not even a benevolent one; the plot centers on his vulnerability, on his need to solve a riddle.

Does the lady's wish to marry Gawain sound like something out of an old Disney movie? Keep in mind that in story language, a marriage is a symbol of fulfillment for body and soul. For the lady to express her wish to marry Gawain is for her to claim her full dignity as a human being, to own her own desire.

Notice that the lady does not win Gawain by pleasing him. She wins him not because of her beauty but in fulfillment of a promise. Her wanting is honored. But hers is not a victory by force, like that of the giant's over the king. Although the king has made her a promise, he points out that he cannot *compel* Gawain to marry her. The marriage is not made until Gawain chooses to go through with it. Once they are married, it is Gawain's willingness to recognize the lady as the subject of her own life—to realize that *she* must be free to choose, that she is not an object of beauty for his pleasure—that frees her to claim her natural radiance. Only if we each hold onto the power to want can we relate to one another as whole human beings.

Why mothers' wants matter. "Gawain and the Lady" is an interesting and surprisingly contemporary commentary on the connection between wanting and gender. Why is the answer to the riddle a lifesaver for the king, and by implication for the whole kingdom? Why is it so important that the lady's wants be recognized? Too often women, caught up in societal expectations of what it means to be a "good mother" and in lifelong patterns of putting the needs of others ahead of our own, are willing to give up so much that is precious to us—time and space to relax, to pursue our own interests, to do the things we really enjoy—because we think that's the best thing for our kids. To sit on a log and tell a king what we want would make us feel ugly indeed; our culture equates loving motherhood with self-sacrifice. "I can't remember the last time I did anything just for *myself*," one mother told me recently, and it was the third time I'd heard that sentence spoken aloud by a woman in the past month.

What does a child learn from having a mother who "would do anything" for him or her, who not only honors his or her needs and wants, but regularly fulfills them in place of her own? If the child is a boy, he learns that a woman's wants are apparently less important than his own. He expects to be catered to. He only knows his mother as the "beautiful lady," the Good Mother. What he misses is a valuable opportunity to learn to recognize and respect the wants of another whole person, even when she is the Bad Mother who looks pretty ugly, and to negotiate with her. He learns that he comes first.

If the child is a girl, she learns by identification with her mother that women's wants don't matter. Whether she grows up believing mother is a "lady" or a "saint" or a "martyr" or, most recently, "superwoman," what she *doesn't* learn is that real women have desires of their own as well as the power to seek what they want and often get it. Unfortunately, this impression is frequently reinforced in the classroom, where recent studies show that teachers tend to call on girls less than boys. Ironically, girls, who tend to be less assertive than their male counterparts, may need to be *more* so in order to get what they want. For girls to achieve their full potential, they need to learn, by example and with coaching (see pages 88–89), how to decide on their goals and work toward them.

Wanting and peer pressure. "Sir Gawain and the Lady" is an especially helpful story to share with a preadolescent, because it helps parents and kids draw a connection between erotic desire and human wholeness. It's all too easy for kids this age to let their wants be dictated by peers and the fashion industry. If it's cool, they want it, and that applies to clothes, friends, and ways to have fun. Sadly, activities or playmates a child once enjoyed may fall by the wayside, labeled "dorky" or stupid. Many of the parents I meet worry that when kids' sexuality blossoms, they lose touch with who they really are. That goes double for parents of girls.

"Remembering what I was like at my daughter's age, I'd like to lock her up until she's thirty-five," one mother told me. "What else can I do?"

In our culture, where women's sexuality is distorted to focus on girls as *objects* of desire, and where girls learn to value themselves and their bodies for the capacity to conform to media ideals of what is appealing, "Sir Gawain and the Lady" offers a fresh perspective. The ugly lady in the story does not have the "privilege" of valuing the image others have of her. Because she is ugly, she is not the mere object of men's desire. She is free to know her own mind, to sit on a log and speak of her desire for a relationship with someone brave and kind. By holding fast to what she really wants, she is the *subject* of her own desires and the active agent in her own life.

It's helpful to try to understand an adolescent's focus on his or her sexuality as an expression not only of active hormones, but of a wish to be grown up. You have the life experience to help your teen find other healthy, life-giving ways to feel more adult.

Learning to stay in touch with their own wants, to respect those of others, and to work toward compromise are some of the most important things children learn in healthy families. But, as we've seen, it doesn't happen overnight. (Remember that Sir Gawain ended up with the beautiful lady because he was willing to respect the ugly one.) In the section below you'll find some ideas on how to help build awareness in your household.

Family Time
"SIR GAWAIN AND THE LADY"

How would your child answer the giant's riddle? What does he or she think women desire most? What answers does he or she think make sense in today's times?

Some kids find it easier to focus on a particular person's wants: What do they imagine Mommy desires most? How about a teacher? a neighbor? Grandma? This "game" is very revealing of your child's often uncanny insights into the people she knows best. For a young child, who is still egocentric, it helps her develop an awareness of others as real people with wants of their own.

Youngest kids enjoy answering a slightly different riddle: "What is it *kids* want most?" Whether your child mentions hugs or merchandising toys or ice cream, try to open a dialogue. What does he like about the answer he gave? Does he think he'd enjoy getting it every day? Would he ever get sick of it?

Invite your child to imagine being the ugly lady. What other favors might she have asked of the king? Would she have wanted a room at the castle or a log cabin in the forest or a prettier face? Why does your child think the lady chose to ask for Gawain as her husband? How would she feel waiting for Gawain to choose which time of day she would be lovely? Why does his answer break the spell? Because this is a long story, this activity and the one that follows can help a child connect with the characters and get a real sense of their struggles.

Encourage an older child to think of himself as Gawain. How would he feel if the lady were ugly by day and lovely by night or vice versa? What if the situation were reversed? Why does he finally tell the lady the choice is hers?

Explore stereotyping in the media. This is a project for you and your preadolescent, but it works best if you avoid making it too "formal." When you're reading the Sunday paper, point out a few photographs of people that catch your attention, perhaps ads for jeans, makeup, diet food (the trendier the better). What does he or she think of your selections? How real do these people look? Does he notice patterns in the body types, facial features, races, and ages of the people featured in ads?

Are there any ads that have caught his attention and he would like to show you?

If he seems interested, take the discussion a step further. Now (or at some other time, when you're walking the dog, doing the dishes, or shooting hoops in the driveway), bring up the subject again: Does he see any connection between what he's noticed in these ads and the way kids think about themselves and one another? How pressured do kids feel to look or act a certain way because of what they see in magazines and on TV? Do kids who might be nice to get to know but who don't have the "right look" get left out?

Your child is more likely to respond if you avoid asking too directly about his own feelings, but instead approach this as information gathering—Mom's or Dad's genuine interest in learning about his generation. Try not to get preachy; let your child come to his or her own conclusions, and drop it when he's had enough. If you don't push your child, this can be an effective way to open an ongoing dialogue about sexual stereotyping, and to suggest a broader perspective than he or she is likely to get from school friends.

Help turn your child's attention from the advertisements to the *articles* in the paper. Point out reports of people who achieve goals—signing treaties, rescuing others, graduating from college or high school, setting records for the high jump. In doing so, you reinforce at this tender age that the world values not only people who look a certain way but also those who pursue their own goals and dreams.

The Parent's Path
"SIR GAWAIN AND THE LADY"

How did adults respond to your childhood wants and wishes? Think back to holidays or times you went to a toy store or on outings with your parents, and try to remember what they were like when you wanted something. The things we wished for as children are important, because the *way* we learned to think about our wants stays with us for a lifetime, long after we have given up on Tiny Tears or a ten-speed. Chances are you respond to your own wants, and your child's, in much the same ways your parents did to yours.

How were gifts picked out in your family? Did you make a list before birthdays or holidays? If you expressed a wish to a parent or caregiver, what was the response? If you wanted something your parents couldn't or wouldn't give you, how did they handle it? Were you told you were selfish for wanting things?

Was there an unspoken rule about which kinds of wishes were appropriate in your family, and which ones weren't?

Did grown-ups make big promises and then "forget" to follow through?

Was it easier to get things, or food, from your parents than time or affection? Did you get more presents than you knew what to do with?

How are your childhood "wanting lessons" influencing you today? Are there certain wants you're still uncomfortable with? Do you stifle your real wants by compulsive shopping or overeating or overwork?

Were boys' or girls' desires treated differently in your childhood home? Even today, it's not unusual for parents to implicitly discourage a girl's interest in sports, learning, or achievement, or a boy's emotional expressiveness. If in your family the stereotyping was confirmed in your parents' behavior, and for example, your mother downplayed her assertiveness or your father was the "silent type," you may have struggled to express wants that were anything but traditional. "In my family the boys got to ride bikes and stay out in the neighborhood late, and the girls had to 'act like ladies' and do all the chores in the kitchen," one woman told me. "From the time I was seven until I went to high school, I was a tomboy. I kept my hair short, wore pants every day, and spent all my time after school following my brother up and down the street."

If that sounds familiar, chances are you've found ways to compensate. Nonetheless, it's not unusual for adults who have overcome sexual stereotyping to feel slightly disconnected or uncomfortable, as though they were made up of different parts that did not quite fit together, or as though they were cut off from part of themselves. "When I was in my twenties, people would tell me, 'You think like a man,' " another woman, who was highly successful in a predominantly male profession, recalled. "No one would talk like that today, but in some ways I think they were probably right. When I'm really going after something I want, I do act like the men I work with. Actually, I'm probably so abrasive I scare them. When I'm at home I love to bake pies and listen to the birds. I'm not sure how to get the two sides of me together."

Recognizing that inner "disconnect," which is often less dramatic than this woman's experience but no less uncomfortable, is an important first step toward reclaiming your wholeness. It's also extremely important in nurturing your child's motivation, because if a child grows up feeling that only certain parts of herself are valued or appropriate, it's hard to focus all her energy on meeting her goals. As you begin to accept and value the different parts of yourself, you can see and accept your child as a whole person.

A child whose autonomous motivation is honored and supported has a powerful engine to move forward through life. Now let's look at one of the feelings that can hold her back—fear—and see how stories can offer the frightened child wisdom and courage.

$\mathcal{S}ix$

Helping Your Child Face Fear

✦

As I write this, kids in my part of the country are wearing T-shirts embla-zoned with the bold trademark: "No Fear." It's an exhilarating mes-sage, isn't it? It expresses the adolescent idea that the wearer will try anything, that he's invincible, that he leads a charmed life. By adult-hood, though, most of us have learned there's more to it. The opposite of fear isn't fearlessness. It's courage. Fear is not the opposite of self-confidence, but an essential part of it. Fear is the human "early warning system," one of the basic, healthy instincts that equip our children to sur-vive safely in the world. Consider the way your body responds when you're frightened, clearly an inheritance from our earliest ancestors. Your brain triggers a rush of hormones that stop you in your tracks, alert you to pay attention, and send blood to your legs for a quick escape. If a child's motivation is the motor that powers him to act, fear is the alert that sig-nals danger. That's the message you'll find in "The Story of a Young Man Who Set Out to Learn What Fear Was" and "Molly Whuppie."

That's one reason it is not helpful to tell a frightened child, "Don't be scared. There's nothing to be afraid of." By doing that, you only teach him to mistrust or deny his instincts. His fear isn't the problem. It's the way he *reacts* to his fear—his anxiety, pressure, worry, nervousness, or stress—that's holding him back. Since the 1960s, when "test anxiety" was first studied, researchers have found that most students feel pressured before a test, but some seem to respond to the stress by actually doing better, while others are undone by it. And in his autobiography, *Music Is My Mistress*, Duke Ellington wrote about how he felt sitting down at the piano on stage: "Scared! You have to enjoy a little stage fright to get that extra punch."

Why some kids are more scared than others. Why does one person get an an "extra punch" when he's nervous and another give up? What distinguishes the kid who's eager to join all the kids on a new playground from the one who shyly leans against the fence until it's time to go home? Why does one child feel excited about going away to camp, packing his bags and looking forward to all the new activities he'll try, while another worries, "I won't make any friends"?

As you might guess, some of the difference is temperamental. Even infants show different responses to loud noises, changes of scenery, and physical sensations. As they grow, some kids seem to be outgoing, others naturally more timid. But there's a great deal of evidence that parents can help any child feel confident and hopeful, even in scary situations.

Help your child express fears appropriately. Everybody feels afraid sometimes. What a child whose parents often say "there's nothing to be scared of" learns is that *it's not okay to be afraid* in his or her family. Fear becomes something to be ashamed of, and instead of serving as a warning signal, it becomes a feeling to ignore or stifle. A naturally timid child who learns not to express fear is likely to avoid trying new things—diving into the pool, studying algebra—because they're too scary. (Churchill probably said it best when he told the English people, "We have nothing to fear but fear itself." An overstatement, but an eloquent expression of how fear can debilitate.)

On the other hand, the temperamentally braver child who ignores fear loses touch with the vulnerable part of himself where fear resides; he turns into a daredevil who finds it hard to empathize with others who are less outgoing, and blunts his body's inborn protection system. (More about this in the story that follows.)

I am not necessarily recommending encouraging kids to express fear as much or as often as possible. Sometimes parents who are sensitive to a child's scared feelings go overboard with "comfort" until it overwhelms a child, opening up the anxiety like a fire hydrant without a plug. Despite the Hollywood notion that "getting out the feeling" through dramatic catharsis is a helpful coping mechanism, that's not generally true when it comes to fear. The key to helping is to teach kids to use words to *contain* and *manage* fear, and to express that fear in ways that will help them gain the support they need. A child who hangs back from a new activity, or who sits and sobs in terror, is feeling isolated and helpless. If your child often says, "It's too scary" or "I can't do it," teach him or her some more empowering ways to express the feeling:

> I'm nervous about this.
> I haven't tried this before.
> This is a whole new experience for me.
> I'm worried.
> I'm working on this.
> I'm scared, but I think I can handle it.
> I'm afraid. Will you help me?

Offer support and encouragement. The word *courage* comes from the Latin *cor*, meaning "heart," a metaphorical way of describing mind and spirit. Courage doesn't come from ignoring fear but from bringing one's whole self to the challenge at hand. A child gains courage by relating heart to heart with an adult who offers caring and help. Recognize that your child's expression of fear is a way of calling on your strength and presence. With time and appropriate support from caring adults, his or her fears will ease.

Children's needs for support change at different ages, of course. In the earliest months of life, a frightened child needs *holding*. When your infant suddenly wails at the sound of a fire siren, and you pick up and soothe her, you're letting her know she is not all alone with her fear, that she can find comfort. Through her reassuring connection with someone strong, stable, and loving who can tolerate her fear, she learns to contain the feeling and, eventually, to soothe herself.

With an older child, holding is a little more complicated than a hug. Now that your child feels more separate from you and has more resources of her own, *holding means helping her feel sustained by your whole relationship*. One example of a time parents naturally learn to do this is when bringing a child to the doctor or dentist, when physical holding often isn't an option. When Laura, my nine-year-old, needed root canal work after a playground accident, I told her I'd sit near her feet throughout her dental visit and massage her legs. I invited her to make a short list of questions to ask the endodontist. This not only engaged her intelligence but also helped her to gain a sense of control and to build trust between herself and the dentist. I sat with her while she expressed her anger about the accident. And I held her while she cried about her fear of the dentist's drill.

It's important to keep in mind that holding doesn't mean passively listening to a child's feelings. The word *holding* implies limits; think of a bottle that holds a liquid. When you offer a hug to someone who's scared, you absorb some of the feelings and keep them from spilling out all over. Sometimes a child needs to talk. Sometimes, especially if you sense that expressing a fear is only making your child more upset, he or she needs *not* to talk, or to hear kind but firm words from you that are calming. If your child lets you know he doesn't want to discuss a fear, respect that. Or if you recognize that talking isn't helping, say so. I listened to Laura's feelings about her root canal work, but I also stopped her when I sensed she had expressed her fears enough and might be overwhelmed.

Keep in mind that often, and especially if your child is under four, you need to pay attention if your child's fear indicates a need for a change in her routine or in your approach to something that's going on in your own life. For example, in our culture we expect our children to achieve a great deal at increasingly early ages. If your nine-month-old regularly fusses during a water babies class, he may be letting you know it's not for him right now. A child who is a chronic worrier, whose fears get in the way of ordinary childhood activities—school, play dates, sleepovers (third-graders and up), learning to swim (over age eight), sleeping alone in bed by toddlerhood (except during thunderstorms, nightmares, and other unusual circumstances)—may benefit from professional help.

Be alert to sudden *changes* in your child's behavior, such as fear of being alone, fear of going to bed at night, fear of visiting a particular adult friend or relative. Any of these may be possible signs that your child is upset about something. Gently express your concern. If there are intense concerns in your home—problems in your marriage, money worries, the care of an older relative—keep in mind that your child is likely to respond intensely but indirectly. Don't expect him to tell you, "I'm worried about Dad's job." Until adolescence, he's more likely to express his concern by suddenly getting clingy or being afraid to sleep in the dark.

Avoid overprotecting. With any child, but especially with a timid or sensitive one, it's easy to fall into the trap of soothing a child, and removing causes of stress, instead of teaching him to cope with fear. Studies by the developmental psychologist Jerome Kagan at his Harvard University laboratory have found that, although there is an indication that some children are naturally more timid than others, parents who protected toddlers from everything upsetting seemed to end up with children who were more fearful. Those who believed it was important to help children learn to cope with life's struggles and overcome their fears produced more confident kids. The overprotective mothers picked up their infants and held them for long periods of time when they were upset. Rather than growing bolder with time, these timid children who were overprotected continued to shy away from novelty and be upset by challenges. Kagan concluded that when children are highly sensitive and mothers try to protect them from frustration and anxiety in hope of calming them, the kids ended up more fearful than they were in the first place.

One day I was visiting a county beach along the Hudson River, a few minutes away from my home. It was the second day this particular beach had been open to the public, after a multimillion-dollar cleanup to remove toxic waste and garbage and restore the riverfront to its natural scenic beauty. Strangers sitting on their blankets gazed at the mountains in the distance, and smiled at one another, exclaiming, "Isn't this great?" A local TV news team videotaped kids building sand castles, toddlers with pails and shovels, and families playing catch among the waves. Suddenly a girl who looked to be about twelve years old came running out of the water wailing. "I'm scared!" she cried to her mother. "That frightened me!" She sobbed and hiccuped for more than half an hour. As her mother clung to her and stroked her, I wondered what on earth could have possibly frightened this preadolescent so much, when finally I heard her gasp between sobs: "It scared me so much—when—that fish—swam near me." Although it was understandable that the child had been startled, her fear was way out of proportion to the reality of the situation, and by holding her without speaking for so long her mother, who thought, no doubt, that she was offering comfort, was only confirming that something terrifying and dangerous had happened.

How much more helpful it would have been if the mother had hugged the girl, shared her understanding in an understated way ("That must have been a surprise!" or "You must have had a fright"), and helped her daughter gain perspective on the event. She might have pointed out—as did most of the sunbathers nearby who, overhearing this exchange were grinning, "Wow, *fish!*"—that the fish's presence was a sign that the beach was clean and healthy for swimmers. She could have asked the girl to describe the fish and then ask the lifeguard what kind it might have been. She might have listened to the girl's *imaginary* fears—that the fish had been a man-eating shark, for example—and helped her distinguish these from reality. And instead of hovering over her on the beach blanket, she could have encouraged her to go back in the water. The child would have had a positive emotional lesson, not to mention a much happier day at the beach.

Help your child put fears into perspective. Because children under six tend to think in mental pictures and bodily sensations, the things and situations that scare them tend to loom like monsters or invisible forces. They're magical. In many cultures, including Europe through the 1850s, parents took advantage of young kids' impressionable natures by using "scaring" as a *discipline* technique. Maybe you can remember being threatened as a child with imaginary dangers left over from those days: "If you're not good, the bogeyman's gonna get you."

Obviously, adding to a young child's fears is no way to calm him down. Instead, by helping your child begin to grasp the concrete reality of a situation, you help trim it down to manageable dimensions (even though he can't really understand it the way an adult would). Here's an example. A two-year-old sat on a potty seat, and it started to slip out from under him. His dad caught him before he fell on the bathroom tile, but the little boy was scared, and the next time they suggested he use the seat he balked. After that his mother insisted they drop potty training completely. Although taking her child's fears seriously was important, by behaving as though they were real, she unfortunately only reinforced his magical fears that the potty would move out from under him of its own volition, or even attack him.

That doesn't mean she should have *forced* him back on the potty or told him his fears were silly. If instead she had reassuringly pointed out that Dad or Mom was right there to help him stay on the seat, tapped the potty to show how stable it was, put his teddy on the potty first or let the child hold him, and given him a chance to try it in a room where he would feel safer, she would have helped him overcome his fear.

Warning him not to wriggle around or jump up and down might have also been helpful. Kagan's studies also showed that protective mothers were more lenient and indirect in setting limits for their toddlers when they were doing something that might be harmful, whereas the mothers of toddlers who ended up learning to face challenges gave direct commands and set clear limits. Kagan's thesis is that the warning itself is a manageable dose of uncertainty, and when the parents who, though loving, did not rush to pick up and soothe the child constantly, he or she learned independently to manage the upset.

In helping your child get a more realistic understanding of a frightening situation, don't forget to talk about *time* in ways that are understandable. To children under eight, abstract notions like "It will only last half an hour" have little meaning. Remember how the summer or the afternoon or the evening seemed to last forever when you were a kid? That's how most experiences feel to a young child—endless. To help your child realize that a scary experience will not go on indefinitely, include it as part of a "list" of other events (preferably with one or more to forward to): "First, we're going to the doctor for your exam and vaccination, and then, we'll go to the supermarket, and then, we'll go home and have dinner, and then, you can watch a video."

With a child of school age or older, encourage him to use his cognitive abilities to understand a scary event or situation. When Laura needed her root canal work, she and I sat down together and looked over a brochure from the endodontist that contained drawings and a simple explanation of the procedure. Keep in mind that explanations help only insofar as your child is capable of understanding them, and that anxiety is bound to color her capacity to comprehend. One endodontist, who apparently had little experience with child patients, tried to explain the procedure to Laura. As he held up a battery of tools, including a dentist's drill, and said, "I'm going to use these and you're not going to experience very much discomfort," I could see Laura tremble in the chair. It was a whole different story when we visited another endodontist who knew how to talk to kids. Without actually showing Laura the drill, she casually "introduced" it at the appropriate time. "This is Mister Whistle," she said, and she let it whir in the air for a split second. "When you hear that sound, that's Mister Whistle cleaning out your tooth." Laura was still scared, but now she could understand the procedure and could see that the endodontist understood *her*.

Remind your child of scary things he's successfully faced in the past. There was the fear of the dark that seems silly to him now or a reluctance to go in the pool's deep end or the worry he'd never learn to write in cursive. Remind him of how he felt then. "Remember how you never thought you'd manage to hold a pencil and make all those squiggly lines? And now look how nicely you write." Let him know you're proud of the way he's growing. And help him recognize his own resources: "You were scared you couldn't, but you kept on trying and trying, and Mommy and Daddy told you you could do it, and after a lot of practice—and a little growing—you did it."

Model effective ways of coping with fear. Not surprisingly, the way parents respond to fear has a powerful effect on the way a child does. For example, there is evidence that parents who are afraid of animals, or excessively concerned with physical injury, tend to have children who develop the same fears and hold onto them into adulthood. By showing your child how you cope with things that you find frightening or stressful (giving a pitch at work, learning to work a new VCR, hiking in a new area), you offer important lessons in dealing with fear.

Pay attention in particular to the way *you* respond when your child tells you he's scared. If you are so anxious that you can't listen calmly, know that you may be sharing your own "anxiety overload" with your child. Parents do this in all different ways. Maybe you're a "venter," the type who "runs around like a chicken with its head cut off," inflicting your anxiety on everyone around you. Or you may be a "denier" if you tend to quickly squelch your own fears or your child's by "solving" it—"No big deal," "Piece of cake," or "It's not going to hurt"—so that you won't have to experience your own anxiety or listen to his worrying. (Unfortunately, that gives your child the impression that worrying isn't okay, and it shames him into believing that grown-ups aren't afraid of anything.) Because children pick up so much from their loved ones by intuition, even without saying a single word, you can communicate your terror or stress about a particular situation just by feeling overwhelmed and not dealing with it. If you find yourself either too expressive or with the dead calm of a surgeon, then you probably aren't coping effectively with your fear.

Let's go back one last time to Laura's root canal work, because I think my own struggle was typical of the ones most parents face in dealing with children's fear. This was a particularly nasty and painful procedure, on a chipped front tooth with an exposed nerve that proved nearly impossible to numb with Novocain. What mother wants to see her child in agony? At first I tried the stoic approach. It was essential to stay calm so I could be reassuring, I told myself. Unfortunately, once the endodontist explained that the procedure was likely to be painful, the only way I could manage that was to forceably maintain a calm expression on my face. I was calm, all right, but emotionally unavailable to a child who needed comfort. Before our second appointment I read up on the procedure, talked with the endodontist about pain management, cried a little in my husband's arms, and meditated for a while. By the time we returned to the endodontist's office, I had managed my anxiety enough to hold Laura's hand throughout the work—without flinching.

If you sense that you're so anxious that you can't really sustain your child, the best way to help him is to take some time for yourself. Talk to your partner or a good friend. If a problem feels overwhelming for an extended period, and especially if it's an ongoing situation like a serious illness in the family or marital discord, you may benefit from the help of a support group or counselor.

Teach your child to approach fear by problem-solving. On page 135 we'll look in detail at ways to help a child learn this. For now, keep in mind that one of the most important ways children learn problem-solving is through play. Adults often think of play as a time to escape from our worries, but for a child the pressure of anxiety often leads to re-enactment of scary situations in fantasy. A doll gets kidnapped on the way to school. A monster comes into the dollhouse when everyone's asleep. An evil knight challenges the good knight to a joust. Not only does this kind of play give a child opportunities to tolerate feeling fear and expressing it, thereby making it more manageable, but it is a chance for a child to experience himself in his imagination as someone resourceful enough to cope with fear.

Help your child explore fears by sharing stories. By sitting down with a child to share a story, you've created a safe, reassuring space in which her feelings can emerge, be expressed, and be held. Shared with a caring adult in a comfortable corner of home, a story promises a safe journey through a dark wood. Some of the most important work on the way stories help children cope with fear was written by the psychoanalyst

Bruno Bettelheim in *The Uses of Enchantment.* Through imaginative tales, children can "work on" fears they can't talk about in realistic terms, often because to think about them consciously or to discuss them aloud would be too direct.

Stories speak directly to children's fears, drawing as they do on vivid images. For young children, who have trouble expressing many of their fears in words, stories embody fears in the form of characters who can be talked about, and who act with courage, cleverness, and nimble feet. For example, a young child might find it terrifying to talk about her fear of being kidnapped. But reading about Red Riding Hood gives her an opportunity to vicariously experience that scenario in her mind—and have a hunter put an end to the wolf. A story makes fears concrete and manageable, and now they can be shared. By dramatizing fears as characters, you help your child feel understood. You let her know that she is not alone with her fears. It is that realization, and not the absence of fear, that helps a child grow up confident.

The importance of fear. The following is a comical tale, adapted from the Brothers Grimm, that depicts a boy so foolish he is without fear. Being fearless, he stumbles through a series of disasters that would terrify anyone else. Yet he senses that something is missing from his life. Is it common sense? emotional depth? awareness? All of these, I think. If you're like many parents I know, this tale is likely to strike you as outrageous and slightly inappropriate for kids, but children over the age of eight usually find it hilarious and exciting. And if we read them stories that are too tame, should we wonder why they lose interest and turn instead to television, superhero comics, and video games that connect with them more intensely?

✧　✧　✧

THE STORY OF A YOUNG MAN WHO SET OUT TO LEARN WHAT FEAR WAS

Once there were two brothers who lived with their father. The older brother was clever and the younger one was a fool.

Whenever the father wanted a chore to be done, he asked the older son. But there was one kind of chore the older brother wouldn't do. If the father tried to send him out on an errand late at night, asking him to walk through the village graveyard or anyplace very dark, the older brother refused, because he was afraid.

The younger brother had no fear. If he was sitting by the fire listening to people tell ghost stories and someone said, "Oh, that story sent chills up and down my spine," he had no idea what the person was talking about. "People are always saying, 'That sent chills up and down my spine,' " he would tell himself, bewildered. "Nothing sends chills up and down *my* spine. I just don't know how to get chills up and down my spine."

One day the father said to the younger brother, "Look how hard your older brother works. It's time for *you* to earn a living. You don't know how to do anything useful."

"There is one thing I'd like to learn," said the younger brother. "I want to learn how to get chills up and down my spine."

Well, the older brother laughed and laughed at that, and the father sighed and shrugged. "You'll learn how to get chills up and down your spine before long," he said. "But I don't think that will help you earn a living."

Soon the church sexton came by for a visit. "Do you know what my younger son asked me?" the father burst out. "I asked him to learn something useful so he could earn a living, and he wants to get chills up and down his spine."

"Hmmm," said the sexton. "If that's what he wants, why don't you just send him to me? I'll teach him how to get chills up and down his spine."

And so the sexton took the younger son into his house and told him it would be his job to go up into the bell tower every hour and ring the church bell. After a few days, the sexton woke up the boy at midnight, told him it was time to ring the bell, and slipped away and hid in the bell tower, with a white sheet over his head. "Now I'll teach you how to get chills up

and down your spine," said the sexton to himself. As soon as
the boy grasped the bell rope, the sexton jumped out in front
of him.

"Who's there?" asked the younger brother, but the figure in
white didn't answer. "Who's there?" he asked again, but the
figure stayed perfectly still, so that the boy would think he was
a ghost. "Who's there?" asked the boy again. "Answer me,
or I'll knock you down the stairs." And when the sexton didn't
answer, the boy knocked him down the stairs with all his
might, then went back to bed.

The sexton's wife was waiting and waiting, and when her
husband didn't come back to bed she went to the boy's room,
shook him awake, and asked, "Have you seen my husband?
He went up to the bell tower with you and he's not back."

"I haven't seen your husband," answered the younger
brother, "but there was someone standing on the stairs when I
was about to ring the bell, and when he wouldn't answer me I
knocked him down." The wife ran to the bell tower and found
her husband at the foot of the stairs with a broken leg. She
carried him back to their house and went straight to the young
man's father to tell him the whole story.

"Take that son of yours out of our house," she shouted.
"He's a fool!"

And so the father came to get his younger son, handed him
fifty crown pieces, and told him, "Get out of my sight! And
don't tell anyone who your father is. You're such a fool I'm
ashamed of you!"

And the younger brother nodded and said, "Yes, father,
whatever you wish."

Daylight came, and the boy was walking along the high
road, muttering to himself. "If only I could get chills up and
down my spine!" he said. "If only I could get chills up
and down my spine!"

Along came a traveler who heard his muttering and began
to walk alongside him. The two of them came to a town
square, where seven criminals had just been hanged. The

traveler pointed to them and told the boy, "Sit down under those people until morning, and you'll get chills up and down your spine!"

"I will," said the boy. "And if I learn to get chills up and down my spine, then I shall give you my fifty crown pieces. Come back here early tomorrow morning." Then the younger brother sat under the hanging corpses and waited. Before long he felt cold and decided to light a fire. "The people up there on that tree must be even colder than I am," he thought, and he climbed up, took them down, and arranged them around the fire. Soon their clothes were in flames, and the youth began to scold them: "If you don't get out of the way," he said, "I'm going to have to hang you back up." But the corpses didn't budge. The young man got so angry that one by one he hanged them again.

Next morning the traveler came back for his fifty crowns. "Well," he asked the young man, "have you learned to get chills up and down your spine?"

"How could I?" asked the young man, disgusted. "Those fools never moved an inch, and they were so lazy and stupid they let their clothes catch fire." The traveler realized he wasn't going to get his fifty crowns that day, and he continued on his way.

And the younger brother walked along the road, muttering, "If only I could get chills up and down my spine! If only I could get chills up and down my spine!" A messenger came along who heard him muttering and said, "Come with me and I'll help you get chills up and down your spine." And he took the young man to a haunted castle. "Keep watch here all alone for three nights, and you'll easily get chills up and down your spine," said the messenger. "Besides, the king has promised that any man who dares to do this can marry his beautiful daughter and have the secret treasure that is hidden inside the castle."

"That's easy," said the young man, and he went to the king and said, "I would like to keep watch in the haunted castle for three nights."

The king agreed and told the young man, "You can bring three things, none of them alive, with you into the castle."

"I would like a fire, a lathe, and a carving bench with the knife attached," said the young man. The king had these three things brought to the castle, and the young man went into one of the rooms and lit a fire. "Oh, if only I could get chills up and down my spine," he said with a sigh, "but I don't think I'm going to get them here, either." At midnight he heard two voices howling in one corner of the room. "You fools!" he cried. "If you feel cold, why don't you come and sit by the fire and warm yourselves?"

Two black cats with blazing eyes sprang forward and asked, "Want to play cards?"

"Fine," said the young man, "but first give me a look at your paws." And as they stretched out their paws, he lifted the cats onto the carving bench. He cut the paws off with the knife and tossed them into the castle moat. Then he went back to his room and was about to sit back down by the fire when a stream of howling black cats and dogs came in through the door. The young man watched them calmly for a few minutes. When he got tired of that, he chased them with his carving knife until he had killed every last one and thrown them all into the moat.

Now the young man went back to sit by the fire and warm himself. Soon he decided to go to sleep. He went to the bed in the corner of the room and lay down. Just as he closed his eyes, the bed began to fly around the room. "Well, this is interesting," said the young man. "But it would be better if it were a little faster." Now the bed was flying all over the castle, up and down the stairs as fast as a coach, until it over-turned and landed with a loud thud on top of the young man. Out he crept from underneath, tossed aside the blankets and pillows, and shrugged. "I guess it's someone else's turn now," he said.

Next morning the king came and was amazed to find the young man alive. "That was easy," the young man told him, "and I'm sure I shall get through the next two nights as well. But I still have not learned to get chills up and down my spine."

The second night the younger brother sat down by the fire and muttered, "If only I could get chills up and down my spine! If only I could get chills up and down my spine!" At midnight he heard loud screaming, and suddenly a man's legs dropped down the chimney and fell at the young man's feet. "Well now," said the young man, looking at the legs, "this isn't enough. We need another half of a man down here." Then there were more screams, and the other half fell down. The young man got up to put a log on the fire, and when he turned around he saw that the two halves had joined together. Now there was a horribly ugly man sitting right in his seat. "That's my seat," the young man said as he shoved the ugly man away, and he sat back down.

Just then more men started dropping down the chimney, and they found nine skeleton legs and two skulls in the corner and began to bowl. "Can I play?" asked the young man, and they nodded yes. "These balls aren't round enough for bowling," he complained, and he picked up the two skulls, put them on his lathe, and turned them until they were perfectly round. He bowled with the men until midnight, when everything disappeared, and then he lay down and slept till morning, when the king came.

"How was your second night?" asked the king.

"I bowled," said the young man with a sigh, "but I still haven't learned to get chills up and down my spine."

On the third night the young man sat down by the fire again and said, "If only I could learn to get chills up and down my spine!" In walked six men carrying a coffin. When they set the coffin down on the ground, the younger brother looked inside and saw a dead man. "Let me warm you up a bit," he said. And he lifted out the dead man, sat him on his knee by the fire, and rubbed his arms. But the dead man didn't warm up, so the young man put him in the bed and lay down beside him, and before long the dead man grew warm and sat up, growling, "Now I'm going to strangle you!"

"Is that all the thanks I get for warming you up?" asked the young man. "Back you go into your coffin." And he lifted up the dead man, stuffed him back in, and shut the lid. The six men came back and carried out the coffin. And the young man sighed. "Even if I spend the rest of my life in this castle," he said, "I shall never learn to get chills down my spine."

Just then an old man with a white beard appeared in the doorway. "Now you will learn to get chills up and down your spine," he said. "It's time for you to die!"

"First you'll have to catch me," said the young man, "and I'm stronger than you, and I can run faster."

"We'll see about that," said the old man, and he led the young man to the castle forge, took an axe, and with a mightly blow drove an anvil into the earth.

"I can do better than that," said the young man, and he seized the axe, struck the anvil, and split it. Then he grabbed the old man's beard and stuck the axe into it until the old man begged him to let go, promising him enormous riches. The young man let him go, and the old man brought him to the castle cellar and showed him three chests filled with shining gold. Just then the clock struck twelve and the old man vanished, leaving the young man standing all alone in the dark.

Next morning the king came. "Have you learned to get chills up and down your spine yet?" he asked.

"No," answered the young man. "Some men brought in a body, and there was an old bearded man who showed me three chests full of gold, but nobody has taught me how to get chills up and down my spine."

"You have been here for three nights and freed the castle from its curse," said the king. "And now you shall have my daughter's hand in marriage."

"That's very nice," said the young man, "but I still don't know how to get chills up and down my spine."

The young man received the chests of gold, and he married

the king's daughter and loved her dearly. But still he kept on saying, "Oh, if only I could get chills up and down my spine! Oh, if only I could get chills up and down my spine!" And one night his wife and her maid went out to the stream that flowed through the garden, and they filled a pail with minnows. That night, when the young man was fast asleep, his wife pulled off his clothes and poured the pail full of minnows on him, and the little fish swam and flapped all over his whole body. And the young man woke up, crying, "Oh! I have chills up and down my spine! I have chills up and down my spine! Now I know what it is to have chills up and down my spine!"

In this story the younger brother has no fear, or at least he doesn't feel any. Of course, he doesn't feel much of anything else, either, like anger when his father sends him away or joy when he hears he is to marry the king's daughter. Seeing the criminals who have been hanged, he doesn't recognize death or evil. As this tale points out, to have no fear is to lack awareness. It is to have lost touch with instincts, with "gut feelings." It is to be invulnerable to fear and to every emotion we recognize as human. That's why the younger brother is a fool.

These things are important to keep in mind when you find yourself worrying that your child's fears might hold her back in life. She needs to learn to cope with fear—no doubt about it—to share it with a friend, to tolerate it in herself, to find the courage and cleverness to face it and triumph, but never to conquer it altogether. She needs to develop a healthy relationship to her fear, not ignore it. Fear is a sign of being alive, of having your eyes open to potential danger, of being vulnerable enough to ask for help when you need it.

To hold onto fear as a helpful part of their emotional "tool kit" isn't something kids can do alone. The two brothers in the story are an interesting pair who illustrate this very clearly. No one seems to be willing to walk alongside them on those nighttime visits through the scary graveyard. And so the hardworking older brother, aware of the fact that death lurks there and unwilling to face the fears that loom large in his mind, refuses to go. He retreats from life. The younger brother, on the other hand, blithely walks anywhere at all. A child who lacks the support and encouragement to conquer his fears often grows up like the older brother, afraid to venture beyond the familiar, to take a risk. But a child who, like the younger brother, is exposed to overwhelming stimulation—from the media, the schoolyard, and, all too often, home—learns to stop feeling anything at all.

In the story the younger brother doesn't experience fear until he has someone who loves him, his new bride. Safe with her, he can let his defenses down (symbolized by her pulling off his clothes). Likewise, a child needs to face fear in the company of someone who really cares, someone who can listen and help him or her hold onto the feeling. And even then, he needs to experience his fears in doses he can tolerate without being overwhelmed, maybe as gently as a pail of flapping minnows. Those "doses" vary at each stage of childhood, because your child's fears at each age reflect his or her way of relating to you and the world.

Fear and Your Child's Growth

Infants. Your infant can travel only when carried; no wonder she startles when she begins to fall. At birth she is the most helpless animal on earth; it's not surprising that loud noises make her cry. Held in your arms, she feels at one with you and with life; of course she cries when you put her down. As the two of you get to know each other, you come to understand what helps her feel soothed and held. Some babies are reassured by the safety of snuggling in a front carrier, others by the vibration of a stroller's wheels, others by a ride in the car. Still others are so sensitive that they seem to get *more* upset by stroking and touching; these vulnerable souls are often calmed by some quiet time alone on a rug, face down in your lap, or in a crib.

But keep in mind that even in these early months, responding to your child's fears does not necessarily mean quieting her. By nine months when you're ready to leave her with a strange caregiver, she is likely to sob or howl as you kiss her good-bye. Although it's wise to avoid changing sitters unnecessarily at this stage, sometimes it's unavoidable. Even now you cannot soothe or eliminate all her fears. With your eyes and voice and caresses, you are showing her that you are a sustaining presence, someone she can rely on for comfort and support through transitions.

By eight or nine months your baby enjoys the familiar faces, voices, and smells of the people who love her best; it's easy to understand why she's upset when strangers get too close. Your baby has learned to respond not only to outside stimuli, such as a separation from you or a honking horn, but to feelings and understandings of her own. Now she can recognize scary things that are *about* to happen—Mommy taking out the keys to show she's leaving in the car or Daddy filling the bath—and feel the fear ahead of time. That makes it hard for you now, but it's an important development for your baby; she's beginning to be able to use fear as a warning signal.

Toddlers. Newly able to explore the world around them, toddlers are frightened by the strange sights and commotion they encounter in their travels—the vacuum cleaner, the clown at a birthday party, the neighbor's toilet. At this stage children need to know that they can gain some measure of *control* in situations that seem overwhelming.

Help your toddler cope with fear by:

- Offering opportunities for children to adapt gradually to scary situations. A party clown may be less scary if the kids watch him put on his face paint, wig, and red nose. But don't be surprised if your child watches the makeup process calmly from start to finish and bursts into tears the moment the clown smiles.
- Encouraging children to be active participants. The vacuum cleaner is less frightening if your child has the chance to turn the switch on and off, or run it across the carpet.

Preschoolers. A preschooler is afraid of things that aren't there— ghosts, monsters under the bed, nightmares that seem real. Because he can't always tell fantasy from reality, imaginary creatures and stories come alive in his head, the stuff of delightful fantasy play—and of very real fear. Snow White lives in the doll corner of her room, and the evil witch sleeps in the closet.

Telling your preschooler that it's not real is occasionally helpful when she is frightened of something imaginary, but often this is ineffective. It *feels* real to her. As at any age, your child needs to know you're willing to listen, and that you care about her fears even if you don't share them. *Playing along with the fantasy is one way you can help transform it.* Here are some simple ways to do that:

Tell your child that he or she has magical protection from fearful fantasies because you're there—along with the fairies, guardian angels, leprechauns, and her imaginary friend.

Leave the light on.

Play soothing music that keeps monsters away.

Hang a mirror beside your child's bed to "reflect" a monster back to its faraway home.

Make up a sorcerer's spell, with plenty of magic words, to keep away bad guys ("Sweep, sweep, enchanted broom, sweep the monsters from this room!").

Give your child traditional Guatemalan "worry dolls," so she can whisper her worries to them and then hide them away—along with her fears—under her pillow at night.

"Supply" your child who gets nightmares with a pleasant dream for the night, or at least the beginning of a dream scenario. "Once there was a girl named Rachel who went for a walk in a beautiful flower garden and met a kind fairy," you might begin, using your child's name and a favorite imaginary or special place.

School-age children. By school age, as your child gains a stronger capacity to distinguish reality from fantasy and focuses increasingly on life outside your home, her fears are more likely to include events in the wider world—divorce, kidnapping, death, street violence, earthquakes. You can help your child feel more powerful by building on her increasingly sophisticated capacity to learn. Be prepared to answer questions truthfully but simply, and point out how grown-ups are working to solve the problems that frighten her. If she's afraid of thunderstorms, for example, teach her basic safety rules. Together you can research the weather, not only how storms happen but how the National Weather Service works to protect life and property from storm damage.

If you're tempted to avoid talking about the news because you don't want to upset your child, keep in mind that during a crisis it is often less upsetting for a child to learn the facts by reading the paper with you rather than seeing violence or destruction in full color on the television screen or hearing about it secondhand on the school bus. If you donate money or clothing to a rescue effort, enlist your child's participation; have him lick the stamp when you send a donation or help deliver clothing to a collection bin.

Stories of your own personal struggles and the ways you and others in your family and community have worked to solve some of the problems that frighten your child will mean a great deal to him at this age; to jog your memory, see Parent's Path on page 126.

Adolescents. An adolescent's fears often center on his or her fragile sense of self. He worries about rejection and humiliation, which he is likely to describe as "looking like a dork" or "looking stupid in front of everybody." He needs friends to share these fears with, to help him put them in proportion, to let him know that even "everybody" feels insecure now and them.

At the same time, your adolescent worries that he won't live up to your expectations of him, that he won't be able to make it in the wider world. As he looks toward the future, he will benefit from opportunities to make connections, try new things, and grow more confident of his abilities.

As if that weren't complicated enough, sometimes your adolescent seems to be an awful lot like the younger brother in the story on page 115. As a parent entering a new phase of independence, with all its dangers, *you* may be feeling more fearful than you have since he was a baby. He may seem fearless or just amazingly "out of it," but he is likely to need reminders from you about the importance of caring for himself.

As always, even though he may *act* as though he thinks you have nothing worthwhile to say, he very much needs your listening presence. He needs to know that you take him seriously, that you care about his fears and respect his efforts to deal with them, whether that means he's combing his hair in the "right" style twenty-eight times before school or refusing to wear the outfit you bought him that makes him "look like a freak." Don't pump him for information, but let him know you're available to talk about things that may be on his mind. Sharing stories and talking about the movies and books that interest him is often a non-threatening way to connect.

Family Time
"THE STORY OF A YOUNG MAN WHO SET OUT TO
LEARN WHAT FEAR WAS"

Make your own bag of scary stuff. Re-create the minnows scene with a traditional Halloween party trick. Collect items with interesting, slimy textures—cooked spaghetti, skinned grapes, gelatin—and put them in plastic storage bags or small containers. Make up names for what they "really" are—monster brains, eyeballs, slime. Stick your fingers in and imagine. Now invite other people to close their eyes and reach in. This is most fun in dark places. This is a memorable way for your child to play at experiencing a scare with you. Like sharing a story, this is an important part of learning to tolerate fear. A kid who might be easily upset when somebody *else* plays a trick like this is often more comfortable doing it himself. If your child is really reluctant to participate, don't force the issue. Maybe he's willing to try one particular item, like the skinned grapes. Maybe he wants to make up his own ideas. Or maybe he needs to let you know when he's ready.

One eight-year-old shied away from anything "spooky" until one Halloween she came to a neighbor's house that was bedecked with ghosts, monsters, and a "live" corpse. The "witch" who answered the door told her that to get a bag of candy she'd have to reach into a bag of monster eyes. She reached in so many times that her parents were hard pressed to get her to move on to the next house.

Name your fears. Invite your school-age child to name all the things that give him chills up and down his spine—a particularly scary movie, a standardized school test, the first day in a new camp. Now together reminisce about some of the things he *used* to be scared of—the toilet flushing, the bathtub drain, the ghosts in the closet. (If he seems embarrassed, don't push it.) Talk to him about the things you used to be scared of when you were a kid (see page 126 for memory jogging), and how you got over it. Turning our own old fears into short stories is a way to open up communication about fear, and to begin to recognize how far we've come.

Although venting your anxieties today is likely to overwhelm your child, talking in a natural, low-key way about everyday worries—the big meeting coming up at work, the slippery roads on a snowy day, an audit by the IRS—helps your child identify with you as a real person who grapples with the same kinds of feelings he has. By pointing out the ways you deal with your fears—planning ahead, imagining a nerve-wracking situation ahead of time, being cautious—you give him a real-life model.

The Parent's Path
"THE STORY OF A YOUNG MAN WHO SET OUT TO LEARN WHAT FEAR WAS"

What are you most afraid of? If someone woke you up in the middle of the night and asked you what frightened you, how would you answer? If you have trouble coming up with something, breathe in and out slowly and deeply for a few minutes and imagine a knot in your stomach. What's in the knot? Let your mind wander to events or occasions when you felt anxious or afraid. What are the worries that make the knot tighten? Read some of the suggestions below out loud to yourself and pay attention to what your stomach tells you:

Money. Bills. Mortgage. Taxes. College.
Deadlines at work. The economy. Fiscal restraint. Layoffs.
My partner. Criticism. Judgment. Illness.
My child . . . feeling lonely or sad. Not comfortable talking to me.
   Sick or hurt.
My child's future. His career. Sexuality. Alcohol and drugs.
Violence. Street crime. Mugging. Rape. Murder.
Airplanes. Earthquakes. Hurricanes. Tornadoes.
My body . . . sagging. Weakening. Graying. Wrinkling. Illness.
Time passing. Getting older. Parents aging. Kids growing up and
   leaving.
One day it's time for me to die.

Going through this exercise may be hard on your stomach, but it's a vivid way to recognize the role of fear in our lives. Our fears reflect the powerful forces around us, and the things we hold most dear. It would be hard for any adult alive in this country today to read through this list without feeling some fear. If you didn't, you'd be like the younger brother in the story, out of touch with reality. Keep that in mind when you're tempted to think of your child's fears as silly.

Notice the way your body responds as your fears come to mind.

Is your heart beating faster? Are you tearful? Are you trembling? Is your mind racing? If your feelings are overwhelming, you may have a hard time coping with your own anxiety. Could it be that you find it difficult to soothe and comfort your child? Pay particular attention if your child seems to be more fearful than his playmates or often seems to be trying to comfort or soothe you.

On the other hand, you may notice very little physical response to the words above. Maybe you're in the habit of trying to be low key. Or maybe you don't feel much at all. Discovering that you have learned to disconnect from your instinctual fear is important, because chances are you have a pretty hard time tolerating or empathizing with your sometimes scared little kid.

Let's continue to explore how you got the way you are today, and how it may be influencing your approach to your child's fears, by doing the exercises below.

What were your biggest childhood fears? Try to remember the things that really scared you when you were a kid. What was it like to lie in bed at night and try to fall asleep? Do you remember an especially dark, scary corner of your room where the shapes of objects made them look mysterious and alive? Who or what did you imagine was lurking there? What could they do to you?

Was there a certain house in the neighborhood that all the kids "knew" was haunted? What did it look like? Were there dark branches hanging over the windows? Who was supposed to live in the house? What would happen if you rang the doorbell? Was anyone rumored to have disappeared there?

Did a particular relative give you the willies? What made him or her so scary? Was it a certain way of chewing food at holiday dinners? a bizarre style of clothing? a gloomy apartment? a weird laugh?

Were you nervous in the ocean or worried your bathing suit would fall off? Did you have a particular recurring nightmare that sent you crying to your parents' room?

Did you dread getting into trouble with parents or teachers? What happened if you got caught breaking a rule? What was it like staying after school, or having to sit in a corner?

Recalling some of these experiences in your own life helps you get in touch with the way a child's fears *feel*, even the silliest ones. Information about child development and knowledge about your child's struggles toward courage are helpful, but there's no substitute for your own memories when it comes to empathizing with your child's anxieties.

Maybe you remember worrying about something more deeply upsetting. Was there a family problem—a relative's drinking, not enough money to pay the bills—that grown-ups talked about after they thought you were asleep in bed?

Did you worry that friends would know the house was a mess, or that you'd have to move because the mortgage was late?

Did you worry your parents would split up? If they did, what did you fear would happen to you?

Were you afraid one of your parents wouldn't be OK if you weren't good or helpful?

What did you do with your childhood fears? Keeping in mind the fears you've just been thinking about, how did you learn to handle them? Was there someone you could talk to, a comforting parent, neighbor, or teacher? Can you remember a particular time you were scared when a friend or adult really helped? What do you think touched you, his or her advice or a certain way of listening or an arm around your shoulder?

Did you tend to find a diversion from your fears, something to get your mind off things? Did you hang out with friends, go for a long walk, or toss around a ball? Did you draw pictures? watch television?

If you didn't usually talk over your fears with an adult, what do you think it might have been like to try? What stopped you?

Did your mother or father seem too busy?

Would they have thought your fears were silly or unimportant?

Did they think you should "get over it" or stop being a "baby"?

Would they have insisted on "solving" the problem, or become so upset that you might have felt worse than if you kept it to yourself?

Thinking about these questions is important, because it helps you grow more aware of how you developed your approach to fear. By recognizing what you appreciated about the way adults responded to your childhood fears, you gain a clearer sense of what your child might need. By realizing what you missed or found upsetting, you get the opportunity to avoid repeating the pattern with your own child. You also avoid another common pitfall—trying to unconsciously "make up for what you didn't get" by giving your *child* something he or she doesn't want or need.

Making fears manageable. The story that follows is a lively English tale that dramatizes the importance of breaking down a fear into manageable pieces and tackling them one by one. This is one of the most important ways a child, or an adult, copes with fear. Molly Whuppie, the story's heroine, has got to be one of the world's all-time great problem-solvers.

✧   ✧   ✧

Molly Whuppie

Once there was a couple who had so many children they couldn't feed them all, and one day they gave each of the three youngest a crust of bread, led them into the woods, and left them there.

The three children walked and walked until they got lost. By then it was dark, and they sat down and ate the crusts of bread. Then they walked farther on until they reached a house. The youngest child, whose name was Molly Whuppie, went up to the front door and knocked.

"What do you want?" said the woman who answered the door.

"Something to eat," answered Molly Whuppie.

"You'll *be* something to eat if I let you in," said the woman. "My husband is a giant, and if he comes home and finds you here he'll have you for dinner."

But the children begged and begged until she let them in, offered them seats by the fire, and gave them bread and milk. But then the giant came home.

"What have we here, wife?" he roared as he saw the children.

"Only three poor lost girls who will soon be on their way," said the wife. "Just eat your supper and leave them alone." The giant gobbled his dinner and ordered the children to stay for the night.

Now, the giant and his wife had three daughters of their own. Hoping to keep the strangers safe, the giant's wife decided to put all six children together in one bed. But just before they went to sleep, the giant slipped three gold chains around his own daughters' necks. Around the necks of Molly and her sisters he slipped three straw ropes.

Molly, who was a very clever girl, saw what the giant had done. As the other five dozed off she lay awake, waiting and listening. As soon as they were all asleep she crept out of bed and, one by one, switched the gold necklaces with the straw ropes. Now Molly and her sisters were wearing the gold necklaces, and the giant's three daughters had on the straw ropes. When she was finished, Molly climbed back quietly into bed.

Just a few moments later, in came the giant carrying a heavy club. In the darkness he felt for the necks with the straw ropes around them, beat the three children who were wearing them until they were dead, and carried them downstairs to the cellar.

While the giant was downstairs, Molly woke up her sisters. They all ran out of the house and kept running and running all night until the sun came up. Now they found themselves standing in front of another house. This one was very grand, with many windows and lovely gardens and fine statues. It belonged to the king.

Molly went inside and told the king everything that had happened in the giant's house. The king listened, and when Molly was finished he said, "Well, Molly, you have done a good thing. But a better thing would be to go back and steal the sword that's hanging on the back of the giant's bed. If you do that, I'll give your eldest sister my first-born son for a husband."

Molly said she would try. That evening she went back to

the giant's house, slipped inside, and hid under his bed. Soon the giant came in, lay down, and began to snore loudly. Molly slowly crept out and unhooked the sword from the wall. But it was so heavy that when she took it down, it rattled in its scabbard and woke up the giant.

Molly ran out the door carrying the sword, with the giant at her heels. They ran and ran until the came to the Bridge of One Hair, and Molly ran across the bridge but the giant could not follow her, because he was too big. He stood at the side of the bridge and shouted: "Woe betide you, Molly Whuppie, if you ever come back again!"

But Molly only laughed. "Maybe again I'll come to see you, if I should come to Spain!" And off she ran to the king's house, still carrying the sword, and her eldest sister married the king's first-born son.

When the wedding feast was over, the king said to Molly, "Well, Molly, you have done a good thing. But a better thing would be to go back and steal the purse that the giant hides under his pillow. If you do that, I'll marry your second sister to my second son."

Molly said she would try. So that evening she went back to the giant's house, slipped inside, and hid under his bed. Soon the giant came in and lay down, and Molly heard him snoring. Slowly she crept out and put her hand under the pillow to feel the purse, but the instant she pulled it out the giant woke up. Molly ran out the door carrying the purse, but the giant ran, too, and they both ran till they came to the Bridge of One Hair, and Molly ran across but the giant could not. Across the bridge he shouted, "Woe betide you, Molly Whuppie, if you ever come back again!"

But Molly only laughed. "Maybe again I'll come to see you, if I should come to Spain!" And off she ran to the king's house, still carrying the purse, and her second sister married the king's second son.

After the wedding, the king said to Molly, "Well, Molly, you have done a good thing. But the best thing of all would be to go back and steal the giant's ring. If you do that, I will give you my youngest son to have as your husband."

Molly said she would try. Back she went to the giant's house, and again she hid under the bed. When the giant came in, she waited until she heard him snoring, and then she reached up, grabbed his finger, and tugged and tugged until the ring came off. Just then the giant woke up with a roar. "Now I've got you, Molly Whuppie!" he said. "And if I had done as much ill to you as you have done to me, what would you do to me?"

"I would stuff you into a sack," said Molly quickly. "And I'd put the cat and dog inside with you, and a needle and thread and a huge pair of scissors, and I'd hang you up on the wall. Then off I'd go to the wood, cut the thickest stick I could find, come home, take you down, and beat you till you were dead."

"And that, Molly Whuppie," said the giant, "is just what I'm going to do to you." And he got a sack, put Molly inside with the cat and dog, and a needle and thread and a pair of scissors, and hung her up on the wall. Then off he went to the forest to cut a thick stick of wood.

As soon as he was gone, Molly began to sing from inside the sack: "Oh, if only *everybody* could see what I see!" The giant's wife begged and begged to see what Molly saw, and Molly took the scissors, cut a hole in the sack, jumped out, helped the giant's wife climb in, and sewed up the hole as fast as she could with the needle and thread.

The giant's wife couldn't see anything inside the sack, because it was pitch dark, and she called to Molly to let her out. But Molly only hid behind the door. When the giant came home, carrying his big stick, he took down the sack and began to hit it. "Stop it, man! It's me!" cried his wife, but the cat and the dog were making so much noise that the giant couldn't hear her.

Out came Molly from behind the door, and when the giant saw her he roared. Molly ran out the door with the giant chasing her until they came to the Bridge of One Hair, and Molly ran over but the giant could not. Across the bridge he shouted, "Woe betide you, Molly Whuppie, if you ever come back again!"

"Never again will I come to see you, even if I come to Spain!" said Molly, and off she ran with the ring in her pocket, married the king's youngest son, and they had a magnificent wedding feast.

✧   ✧   ✧

Molly Whuppie has courage. Even in the scariest of situations, she holds onto her wits and presence of mind long enough to get what she needs for herself and her sisters. Molly is just a little girl, but she's always a few steps ahead of the giant chasing her. She even uses her small size to her advantage by crossing the Bridge of One Hair, which the giant is too big and clumsy to manage. And before she's had time for more than a sigh of relief at her narrow escape, back she goes to the giant's house, willing to take a risk for the promise of a reward from the king.

"Molly Whuppie," like "Hansel and Gretel," is one of many stories whose child heroes and heroines win out against giants, witches, and other evil creatures through their own bravery and cleverness—usually with the encouragement of a friendly grown-up and the help of a magic potion or trick (in this tale, the narrow Bridge of One Hair). In this story, as Molly Whuppie faces a series of tasks, each one a little bit scarier than the last, her courage grows. (Real kids learn to face fearful situations gradually, too; they need time in advance to talk about what to expect and how to deal with it, and also to talk about it over and over afterward until they can make sense of it.) Notice how Molly seems to enjoy all the challenges she faces. She takes great pleasure in her own competence. The more competent your child feels and the more she develops a sense of *mastery* over the tasks in her environment, the taller she will stand in the face of fear.

Let's take a look at the development of Molly's courage, and how it's different from other ways characters in this story cope with fear. The sleeping girls, Molly's sisters and the giant's daughters, are voiceless and interchangeable. The giant's daughters are powerless; Molly's sisters, abandoned. No one cares about their childish feelings. They adapt by going along with whatever happens; their fears are numbed. Only Molly stays awake.

The giant's wife knows how dangerous her husband is, and she responds to her fear defensively. Instead of standing up for what she wants in the face of fear, she cowers and manipulates. She tells the giant to leave the girls alone, but mostly she appeases him, and she is too weak to even safeguard the lives of her own daughters. Spineless and gullible, and with her natural, instinctive fear dulled, she lacks healthy caution. No wonder she ends up in the sack with the cat and the dog.

The giant's wife isn't much of a model for teaching kids to cope with fearful situations. When the giant comes in, she half-heartedly "hides" them in chairs by the fire, where he can easily see them. She puts all the girls in bed together, thinking to keep them safe, but she doesn't even warn her own daughters that they ought to stay awake. Instead of equipping them to deal with challenges, the giant's wife overprotects.

Molly starts out feisty. She's the one who knocks on the giant's door, who asks for food, who stays awake and switches the necklaces while the other girls doze. Unlike the giant, who is fearless because of his brute strength, and the giant's wife, who goes along with him, Molly holds onto her instinctual fear. She's awake, alert, always ready to use her cleverness to get out of a scrape. It's the king who challenges Molly to grow even braver. He lets her know he appreciates and respects her for escaping from the giant. But he goes a step further. The king tells Molly to take *for herself* some of the giant's prized possessions. In order to truly develop courage, she needs not only to run away from the giant, or to pay close attention to his trickery, but to incorporate his *strength* (symbolized by the sword hanging on the bed), his *power* (the purse she pulls out from under the pillow), and his *honor* (the ring, which stands for marriage, fulfillment, and wholeness).

Helping kids develop courage. Parents, like the king, need not only to be proud of kids for facing up to the fears that confront them but to encourage them to meet new challenges. Trying new activities—sports, challenging games, a new class, a difficult book—helps build your child's sense that she can try things and succeed, the lesson Molly learns when she steals the giant's belongings. If your child often withdraws from new situations, protesting, "I'm too scared" or "I'm no good at that," teach her some less-timid ways of expressing herself (see page 105).

Courage develops slowly, and there are always times when your child surprises you by being more timid, or braver, than you expected. Most kids move back and forth, like Molly does, between stealing from the giant's room and going back to the king for encouragement and rewards. It's not always easy to tell when your child needs empathy ("I know it's scary; you don't have to try if you don't feel ready") or a friendly nudge ("You can do it"). One way to find out is to *ask* him or her: "How can I help you try this new thing?" or "Is it that you're too scared to try, or that you're scared but you want me to help you try anyway?" If in doubt, check your own motives. If your child is resisting, ask yourself, "Is this something my child really *wants* or needs to try, or am I pushing him into it because it's important to me?" If he's nervous and you're not sure about how much encouragement to offer, here's another question to think about: "Is this something my child is ready to try, and am I holding him back out of my own fears?" If the answer to either of these questions is yes, be sure to spend some time on the Parent's Path on pages 125–27, where you'll find questions to help you gain insight into your own relationship to fear.

Family Time
"MOLLY WHUPPIE"

Make a "Fear Buster" poster. Too many "self-esteem" programs involve superficial labeling of kids, as though these could magically transform them: "I am lovable" or "I am competent." In fairy tales, magic words work not just by being spoken aloud but by helping heroes conquer fearful situations. In real life, kids develop confidence the same way. They need to successfully face challenges with the aid of loving encouragement from adults.

Here's a rainy-day project that will help you work that kind of magic in your household. Glue a snapshot of your child to the top of a sheet of posterboard. Title it "Fear Buster" if you like and hang it in a prominent place—on the refrigerator, the wall of his room. Each time he or she successfully faces a scary situation—a first trip to the barber, a tough test at school, an overnight when parents are out of town—make a note of it on the board. Don't limit notations to things you think are frightening; the only criterion for including an event on the board is that your child was worried about it.

Be sure you're not rewarding a "stiff upper lip." Each time you mark an achievement, tell your child you appreciate his courage. Let him know you recognize how challenging this event was for him. Invite him to talk about the experience if he wishes. This way, you use the poster to keep communication open.

Set up an obstacle course. In a hallway or backyard, lay out a path of appropriate challenges—physical, mental, social—for your child.

A toddler will enjoy a short series of simple tasks such as dropping a small toy into a pail, rolling a ball, and telling you the name of one of her favorite foods.

Your preschooler can try running, hopping, skipping, naming colors, and bowling.

A young school-age child is ready for a treasure hunt with clues written on slips of paper that lead to prizes such as apples and oranges, toys and trinkets ("Find something behind the maple tree near the big rock").

By nine or ten, your child is likely to enjoy some tougher physical challenges—shooting hoops, sit-ups, jumping jacks, running up and down the stairs or the driveway as many times as possible in five minutes.

As your child reaches adolescence, he will want to face obstacles in the wider world. Together you can agree on goals and draw an "obstacle course" marked with life challenges—getting an "A" in math, making a particular team, finishing his summer reading list. The reward for "winning" is a special outing where the two of you can spend some time together—a ball game, a fishing grip, the theater.

The Parent's Path
"MOLLY WHUPPIE"

How have *you* learned to cope with fear? Through the years you've probably developed some effective ways of coping with anxiety. Recognizing these techniques helps you know how much you have to offer your child. Take a look at the fears and worries you listed on page 125. Now focus on how you deal with them by seeing if any of the following approaches to anxiety describe your personal style:

I manage by doing research, educating myself about whatever's on my mind.
I'm funny. I break the tension with humor and then get down to business.
I usually ask my partner or a friend for advice or support.
I like to set aside my fear for a while. I make time for recreation, or to clear my head, so I can bring fresh energy to the problem. I exercise, play a sport, pray, meditate.

Naturally, the approaches to fear that work for you won't all suit your child's temperament. But maybe there's one strength you weren't aware of that you'd like to offer next time he's worried about something.

What do you need to work on? If few or none of the coping mechanisms above seem to describe your style, what approach to fear *are* you showing your child? Take inventory. (If you're not sure you need to do this, go back to your responses to the questions on page 127. If you didn't tend to talk about your fears as a child, I highly recommend doing this exercise.)

Here are some of the less effective ways of handling fear. Most of us fall into one pattern or the other on especially bad days, but if either is your *regular* approach to anxiety, you may need to focus on ways of handling fear in your own life.

Do you lose your cool and vent your anxiety on the rest of your family? Do you blame others for the things that worry you? Do you tend to half-jokingly refer to yourself as "a basket case" more often than you like to admit?

Or do you go to the other extreme? Do you usually grit your teeth and force yourself to get on with the task at hand? Do you ease the tension with food or shopping or television? Do you give everyone around you the silent treatment? Does your child ever get a chance to know that you're feeling worried or vulnerable?

What if either of these coping styles reminds you of your partner? If your husband or wife tends to explode or ignore anxiety, ask yourself whether *you* fall into the opposite category. "My husband yells about everything," one woman told me. "I'm beginning to realize that I hate yelling so much that I hold everything in. My kids are just like me." This mother recognized that she needed to work on not accepting her husband's blaming, learning to express her own worries appropriately, and creating enough trust and safety in her relationship with her children to allow them to talk about their fears and find support.

Just as stories have long helped children conquer fear, they have also offered lively but safe opportunities to explore one of the most troublesome, complex human feelings: aggression. Let's see how.

$\mathcal{S}$even

Healthy Aggression

Healthy aggression sounds like an oxymoron to many parents I meet, and especially so to those who appreciate the nurture of children as a spiritual path. If you want your child to be *spiritual* (which, to many parents, means "caring, centered, and *nice*"), where could aggression possibly fit in? An "aggressive child" is the bully who hits other kids on the playground and fouls on the basketball court. To many well-meaning parents, aggression, unless it's on the playing field, is a dirty little secret of human nature, the way sex was for our Victorian forebears. "We try to discourage aggression as much as possible," parents often tell me. "Do *you* have any tips for getting rid of it?" Meanwhile, our kids are tuning into music loaded with hate lyrics, flocking to violent movies, and going to schools where weapons are all too common. What's going wrong? "Leftovers," from the Brothers Grimm, and "The North Wind's Gift," from Italy, offer some insights into the problem from times past.

What motivates aggressive behavior? Maybe part of the problem we have teaching healthy approaches to aggression is that the part aggressive feelings play in *normal* emotional development has been explored surprisingly little. Researchers on aggression have tended to focus on its destructiveness, looking for clues to its origin in the backgrounds of tyrants like Hitler and Stalin. Writing his major work on the subject after the carnage of World War I, Freud, whose theory of aggression is highly influential even today, understood it as a death instinct, an inborn urge to harm and destroy that naturally presses to be discharged. He saw the human being as a savage beast who needed to satisfy his drive to destroy by hurting others. If you've watched one child on a playground turn to another and suddenly swat him, you've probably found yourself thinking about aggression much the same way Freud did.

More recent theorists such as the self psychologist Heinz Kohut, taking the more optimistic view that human beings basically want to connect with one another, tend to see aggression as a sign that something has gone awry. They understand it not as an instinctive drive, but as a pathological *response* to wounded self-esteem. All children (and adults) have needs for love and admiration, they point out, and behave aggressively when disappointed, frustrated, or hurt. For example, a child building with blocks and seeing her tower topple over for the third time knocks the blocks all over the floor. Or an adolescent whose parents have grounded him stomps off to his room, shouting, "I hate you!" The psychoanalyst Erich Fromm, in *The Anatomy of Human Destructiveness*, described a sadistic personality such as Adolf Hitler as someone born into an environment so unresponsive that he grew up feeling ignored, powerless, and seething with rage.

Why are boys more aggressive? Much more work is needed to explore the many facets of aggression, and particularly with regard to whether "nature or nurture" is responsible for the fact that males as a group appear to be more aggressive than females. Is the difference biological, that is, the inevitable result of higher testosterone levels and a need for discharge? Could it be that the rough-and-tumble socialization boys get more often than girls all through childhood makes them more likely to express aggression physically? Or is male aggressiveness part of a deeply entrenched "masculine mystique" glorifying violence in our culture, to use the phrase coined by the author Myriam Miedzian in her groundbreaking study, *Boys Will Be Boys*?

Most of the prominent theorists have neglected to recognize any potential for the *positive* use of aggression by males or females—the kind it takes to find a job, start a company, or stand up for what you believe in. Confusion also arises because many people use the word *aggression* in different ways. Sometimes it means extreme competitiveness; at other times, actual violence. For our purposes, some of the most helpful ideas come from the pioneering work with children done by Henri Parens, who spent a great deal of time observing kids and trying to understand what motivates their aggressive behavior. Parens disagreed with the theorists who conceptualized it as a response to frustration or hurt, pointing out that even in apparently well-adjusted children brought up in caring homes, there seemed to be an "overriding unavoidability" about aggressive behavior. Watching kids play, Parens came to see their aggression as a *goal-oriented activity*, aimed at changing situations they found unpleasant. (Think of the way a toddler sometimes kicks and hits someone holding him down for a diaper change, for example.) Parens found that when a child learned he could reasonably expect to meet his goals within a reasonable period of time, he also learned to express his needs in a reasonable way.

Parens's observations also contradicted that Freudian view that the discharge of destructive aggression is a basic human instinct. The only time aggression became a goal in itself, he insisted, was when a child often found himself in unpleasant situations without having the support or guidance he needed to reach his goals, stimulating him to feel aggressive for long periods of time. Ironically, in Parens's view, a child who didn't learn to use aggression appropriately—to meet goals—ended up using it destructively.

One of the most dramatic examples I've encountered in my work was the relationship between a three-year-old girl and her mother, a single parent who had a new baby. The child was regularly sent home from preschool for biting other children. As we talked, I learned that when this mother wanted to talk to a neighbor, she would carry the infant with her and leave the little girl at home alone, sometimes for as long as an hour. When the mother asked for advice on how to stop the biting behavior, I helped her recognize that the three-year-old was expressing feelings about her mother's neglectful treatment of her. Once the mother began to spend more time at home with her little girl and to bring her along on errands, the biting soon stopped.

Dealing with frustration, working toward goals. By recognizing your child's need to experience his own aggression and find appropriate ways to express it, you help him be much more than "nice." You help him *define* himself. You help him grow into an individual who can make a *difference* in the world around him. Aggression has a place in the soul, a place that is home to a child's power and strength. It takes aggression for a child to do a cartwheel, raise his hand in class, join a game on the playground. Learning something new is an aggressive activity; it demands the capacity to push ahead even when the going gets tough. By the teen years, saying no to drugs and alcohol is no simple slogan; a child who is strong enough to stand apart from peers and from the group is mustering aggression.

Healthy aggression isn't something kids learn overnight. As your child develops, you can help him turn his impulsive, angry feelings into an increased capacity to contain his aggression, control it, and use it to meet goals.

Let's take a look at a story, adapted from the Brothers Grimm, that shows frustration, a destructive form of aggression, transformed, as a maiden's rage is contrasted to a servant girl's capacity to persevere for the sake of her goal. The marriage switch sounds off-putting and sexist to twentieth-century listeners, but keep in mind that this is a fairy-tale way of symbolizing the path to fulfillment and fruitfulness.

LEFTOVERS

Once there was a maiden who lost her temper easily. If she was spinning flax and found even a tiny knot in the thread, she felt so frustrated that she would rip out all her work and hurl it to the ground.

The maiden had a servant girl who was very patient. Every time the maiden angrily threw her flax to the ground, the servant girl would pick it up, dust it off, and spin it into fine linen thread. Soon she had woven herself enough fabric for a lovely dress.

Now the maiden who lost her temper easily was betrothed to a young man. The night before the wedding there was a great feast, and the whole village joined in the dancing. The maiden and her future bridegroom watched as the servant girl twirled and curtsied, her brightly colored linen dress swirling gracefully around her as she danced. Suddenly the maiden grew very angry: "How lovely her dress is as she dances around! And the cloth is spun from flax that *I* threw to the ground!" she shouted, stamping her foot.

> When the bridegroom heard these words, he left the maiden he had planned to marry, walked up to the servant girl, and asked her to be his wife.

✧   ✧   ✧

If you look at this tale in simple black-and-white terms, it's all too easy to think of the maiden as the "bad guy" and the servant girl as "good." If you share the story with a young child, he or she is almost certain to respond that way. But keep in mind that the maiden and the servant girl are paired for a reason. If we're honest, we can see ourselves in both of them, because few of us manage to be like the maiden until we've spent some time as the servant girl.

The maiden who loses her temper has a goal; she wants the knots out of her flax. Instead of channeling her aggression into cleaning and spinning, though, she flies off into rages. Following Henri Parens's way of thinking, we might wonder why the maiden isn't getting the support and guidance she needs to learn to cope with her frustration long enough to meet her goal. Where's her mother? Why doesn't the servant girl offer to help?

Empowering a frustrated child. At one time or another you've probably felt as frustrated and angry as the maiden does—ready to unplug a jangling phone, sink an axe into a locked-up computer, walk out on a relationship that seems too tangled to work. Know that your child, who is less competent than an adult at most of the things she tries, feels that way quite a lot of the time. (Right from infancy, some kids, as you've probably noticed, seem to be more demanding or irritable by temperament than others.) If your child is to grow up thinking of herself as someone who can successfully reach her goals, she needs your empathy and help.

Let me offer an example. Four-year-old Maria is having trouble fitting the arms of her small doll into the sleeves of a new outfit. Each time she sticks the doll's hand into the sleeve, the fingers get stuck in the seam. After trying several times, she flings the doll to the floor and dissolves in tears for the third time that morning.

"It's just a toy. Why are you making such a big deal about it?" says Maria's mother angrily, and she takes away the doll. Maria's mother has made sure she won't have to tolerate her *own* frustration anymore today. But her daughter now has the message that she is too clumsy to get the dress on the doll and that her frustration is shameful and unacceptable to her mother.

Maria is locked in the role of the maiden in the story. Her frustration is so overwhelming to her that she can't stay on task, and her mother only adds to it by piling on her own anger. How is Maria going to learn to tolerate her frustration long enough to actually focus on getting the doll's arm into the sleeve? How will she experience what it means to use her aggressive feelings constructively? We can imagine that if this scene is part of a regular pattern, Maria is likely to grow up to be just as impulsive, just as incapable of controlling her aggression, as her mother who grabs the doll. If she is like many girls, she may begin to turn it against herself in depression. That's what the maiden does in the story, looking on in helpless envy as the servant girl dances in a colorful dress spun from the flax that really belonged to her. Instead of learning how to use her own aggression, and owning the assertiveness that is rightfully hers, Maria, powerless and angry, loses her doll.

Let's picture a slightly different scenario. Suppose Maria's mother had offered *empathy*, maybe by saying something like, "It's awfully hard to fit those arms into those tiny sleeves, isn't it?" By acknowledging her daughter's frustration instead of belittling her, the mother would have communicated understanding and enough support to encourage Maria to tackle the sleeve again when she was ready.

Once Maria is calm enough to try again, her mother can teach her to approach dressing the doll in the spirit of *problem solving*. Together they can look at the inside of the sleeve, try to get any hanging threads out of the way, and notice where the doll's fingers get caught. With this kind of support, Maria can come to recognize that she can face a frustrating situation and achieve success.

What if Maria's mother is having a bad day, and is too busy or frustrated herself, to help with the sleeve right now? Instead of taking it out on the little girl, there's nothing wrong with acknowledging her own feelings in an appropriate way. In doing this, she offers her daughter a healthy model for handling frustration: "Honey, it's been a long day, and I don't have the patience to help you with your doll right now. When I've had it, I know it's usually a good idea to set things aside for a while.

Why don't you play with something else, and then we'll try the sleeves again later on or tomorrow."

Aggression and goals. By now, I hope you've seen why the maiden in the story isn't someone we ought to condemn. Now let's go back to the servant girl, whose hard work depicts the way aggression can be harnessed to achieve a goal. In her patient hands, raw flax is spun and woven into a dress that swirls when she dances—and wins her the prince.

Notice that the servant girl spins the flax and makes the dress *for herself*, not for her mistress, and she wins the prince as her own husband. She isn't following any orders from the maiden to spin the flax into a gown. She acts on her own, like the two-year-old who says, "I want to do it myself!"

That's how your child first learns to use her aggression effectively—to get what *she* wants, to meet her own goals, to do it *her* way. Her efforts to experience her own power often threaten to turn into power struggles between you, as though the two of you were fighting for dear life over a colorful dress. As we'll see later on in this chapter, each major stage in your child's development brings new opportunities to help her use her aggression—and new challenges as she practices on those she loves best.

Family Time
"LEFTOVERS"

Invite your child to role-play frustrating situations. Encourage your three- to seven-year-old to pretend to be the maiden in the story. This is her chance to learn to express frustration in words instead of going out of control. How does the maiden feel when she finds a knot in the flax she is spinning? (Supply words and phrases such as *annoyed, upset, angry, frustrated, at her wit's end, fed up, desperate.*) If spinning doesn't engage your child, devise your own scenarios. Let her be a pizza maker kneading dough or a construction worker putting up a wall.

Use the story to compare notes about frustration in your lives. Children seven and up are interested in knowing about the activities that leave *you* feeling like the maiden when she gets to a knot in the flax. Does home repair get to you? a car breakdown? origami? (Be sure to ask your child to tell you what *she* thinks gets you really frustrated, and don't be surprised if you get an instant answer.) Talk about how you usually handle the frustration, and what you find most helpful. Now give your child a turn. Does she get frustrated by a particular computer game? a gymnastics move she can't quite get? long division?

Because it's not always easy to talk about frustration when you're actually feeling it, this is an opportunity to start some low-key conversation in a nonconfrontational way. On pages 152–53 you'll find practical advice on how to help your child cope with frustration at different ages.

The Parent's Path
"LEFTOVERS"

How do you usually handle your own aggressive feelings? During the next few days, make it a point to notice particular situations, problems, or people you often feel angry about—rush-hour traffic, your boss, taxes, your twelve-year-old. What do you do with the feelings? Do you lose your temper? Do you try to ignore aggressive feelings, and busy yourself with food, shopping, jogging, or worrying? Do you blame yourself or others around you?

Because we're often uncomfortable with our aggressive feelings, we tend to try to get rid of them, either by shifting them onto the people close to us or by pretending the feelings don't exist. When you do that, it's hard to use aggression appropriately—or teach your child to— because you're not in control of it. Suppose next time you were to try something different. What do you imagine it would be like to change the pattern and just *acknowledge* the feeling by saying to yourself, "I'm really angry right now" or "I'm frustrated"?

Are there one or two areas of your life where you use your aggression effectively? Think of times when you feel good about your own aggressive feelings and the way you use them to get results—at the office, on the tennis court, in political discussions with friends.

Did your own parents or a special teacher help you channel your aggression into these particular areas? How? Maybe a particular phrase or word of encouragement has stayed with you. "Get *angry!*" one father used to tell his daughter and her teammates when they stood and watched the ball go by at field-hockey games.

Try to recall a "success story" about aggression from your own life to share with your child. Appreciating your child's struggles with aggression is easier if you're aware of your own. Sharing your struggles with your child helps him or her see you as a flesh-and-blood person who knows how it feels to have a hard time now and then. Have you worked at learning to be more assertive? Are you someone with a "short fuse" who has struggled to control your temper?

Now think back on the achievements you're proudest of, and you're likely to find examples of effective use of aggression to meet a goal. Maybe you trained for months to run the marathon or do a six-minute mile. Maybe you got your college degree at night, working full-time during the day, while most of your high school friends settled for less. Perhaps you have recently won a well-deserved promotion. Your child is not always going to be eager to listen to your success stories, but well-timed reminiscences in small doses can be very reassuring.

One middle-schooler came home furious after being falsely accused of copying a research report off the Internet. His mother told me she encouraged him to show the teacher his handwritten outline and library materials, and to point out how hard he'd actually worked. Then she told him about a time in her college days when a professor accused her of paying a graduate student to research a paper he considered "too good to have been written by an undergrad." She went back to her dorm room, pulled her notes out of the garbage (redolent of tea bags and orange peels), dumped them on the professor's desk, and stood there until he gave her an "A."

A developmental look at aggression. In the Italian story that follows, a hapless farmer starts out wimpy and eventually learns to harness his aggression with the help of the powerful north wind. Just as a child doesn't learn to do this easily, Giuseppe the farmer goes through a series of journeys and misadventures, not to mention numerous clubs on the head. This is another one of those stories adults might not consider particularly edifying for kids, which is, I suspect, exactly why they sit up and listen.

✧ ✧ ✧

THE NORTH WIND'S GIFT

Once there was a farmer named Giuseppe whose fields were owned by a rich landlord. The landlord made Giuseppe plant his crops high up on the hillside, and every winter the cold north wind blew across his fields and killed the crops. One day, as Giuseppe and his family sat in their tiny hut with no food, Giuseppe decided it was time to go and speak to the north wind.

He walked and walked until he reached the north wind's castle. "Every year you kill my crops," he told the north wind. "My family is starving."

"What do you want from me?" asked the north wind.

"That's up to you," said Giuseppe.

The north wind gave Giuseppe a small box. "Whenever you're hungry, open this box, ask for what you want, and you'll get it," he said. "But don't tell anyone else about the box, or you'll lose it."

Giuseppe thanked him and started home. When he got hungry, he sat down and opened the box. "I want something to eat and drink," he said, and out of the box came a loaf of bread, a ham, and a bottle of wine. Giuseppe ate his fill and started walking.

When he got home, he sat down with his family, asked the box for dinner, and they all ate happily. Afterward, he warned his wife, "Don't tell the landlord about this box, or we'll lose it."

She promised not to tell, but the next morning the landlord sent for her and she told him all about the box. The landlord sent for Giuseppe. "If you give me your box, you can have all the grain you need," he promised. But when Giuseppe handed over the box, all the landlord gave him was a bag of old seed. Now Giuseppe and his family were poor and hungry again, and Giuseppe decided to go back to the north wind's castle.

"Remember the box you gave me?" he told the north wind, who answered the door. "My landlord tricked me out of it, and now my family is poor and hungry again."

"I told you not to tell anybody about the box," answered the north wind angrily. "Go home!"

But Giuseppe waited until the north wind stopped puffing. "Here's a gold box," said the north wind. "This time, be sure you don't open it unless you're really hungry."

Giuseppe thanked him and headed home. When he felt a little hungry, he opened the gold box and ordered it to serve him dinner. Out jumped a giant with a huge club, and the giant started beating Giuseppe on the head until Giuseppe managed to stuff him back in the box and shut the lid. Then Giuseppe started walking again, rubbing the top of his head.

When Giuseppe got home, he showed his family the gold box, but as soon as he opened it two giants began to beat all of them with huge clubs. Giuseppe stuffed them back inside, shut the lid, and said to his wife, "Now why don't you visit our landlord and tell him that this time I've brought back an even better box."

So Giuseppe's wife visited the landlord, who sent for Giuseppe and asked to see the new box. "I'm not going to show it to you if you try to take it the way you took my other box," said Giuseppe.

The landlord promised not to, but as soon as he saw the gold box he said, "Give it to me and you can have the other one right back." Giuseppe agreed, and as they exchanged boxes he warned the landlord, "Don't open this box unless you're really hungry."

"I'll open it tomorrow," answered the landlord. "I'm having dinner guests." And the next day, as all the guests sat around his dining room table, the landlord proudly brought out the gold box and opened it up. Out leapt six giants with heavy clubs, and they started to beat all the guests. Giuseppe's landlord was so upset that he knocked the box to the floor, and Giuseppe, who was hiding under the table, stuffed the giants back in and shut the lid so that the guests would not be beaten to death. The landlord and his guests had nothing to eat for dinner. And as for Giuseppe, he kept both of the boxes the north wind had given him, never lent them out to anybody again, and always had enough to feed his family.

To see this tale as nothing more than an allegory about how human beings learn to integrate aggression would be to reduce it from the wonderful slapstick story that it is. There's something Chaplinesque about the hapless Giuseppe, who bumbles his way into learning to use his own power. As the story opens, we see aggression depicted as the north wind, an untamed force that destroys everything in its path, not very different from the way Freud understood it. Giuseppe, by contrast, is a passive fellow who summons the courage to go see the north wind but leaves it up to him to do something—anything—to repay him for the harm done to his crops. The north wind does give him a box with the power to feed him, a box containing a powerful giant; now Giuseppe is going to learn to handle his own aggression, and to "contain" it. Unfortunately, he doesn't guard the box as carefully as he should. By the time Giuseppe gets the second box from the north wind, and discovers its power the hard way, he begins to understand that he's at the mercy of the giants in the box. If he is to take care of his family, he needs to learn to *control* the contents of the box, to use it to get what he wants. By the end of the story Giuseppe has learned to do exactly that. He unleashes the box's giants on the landlord's dinner guests, then saves the guests by stuffing the giants back in the box. From now on Giuseppe will hold onto both boxes and use them when he needs to, and his family won't go hungry.

Toddlers. Like Giuseppe, a child learns to integrate aggression by using it to work toward goals and solve problems, and it's a process that happens in stages, some more painful than others. Beginning in the second year of life, as your toddler learns that she can be different from parents or siblings (whether because she doesn't want to eat peas or because she can creep away from Mommy or because she doesn't want to listen to a story you've read), she's harnessing the aggression needed to define herself as *separate*. Instead of just letting things happen to her, like Giuseppe watching the north wind kill his crops every year, she begins to define herself as someone with wants of her own (as we saw in chapter 5), and to assert herself as a different person from you. The energy it takes to do that is a form of aggression; you've probably experienced it that way when she shouts, "I don't *want* to!" and "No!" in situations that don't (from your grown-up point of view) necessarily call for quite so much indignation.

Sometimes she needs to do things her way even when doing so works against her, like Giuseppe who defiantly opens the first box, against the north wind's explicit instructions. Through her anger and defiance your child is developing the aggression it takes to be her own person, a real individual.

Preschoolers. By preschool your child is imagining what it would mean to be as powerful and strong as Mommy or Daddy. Dressing up as Superman, your three- or four-year-old copes with two difficulties he's facing in connection with his own aggression. First of all, imagining himself as someone with supernatural powers is one way to recover from the all-too-realistic awareness he has gained of himself as a thirty-pound weakling surrounded by grown-ups. Second, through fantasy play— killing all the bad guys and slaying them with his sword, for example—he experiences his aggressive feelings in ways that he can't in the real-life social settings he enjoys with playmates and family members.

One mother told me how startled she'd been by an experience with her four-year-old daughter, Lisa, a sensitive and shy girl who was a budding ballet dancer. "Lisa wasn't a demanding baby, and she grew into a kid who got along well with other kids and adults, but sometimes I worried she was just a little too agreeable, a little to nice for her own good," said her mother. "Even as a toddler, she hardly ever got really off-the-wall angry." One day she took the child to audition for a ballet class at a new school. The mother waited in the hallway until Lisa came out of the studio with a somber expression. "She told me the teacher said she was good at the positions but scolded her for not knowing the French names for all the steps," recalled her mother. "She said she'd been accepted into the class, but she'd have to go home and learn the French words before the first day. But the minute we got into the car Lisa burst into tears. They hadn't taught the French names in her old school, she said; why had the teacher been so mean?" As soon as they arrived home, Lisa, still wearing her pink satin leotard and skirt, walked over to the playroom sofa, picked up her brother's toy rifle, and aimed it out the window. "I'd like to *machine-gun* that teacher right through her leotard," she said angrily.

"I was so stunned to see my usually quiet child standing there like Patty Hearst," recalled the mother. "I told her she had a right to be angry, but I was proud that she'd danced so well even though she was upset, and we'd find a nicer teacher." The crisis became a turning point. Once the temperamentally easygoing Lisa had had this opportunity to express aggression with the help of a toy, she seemed ready to learn ways to speak more assertively. "The whole episode was an eye-opener for me, too," said her mother. "Obviously, the teacher was out of line. But I also realized I needed to teach Lisa how to express herself clearly instead of quietly putting up with unfair criticism, even from authority figures."

A child like Lisa, who tends to dissolve in tears instead of defending herself, will end up feeling like a victim unless she learns to use her aggression appropriately. This child may be "good" most of the time, the kind who doesn't "cause trouble" at home. Such a child may have been born with a milder temperament, or may have somehow learned that it's not OK to get angry, and instead learns to turn her aggression on herself, becoming passive or depressed. She may see herself as powerless in the face of more openly aggressive people, the way Giuseppe feels with the north wind. Often it's helpful to supply a child like this with verbal expressions of aggression. "This is my TV time and I'm watching this show," she might need to learn to tell a sibling, instead of whining when he grabs the remote.

Parents are often inclined to be impatient with a passive child ("Stop crying! You never speak up for yourself!"), which often backfires, making him or her more timid than ever. Instead, teach a passive child how to "talk strong." "Can you take a deep breath and tell me what you want?" you might ask. Or, "I think you can tell me what's wrong and how you'd like to fix it." Teach her the words to express her feelings—"I'm annoyed" or "I'd like to discuss a problem."

Your school-age child. Many preschoolers aren't passive at all, of course; they're "feeling their oats," and often are inclined to get into minor skirmishes with playmates. With them and with school-age children, many parents find it helpful to remember the "Stop, Look, and Listen" approach below while dealing with inappropriate aggression:

- **Stop** the hurtful behavior. If a child is hitting, biting, shoving, punching, or otherwise hurting another child, don't attempt to reason or discuss things with him or her. The behavior must stop.

  For a child who has really lost control, use time-out; send him to his room or another quiet place until he's calm enough to be around other people. This is not only an effective discipline technique, but also a helpful way to teach him to contain his aggressive feelings.

- **Look** with your child at the consequences of his lack of self-control. Teach him to empathize with others by helping him see how they feel as a result of his behavior: "Do you see how upset David is that you've hit him?" and "Don't you remember how much it hurt that time Andy hit you?"

  Research shows that parents are more likely to talk about feelings with girls than with boys. When my own son was turning two, I observed a dramatic illustration of the way we too often treat boys. We were standing in a hardware store when an acquaintance walked in with his son Jason, who was around the same age. The boys had never met. "Jason, this is Matt," said the father, and Jason reached out and smacked Matthew in the face. Stunned, Matthew burst into tears.

  As I rubbed my son's cheek, Jason's father looked at Matthew and scowled. "You've got to learn to hit back," he said matter-of-factly. If that's what we think two-year-old boys ought to learn, then it's no surprise when their aggressive behavior only escalates. We end up raising bullies, and our society suffers for it. If, on the other hand, we help them see the consequences of violent behavior and teach them to express their feelings—hurt when someone else hits them, anger when they feel like hitting—then we teach them to own their own aggression. Then, to borrow from Zen, we're raising *warriors*.

- **Listen** to your child's feelings. Saying "Tell me in words what you're so angry about" is a way to teach him to express aggression appropriately. That doesn't mean teaching your child to talk like a character out of a Woody Allen movie or a *New Yorker* cartoon. By encouraging him to talk, you help him learn that words can take the place of grabbing or shoving. And by showing him your willingness to listen, you teach your child to listen to others.

By school age, your child's aggression is channeled into what Erikson called industriousness, an ability and eagerness to apply himself or herself to new pursuits—learning the multiplication tables, memorizing the map of the Western Hemisphere or lists of spelling words, starting collections and hobbies, from stamps to baseball cards to Barbie dolls to magic tricks. He's now ready to use his aggression in organized sports. (Chapter 9 is devoted to the nurture of healthy competition in kids of all ages.) And at this age, children begin to be aware of themselves as part of a wider community. At school or camp, on a team, and at home, they can understand that controlling their aggression is part of their responsibility as community members. And they notice who's a "dirty player" or a "rough kid."

That doesn't mean aggression isn't a problem at home. One of the most annoying ways it shows up is in bickering between siblings. You've overheard the battles from the kitchen: "I'm not emptying the dishwasher. I did it yesterday. You *never* do it!" "That's bull! I do *so!* You think you know *everything!*" How can parents deal with the pattern?

First of all, if you're worried your kids hate each other, try to recognize arguments as a way for each child to safeguard getting fair treatment. Within limits (words only, no hitting), they are—like classroom debates or moot court cases in law school—opportunities for your child to experience what it means to defend his point of view with the people he's closest to.

If the bickering seems to be incessant, it may serve a different purpose. Remember the two-year-old's aggression we talked about, which is his way of letting caregivers know he's a separate person, no longer merged with them as he was during infancy? Siblings who bicker constantly often sound a lot like two-year-olds: "I like vanilla ice cream." "No, *I* like chocolate." "I want to go out." "No, I want to stay in." It's a paradox, but you're likely to hear less discord between your kids if you play up their differences. Don't get caught up in whatever they're arguing about; the so-called problem isn't the point. Instead, look for opportunities to highlight the diversity among family members. "Susie loves hamburgers, and Tommy is a vegetarian," you might say. "I love lobster and Dad's big treat is chicken curry. Isn't it great how much variety there is in our family?"

Adolescents. Unfortunately, as children move into adolescence, media stereotyping of male and female aggression becomes a powerful, and usually negative, influence. Boys line up to see movies that sensationalize violence in war zones and on our streets, and glorify male characters who use brute force, like the Terminator and *Friday the 13th*'s Jason. Girls, on the other hand, are offered images of women as the most frequent *victims* of male violence, unless they are women who either mimic the violent behavior of their media male counterparts or disown their own direct assertiveness and instead use sexual seductiveness to wield power over those around them; sometimes both. According to the National Coalition on Television Violence, children living in homes with cable television and/or a videocassette recorder will see about 32,000 murders and 40,000 attempted murders by the age of eighteen. Stories, books, theater, and the movies have always included unsavory characters, but it makes little sense to make comparisons between their impact and that of the highly graphic television images flooding our children's developing awareness over and over for more hours per day than many of them spend in the classroom. Consider the barrage of violence in popular music and comic books, and it all adds up to overload for today's kids.

What can parents do to stem the tide of violent (and victim) media images? Most important, set limits on the programming and films your child is allowed to see. Check your local listings or the Internet for reviews written with children in mind; these usually include information on the degree of violence and bloodshed in a particular film or show. Some of the premium cable channels note a film's rating at the start of each broadcast, along with a message about the level of violence and obscenity it contains. Keep in mind that many kids think a movie is acceptable to parents as long as it doesn't contain nudity. "Don't worry, Mom, it's only rated 'R' because it has violence in it," one thirteen-year-old assured his mother. "There's no sex or anything."

Most important, be aware of what your child is watching, and make opportunities to talk about it. You probably can't keep your kid away from all media violence, but you *can* teach her to recognize how manipulative it is and to understand its impact on our culture. You can help him develop *values* about aggressive behavior.

Ask your child what she thinks of the way characters act or of how they solve their problems. Does she think all of the violence in a particular show or film was necessary to present the characters or the plot, or was a lot of it included to attract viewers who find it exciting? What could have been cut? If the two of you are watching a film or movie that you find upsettingly violent, let her know how you feel; if she doesn't share your horror or nausea, ask how she *does* feel about it. (Boys, in particular, are encouraged by peers to be macho about media violence, as though not to react was a sign of maturity; by sharing your own responses without preaching, you can offer a different message.) If a newspaper report tells of teen vandalism or violence that looks suspiciously as though it was inspired by a recent film or TV show, talk about it. It's tempting for parents who recognize the dangers of violence in the media to come down hard on kids, but pick your battles. Make it clear that you reserve the right to rule out programming you really object to, but keep the focus on an honest, heartfelt exchange of ideas and opinions.

Family Time
"THE NORTH WIND'S GIFT"

Give a young child chiffon scarves and let her pretend to be the wind, blowing through the trees and across the fields, freezing the plants. This is an opportunity to experience in fantasy the full force of her aggression. Now invite her to imagine being a warm breeze. How could she use her power now?

Invite your school-age child to design her own "box of power," like the one the north wind gives Giuseppe. Provide her with a discarded cardboard box, wrapping paper or aluminum foil to cover it, and stickers, crayons, and markers for decorating. Now invite her to fill the box with symbols of strength—tools, pens, pictures of engines or high-energy soft drinks—anything that could help a person achieve his or her goals. Invite her to think of what she'd put in a gift box for Giuseppe—seeds, fertilizer, rakes, burlap to shelter his plants from the wind.

What if Giuseppe were a comic-book superhero? Ask your preadolescent to imagine (or actually draw) Giuseppe as a cartoon character. How does he resemble other famous superheroes? What magical powers does he have because of his box? Use the opportunity, if you haven't already, to learn about the superheroes your child is interested in. Who are his favorites? Why does he like those better than others? Is there one story he particularly likes?

If you do read one of your child's comic books on his recommendation, try to avoid judging too harshly. Let him know you appreciate his sharing something he enjoys. Rather than phrasing negative comments as criticisms ("That page was awful, loaded with violence"), stick to expressing your own thoughts and feelings: "I was disgusted by all the blood in this part of the story. I was angry at the main character for doing that. I was upset at the way that woman was treated."

The Parent's Path
"THE NORTH WIND'S GIFT"

What do you like *least* about your own aggression? Does the idea of healthy aggression still seem like a contradiction in terms? Spend a few minutes focusing on the pattern aggression takes in your own life. Maybe you have a hard time expressing it; perhaps you've learned to expect negative reactions from other people when you really speak your mind. Maybe others consider you abrasive or tough. Or perhaps your partner clams up or belittles you when you assert your opinion.

On the other hand, maybe you're not happy with your capacity to control your own aggression and use it constructively. Do you lose your temper easily? Or do you go for a run or eat a brownie instead of facing a difficult situation?

How do you and your partner deal with angry or aggressive feelings? This is an exercise you can answer alone, but it will mean more if you and your partner each write down your answers to the questions in this section and then compare your responses.

For couples, taking a hard look at your partner's way of dealing with anger and aggression can help you see your own more clearly and honestly. How does he or she push your buttons? What do you do that drives your partner up the wall? How do you know when your partner is angry? How does he or she know when you are?

Think back to times the two of you have successfully dealt with disagreements. What made it work—talking things out quietly, having a "cooling off" period, taking turns listening? Are there topics that are still too hot too handle? Where would you like to improve?

How does your child respond to your arguments and disagreements? What do you think he or she is learning from the way you and your partner cope with aggressive feelings? If you're not sure of the answers, *ask* your child. You're likely to be surprised at his or her insights.

One couple realized that they rarely disagreed in front of their children at all. "My husband grew up in a household where arguing wasn't allowed, and my parents fought like cats and dogs, so neither of us really feels comfortable even *negotiating* in front of our kids, even on relatively small stuff," recalled the woman. "But we started to realize that we weren't teaching them to work out their differences, and that it would probably be a lot better for them to hear us hash out our disagreements now and then. I guess we didn't get to that point until we figured we could both manage it without flying off the handle, which is something *our* parents never showed *us* how to do."

To gain a fuller understanding of the way you handle aggression, continue on to the next question.

What did you learn about aggression as a child? Did you and your sibling bicker and battle? Were disagreements common or out of control? Or were you "one big happy family" where disagreement was scarcely tolerated?

How were conflicts among family members handled? What happened if you "talked back" to your parents? How did your parents let you know that they were angry? Did they "freeze you out," shout, or physically punish you? How does your childhood experience of aggression seem to affect you now?

So it is we teach our children healthy aggression as we learn to handle our own. Let's see how stories can help us do the same with that universal human experience—loss.

Eight

Helping Your Child
Cope with Loss

✧

Loss is part of every move our children make toward growing up. "My ten-year-old put all his action figures in a big bag, carried them out of his room and put them in the garage, because he said it would be embarrassing if other kids saw them when they came over. He's always loved those toys, and the thought of not seeing him set them up on the floor anymore brought tears to my eyes," one mother told me. "Then two days later I saw him carry the bag back into his room. I think he's finally compromised by hiding the bag under his bed."

For both parents and kids, loss looms over many of the most joyful events of childhood—the first missing front tooth, the first day of kindergarten, the first signs of puberty. Experiences of loss are, inevitably, part of all love, and they are a reflection of the growth of a child's attachment to familiar caregivers. The eight-month-old who cries at separation from you is letting you know that she has developed a healthy bond with you and an awareness that you're a special and unique person in his life. The pang you feel at his cry is a sign that you feel that deep connection, too. The presence of loss in the midst of life is beautifully conveyed in "The Lost Horse" and "The Mouse That Drowned."

No one on earth, not even our children, can be protected from loss. Unfortunately, though, in our culture we don't help them learn how to deal with it or see it as an opportunity to grow. To be a "loser" is considered an insult. (No wonder we tell our kids more about *acquiring*—getting toys and clothes, getting into college, getting a job—than about losing.) In this chapter you'll learn how to help your child handle predictable losses that occur at every stage of childhood, and how to emerge stronger and wiser. You'll also find advice on how to help him cope with major losses—a move to a new town, a parent's job layoff, a divorce, a death. Because so much of what your child learns about coping with loss comes through unspoken communications from those he loves best, I hope you will spend some time with the exercises and questions in these pages, which are designed to help you reflect on the losses in your own life.

Let's begin with a Chinese story I like because it speaks beautifully and simply of the way blessing and sorrow commingle in our lives.

✧   ✧   ✧

THE LOST HORSE

An old man and his son lived in a farming village on the edge of a desert where enemy nomads lived. One day the son's horse ran off and was captured by nomads. "What a disaster," said the people of the village. "We're so sorry."

But the boy's father only asked, "How do you know this isn't a blessing?"

After a few months the son's horse came galloping back with another horse, a magnificent nomad stallion. "Congratulations!" said the people of the village. "What a blessing!"

But the father only asked, "How do you know this isn't a disaster?"

The son loved the nomad stallion, and every afternoon the son went out to the fields and rode the horse as fast as the wind. Then one day the horse stumbled, and the son fell off and broke his hip. "What a disaster," said the people of the village. "We're so sorry."

But the boy's father only asked, "How do you know this isn't a blessing?"

Then came the day a band of nomads galloped across the border, carrying clubs and spears. All the able-bodied men in the village went to fight them, but since the son's hip hadn't healed yet, he stayed at home with his father. By the time the battle was over, every single man who fought had been killed. But the old man and his son lived together for many more years.

Blessing and disaster, disaster and blessing, one turning into the other: This is one of the great mysteries of life.

This story has an unsettling, paradoxical quality, like a parable of Jesus or a Zen koan about the sound of one hand clapping, doesn't it? At the beginning, the villagers see everything as clear cut, either black or white. The stallion is a wonderful gift; the son's broken hip, a loss. That's the way children start out, seeing most things in life as split into all good or all bad. When Mommy gives them what she wants, she is "nice" or "good," like a fairy godmother. When she says no, she's more like a wicked witch, "mean" or "bad." As they grow (usually some time shortly after they turn three), thanks to enough experience of both the fairy godmother and the witch, as well as increased cognitive ability, children begin to stop "splitting" and understand the paradox that it's the same Mommy who is sometimes agreeable, sometimes not. But long after that developmental step forward, in times of loss or painful transition, most of us find it hard to keep a balance. We return to that early state of splitting. Life or the universe or God seems to be against us.

"The Lost Horse" is a story that reminds listeners, through one blessing and disaster after another, to keep our eyes on the whole picture. Each time the villagers pronounce a blessing, the old man sees a disaster, and vice versa. This isn't a tale I would tell or read to anyone who is actively grieving a major loss or in the midst of a painful transition. Those are times for listening and comforting. But it is a story that, through its capacity to startle, helps us both gain perspective on our losses and avoid taking our blessings for granted.

Loss and Development

At every stage of life, coming to terms with loss always goes hand in hand with the growth of *attachment*. Picture a bereaved person. Does he or she remind you of a baby whose mother has left the room—head hanging, eyes brimming with tears, arms reaching out for a hug? A person in mourning may often want to avoid the company of others, but healing comes when he or she feels the presence and touch of someone who cares.

Infants. Much of the research on how human beings experience loss has focused on the intense relationship between mother and baby and on early experiences of separation. Nature equips the baby with just what he needs to hold her close; by sucking, crying, and smiling, he keeps her attention. (Daniel Stern, in his pioneering work with infants at New York University, remarked on the "exuberant" smile an infant reserves just for mother.) As an infant develops an internal sense of this loving bond, he can hold onto it in mother's absence. If she leaves the room briefly and he is faced with the loss of the warmth and scent of her skin, her voice, her milk, he still maintains a sense of his own existence and a trust that she will return. He has a kind of everyday faith, an early resilience, that the British psychoanalyst and pediatrician D. W. Winnicott called "going-on-being."

By six months of age, an infant can hold onto his mother as a *representational image* when she is not with him. He has enough of a notion that she is a particular and separate person, according to the pioneering work on attachment and loss by the British psychoanalyst John Bowlby, to actively yearn for her when she is away from him. If you have a seven- or eight-month-old, you've probably noticed that if you threaten to leave the room, he comes creeping after you. If you leave him behind, you may hear him whimpering or sobbing, and when you come back he greets you with a big smile and a hug. (By toddlerhood he's likely to pretend he's not particularly interested in your return.) On the other hand, if *he* decides to crawl away from you he's probably not upset, but he'll crawl back frequently as though to "check in," and enjoys playing "peekaboo."

That ability to tolerate a separation from someone we love, and to hold onto an attachment in the face of the loss, is one way to describe the process of grieving as it happens all through life. To cope with loss means to hold onto well-being through disappointment or aching sorrow, and to trust that somehow comfort or relief will soon come.

By helping an infant develop a healthy attachment, you prepare him to deal with separations he faces now and losses he will encounter in the future. By letting him use a "cuddly" such as a teddy or blanket, and by offering an older infant or toddler opportunities to get to know a new caregiver before he is left alone with her for a long period of time (the day you return to work, for example), you prevent him from being overwhelmed by the loss and show him that he can find the comfort he needs.

Bowlby studied not only the physical presence of mothers, but their *psychological* availability. He found that if mothers were "emotionally absent" because of depression, worries, or other concerns, the child has great difficulty feeling a strong enough connection to her even when she's there. It's not hard to see how difficulties dealing with grief get passed down from generation to generation.

Toddlers and preschoolers. Between the ages of two and five, children who have formed a healthy attachment to familiar caregivers have learned through experience to trust that the caregivers will return after a separation. If they haven't been cared for outside the home up to now, they're likely to be enrolled in preschool. Many children experience separation anxiety at this point—anger at parents for "deserting" them, a wish to bring along a stuffed animal from home, a fear that if Mom's late she isn't going to come. With time and support from parents, and as he develops new relationships with the teacher and other children, a child learns to tolerate this transition and, in the process, grows a little more independent.

At this age kids often experience the birth of a younger sibling, which brings a loss of "baby status" as well as the separation from mother, who is busy caring for the infant. You're likely to hear the loss expressed obliquely, in questions like, "Why don't you send the baby back to the hospital?" or "Who do you love more, me or the baby?" What your child needs to do is to share his feelings with you without worrying that you will scold or shame him. Ease the transition by spending some special time alone every day with the older sibling, and by getting him or her involved in helping you care for the baby and understand how she's growing (more on this in chapter 10).

School-age children. Reaching school age means moving out into the community beyond home or the child-care center and into the world of peers, school, and organized activities. Although these changes are exciting and positive, they also entail a loss of the safe, familiar world of home or preschool. For many kids, especially those faced with highly academic programs or heavy team sports schedules, experiencing competition (see chapter 9) brings a loss of self-esteem; they may be disappointed at their ability to perform and miss the unconditional acceptance of their early childhood environment.

This is a time of loss for parents, too. "It's amazing the loss of control I feel over my child's life now that she's in school," one father told me. "They assign her a teacher, she's put in a certain program, and except for a teacher conference I have very little to say about how she spends her day."

By the age of seven, your child has lost much of the infantile dependence and the expressiveness of the young child. You may notice that he has grown more private about his thoughts and the events of his day, less willing to chatter. Sometimes, when his new independence is scary, he may express the fear through worries about his health, like asking for Band-Aids to cover barely visible cuts and scratches. Ease this new transition by letting him know you're available. That doesn't mean asking a lot of questions, which he may experience as intrusive. On the other hand, a question like "Are you all right?" is likely to get a simple "Yup" and not much more. Keep in touch in simple, low-key ways—take a walk, toss around a ball, ask him to cook with you, get some help changing the oil. Be sure there's time and enough privacy and connection between you for her to open up when she needs you.

Adolescents. By preadolescence, your child is eager to think of himself as independent, and yet he's not quite ready to give up being a kid. "First my son tells me to get lost. It's 'Don't ask me, Ma, 'cause I don't want to tell you anything, so just leave me *alone*,' and the next thing I know he's back wanting to sit in my lap," said one mother of an eleven-year-old. By adolescence a child is deep in the process that has been called "normal adolescent mourning," recognizing your imperfections, no longer idealizing you, feeling the loss of childhood and of the protected family circle, and seeing that the world is no longer perfect. No wonder he's moody. He's got his whole life ahead of him, and yet to move forward he is facing tremendous loss. He's intense one minute, calm the next, loving and hating, dependent and independent. He feels helpless at times, and angry. Bereft of his childhood, he searches for ideals, and argues and defends them ardently.

Parents of an adolescent often feel acutely the loss of the child who once respected their opinion and enjoyed their company. The way you experienced this tumultuous process during *your* adolescent years can help you empathize with your teen's struggle and recognize what he needs—or, if you have many unresolved feelings, it can bring more anxiety to the separation process. When it seems as though your child "doesn't want to have anything to do with me except when it's time for an argument," know that *the quarrels,* painful though they are, *represent for your adolescent an acceptable form of attachment to you.* Through the arguments, he can get your attention, let you know what's on his mind, and experience the loss of his childhood bond with you, all at the same time. That's why it's important not to give in to his needling or refuse to engage with him.

Family Time
"THE LOST HORSE"

Compare notes on recent "disasters" that turned out to be blessings. Go back over the past few weeks or months. Think of events and situations that you and your child thought were going to be relatively disastrous, yet turned out better than you'd expected. They don't have to be earth shattering. A preschooler might mention a bite into a new ice cream that looked great but turned out to be awful. Maybe your school-age child had too much homework to go with a friend to a particular movie, which turned out to be boring. Your adolescent might talk about getting left out of a clique, then realizing he didn't want to join it in the first place.

If your child seems receptive, share similar experiences from your own life. Maybe you remember something that seemed to mean the whole world at one time, like not getting accepted into the college of your choice and loving the place you did attend, or getting dumped by a big crush and finding out it was an opportunity to grow. You can mention something minor, like forgetting an important ingredient in the dinner last night and finding out everybody loved the dish you improvised.

Look at today's newspaper. Invite your school-age child or adolescent to comb the news columns with you for blessings and disasters. Is there a crisis or conflict between two interest groups that might turn out to be a positive force for change? Does the day's good news in the financial section have a potential "down side"? Could there be anything valuable about a contract dispute reported in the sports section? The editorial or op-ed pages are good places to look for lively pieces that offer a variety of points of view on the day's events.

By encouraging kids to think of more than one side of an issue, you can provide an antidote to the shallow opinions and sensationalism kids are exposed to on the radio and television. As you raise the level of discourse on the news, your children learn to think and express themselves in more balanced, articulate ways.

The Parent's Path
"THE LOST HORSE"

Work with a grief partner. One of the most remarkable survival skills human beings have is our capacity to put our losses behind us and move on. Sometimes, though, we move on so quickly that we never really pay attention to the pain. Without even realizing it, we're the "walking wounded." As a parent, it's important to recognize the losses in your own life that need healing, and to deal with them, or they become a silent but powerful presence in your relationship with your child. One way to do this is by sharing your loss with a friend or other understanding listener.

One woman who came to me for help with depression told me she'd wished all her life that she'd been able to talk with her alcoholic father, and to feel close to him, before his death when she was fifteen. Eventually she became a parent herself. As her son grew toward adolescence she found herself in despair, worrying that now that she was "losing her little boy," their whole relationship was about to come to an end. She was tearful and had trouble sleeping. When this woman came to understand that she was dealing not only with her son's transition to manhood but also with the *past* loss of her father, the first "man in her life," she was able to recognize that much of her worry was connected to unresolved grief from her own adolescence. As she "revisited" that period of her life in our therapy sessions—remembering good and bad times with her father, and exploring what she regretted about him and what he had given her— her despair about her son faded, and she was able to face the challenges and losses and joys of his growth into young manhood.

The exercises in this chapter will help you explore the losses in your life and grow more aware of how they may be affecting you (and your ability to help your child cope with loss). Before you begin, do consider asking your partner or a friend to work on them along with you and share one another's experiences. Thinking about loss and grief isn't something we're meant to do alone. At times the process may even be overwhelming. Although the questions that follow will help you reflect and understand, healing begins when you share your feelings with another person.

If you do decide to work with a partner, choose someone whose confidentiality you trust and with whom you feel comfortable talking. Make a commitment to meet for the first time on a particular day when you can have at least two hours without interruption. If that sounds like a lot more time that you think you'll need, or can fit into your busy schedule, keep in mind that this process is likely to bring up powerful feelings for you that aren't always easy to manage. Because confidentiality, privacy, and support are essential, this isn't a process you'll want to do while chasing your toddler around the room or in a fast-food restaurant.

In the meantime, read "The Lost Horse" and work through this set of exercises, recording your responses in your journal or on separate sheets of paper. You may wish to begin your meeting by reading or telling the story again to one another. Now take turns going over your loss timelines below. Talk about the feelings associated with each event you've written about. Don't take responsibility for soothing one another's pain. Just listen and ask for clarification when you don't understand what your partner is saying or how she's feeling. Try to complete your first conversation about the loss timelines in one meeting.

When it's your turn to talk about your own responses, be aware of feelings of sadness, a tightening in your throat or an ache in your chest or stomach, sudden tears, or a noticeable *lack* of affect that you experience when talking about particular people or events; these are likely to be signs of unresolved grief. Of course, we all feel some sadness at the thought of people we've lost; that's a sign of how much we loved them. Sometimes, though—either because you haven't had enough opportunity to talk about the loss or *because your child is approaching the same age you were when you suffered the loss*—the old wounds are reopened, and you need to attend to your grief.

At your second meeting with your partner (preferably no more than a week later), talk about how each of you felt about the first meeting. What moments were particularly helpful? Now take turns going back to the people whose memories seemed to trigger painful feelings or about whom you felt surprisingly little. Tell your partner how you felt talking about the memories with him or her then and how they have affected you since the first meeting. At this point, stay with the memories if you are comfortable doing so. Talk about your relationship with the person—happy times, sad times, regrets. Finally, schedule another meeting to work on the rest of this set of exercises, or to move on to the next story.

Make a loss timeline. In order to support and comfort a child who is having difficulty dealing with the separations that come with the beginning of preschool or elementary school or adolescence, we need to be able to *connect with her feelings without being overwhelmed by them*. To do this means to walk the fine line between disaster and blessing. It demands that we come to terms with the losses in our own lives. Working on this exercise (preferably with your grief partner) is one effective way to do that.

Starting from birth, you're going to write down all the losses in your life—a move to a new town, the death of a pet, a breakup with a "big crush," the death of a parent. Take a standard sheet of paper, turn it sideways, and using a ruler draw a horizontal line across the page.

A SAMPLE LOSS TIMELINE

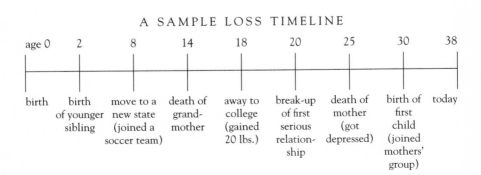

Write down the year of your *earliest memory* (whether or not you perceive it as a loss). Make a notation of how you felt at the time, as well as how you feel now thinking back on the event and people you recall—sadness, envy, embarrassment, joy. Whether you recall the birth of a younger sibling, your mother holding you in the park, or crying in your crib, keep in mind that your earliest memory gives you and your partner an idea of how you experienced your introduction to the world, and how you probably tend to approach life—and loss—today.

Continue along the timeline to the right, noting losses in your life from early childhood to the present day. Include not only obvious losses, such as deaths or relationship breakups, but also positive events that entailed loss, like the birth of a child. Be sure to record the following:

1. Your age at the time of each loss;
2. your feelings about the loss then and now;
3. how you dealt with the loss at that time.

The third item is essential because it helps you recognize not only unresolved grief but also how you tend to respond, or avoid responding, to loss today.

In my own case, for example, I was sixteen when my grandmother, who had lived nearby for most of my early years, died. I was devastated. For me she'd been a nurturing, strong woman who still did her grocery shopping on foot at the age of ninety-two. I treasured memories of the times she'd brought me to the live poultry market, taught me old Italian songs, and made vegetable soup from scratch.

When I saw her closed casket in the center aisle of the church at the funeral mass, the thought crossed my mind that my grandmother could no longer breathe. It was more than I could manage. For the next few days at school I excused myself from class several times a day and ran to the girls' bathroom to cry in private.

Finally, in an art class, I began working on a pastel portrait of my grandmother, sketching from a photograph. It was a good likeness and a way of connecting with her as I poured my grief into the drawing.

Looking back, I realize that the way I responded to my grandmother's death reveals both the positive and the negative aspects of the way I tend to cope with loss. I had found a creative "solution" that helped me hold onto her memory, but I hadn't shared with anyone my sorrow at the reality that she was gone.

As you consider the losses on your timeline, pay attention in particular to what the adults in your life seemed to be teaching you. Were you invited to find a replacement for the loss ("Don't worry, we'll buy you another dog")? Did you get the message that others were distraught that you were *alone* with your feelings? Did you *take care of others'* needs, offering emotional support or taking over chores and responsibilities beyond your years? Were open displays of emotion frowned on, so that you *hid* your grief? Did you, in your childish way of thinking, get the impression that somehow you were to *blame* for the loss? Were you told to "give it *time*"? Did anyone say, "It's all for the best" or "It's God's will"? How did you feel about these "grief lessons"?

Was there a particular adult—parent, teacher, relative, other mentor— who *was* helpful? What meant so much to you about that person's response? What made it different from others' attempts to comfort you?

Now open your journal and write down the things you came to believe about grief and loss as a result of these early experiences. Pay special attention to those beliefs that are no longer useful to you today; for example, "It must be my fault" or "Just keep busy." Putting these in writing will give you an opportunity to refer back to them later, which is important because these are the unspoken "lessons" you're likely to be teaching your child about grieving and loss. (You'll find advice on teaching healthy grieving on pages 182–83.) If you're sharing these exercises with a grief partner, make time now to sit down with him or her, acknowledge these old beliefs, and set them aside.

What losses or transitions have you or your household experienced in the past year? Has there been a job loss? an illness or death? a "big" birthday? your first gray hair?

Has the loss affected your daily routine? Has it made a difference in your child's schedule or expectations? How has the loss caused you to struggle with your sense of who you are?

An athletic father was stunned the first time his son outran him in a race along the beach. "I remember when I was this big guy who used to toss him up in the air," the man told me. "Now he's faster than I am." He paused. "I guess it's time to pass the baton," he said slowly, then brightened: "At least I'm still better at soccer."

Do you see a connection between your response to a recent loss and any of the losses you've marked on your timeline? Did the earlier experience of loss help prepare you to deal with the one you're facing now, or do you avoid your feelings by following one of the negative patterns you described above?

Maybe the recent loss has surprised you by triggering earlier grief about something or someone you thought you had put behind you.

Can you see any good that has come out of the losses in your life? *Do not try to answer this question until you have met with your partner several times to talk over your loss timeline.* This is a question to answer only *after* you've had the opportunity to develop an awareness of unresolved grief and to share your feelings and memories with your partner. (If you skip that painful work, you're likely to short-circuit that healing process by coming up with a "philosophical" rationalization such as "It's all for the best.")

Looking back now, how have you grown as a result of the loss you experienced? How have you come to know yourself better?

Is there a loss or disaster in your life that has yet to become a blessing? *This is an exercise in guided imagery that you can do on your own or with your grief partner.* Who has a life with no regrets? Most adults have had a relationship that didn't work out, a job where we feel stuck, a bad choice that seems to be determining too much of our future. When you feel locked in to a negative viewpoint, when you see nothing but disaster, a first step in changing things is to use your imagination to tip the balance back toward blessing and open you up to fresh possibility. If you're having a hard time connecting a relatively simple relaxation technique with expanding your options, it may help to consider that, in Hebrew, one word, *ruach*, means both "breath" and "spirit." Let your breath bring healing.

Take turns with your grief partner reading this exercise aloud, or if you're alone, make an audiotape to listen to:

Set aside fifteen minutes when you can be alone in silence. Find a comfortable place to sit, perhaps a straight-backed chair or cross-legged on the floor. Close your eyes. Now slowly inhale, letting your breath fill your abdomen. . . . Then slowly exhale, letting the warm air come out through your nose and mouth.

Keep breathing slowly in and out. Feel the air filling your body more deeply with each breath. Let your whole body relax and receive the fresh air. As you draw air in, let your abdomen expand. Imagine that you are opening up a space for blessing to come in. Focus on any pain or tightness you may feel in your chest, your belly, your arms and legs, and try to let it go. Open up to the idea that change might come, that something good might grow out of your pain and loss. Continue to inhale and exhale. And as you breathe in and out, let your deep breathing bring calm to the tightness in your body. And just as each breath you inhale is followed by the one you exhale, allow for the possibility out of the pain you feel now, a blessing may come.

Rest in this awareness, continuing to inhale and exhale slowly. And when you're ready, open your eyes.

Helping Children Cope with Loss

No one is ever "prepared" to cope with major loss, and we all wish we could protect our children from loss during their vulnerable early years. But when a child does suffer a major loss, he needs to know that we can face his grief and help him bear it. A child's losses might include not only those adults easily recognize, such as the death of a loved one or a divorce, but also events that may seem less traumatic yet change his world, like a move to a new city or the departure of a long-term caregiver.

In July 1996, when TWA flight 800 from New York to Paris exploded over the Atlantic near Long Island, I was struck by the way the media dealt with the survivors' grief. Grief counselors were sent to the bereaved families of the victims, and the "predictable stages" of grief were described by TV newscasters. One report announced on the following day that survivors who "would have been going through shock and disbelief" would now be "reaching acceptance." Comments like these create a mistaken impression about grief. Although both child and adult mourners do experience a wide range of the emotions—including denial, shock, and disbelief; anger; sadness, regret, and a feeling of abandonment; guilt; and acceptance—described by Elisabeth Kübler-Ross in her pioneering work with dying people, these don't happen in neatly compartmentalized stages that can be marked on a calendar. "People keep asking me when I'm moving on to 'acceptance,' " one adolescent, whose mother had died, told me with a sigh. "I think I go through just about all those stages every day."

The way we grieve a particular loss, such as the death of an immediate family member, has a great deal to do with the nature of our relationship with him or her; as we remember the person, we experience the full range of feelings we had when that person was alive. If there were many conflicts or disappointments, it's that much more difficult to recover. We blame ourselves or give ourselves more responsibility than is realistic: "If only I'd realized he didn't look well, I might have talked him into going to the doctor sooner." If the death came after a long illness, we're likely to feel some relief. ("Yay! Mommy died!" said one three-year-old, to his father's horror, after a mother's two-year battle with cancer.)

Grieving children experience many of the same emotions as adults, yet they are much less equipped to handle them for several reasons. First of all, kids don't always express their feelings and needs in ways adults can understand. Second, parents may unintentionally communicate attitudes that block a child's capacity to express grief: "It's not OK to talk about it," because it gets grown-ups too upset; or "Everything will go on the same as it always has," no matter how awful you feel; or "Everything has to be under control," including you. If there isn't a regular pattern in the family of expressing feelings, or if sadness, anger, and hurt are usually dealt with by finding someone to lash out at, then children may not have learned to talk about pain over an event that can't be blamed on anyone, as a death often is.

When the loss involves a parent, there's likely to be a disruption of the child's normal development that can leave him or her less capable of coping with his feelings. Naturally, a child's responses reflect his own particular level of maturity and all that this implied about their connection. How dependent was he on the parent to meet his physical and emotional needs? Did he look to the parent as a role model? Was he going through a period of anger or "testing"? The answers to these and similar questions all have an enormous effect on the child's capacity to come to terms with the loss, and on the kind of support he needs.

Let's look at some of the particular struggles children face when they experience a major loss, such as the death of a parent or grandparent, at different ages.

Infants. An infant's capacity to continue healthy development depends a great deal on how the adults in his life respond to the loss. Do they continue to meet his basic needs for feeding, sleep, and affection? Can the adults face the baby's loss, or do they identify so strongly with the helplessness and pain he will face that they try to pretend the relationship never existed? Do they recognize that even an infant knows his mother as a unique, irreplaceable person? Are the adults in his life dealing with *their* grief, or are they trying to set it aside? Because babies are so "emotionally permeable," they take in the feelings their caregivers don't consciously process—anger, sadness, abandonment—all the emotions that are part of grieving. (The baby may not directly experience the loss of a grandparent, but he will respond to his own parent's bereavement.) Do the adults around him recognize that, although infants can't talk about what's happening to them or the people around them, they process the loss *bodily*, sometimes "expressing" it through difficulties with feeding or sleeping?

Toddlers and preschoolers can communicate about a loss in words. But although they talk about death, dying, and heaven, they use these words in ways that reflect their magical understanding of the world. A child under five, told that a grandparent has died, cries in your arms and says how much he'll miss Grandpa. He may ask where Grandpa is and, if parents say he's gone to heaven, wonder whether Grandpa will be able to go to baseball games there. Two days later he asks eagerly when Grandpa is coming to dinner.

This lack of reality testing can be frightening to a young child, who may turn his active imagination to wondering whether a death was the result of his own wishes. He'll recall the time he had to go to Grandpa's house instead of a playmate's birthday party, for example, and got so angry he told his parents, "I wish I didn't even *have* a grandpa!" Or he'll remember the day he jumped out from behind the door and yelled, "Boo!" at Grandpa, and the old man said jokingly, "You'll be the death of me yet!"

If he is "protected" from the reality of the death and kept home from the funeral, he may have little to think about except his fantasies. Keep in mind that he isn't only coping with the death itself, but with the distress of parents and other family members. Then there are the visits from strangers and other disruptions to his routine, probably including extra time with babysitters. What he needs are opportunities to share his grief with you in his own way, and to ask questions. You can help a grieving preschooler by offering clear, concrete explanations. When someone dies, give him the biological facts first: the person can't eat, breathe, talk, feel, walk, see, taste, or smell things. This is a curious age; expect your child to ask the same questions over and over again, some of them rather fantastic sounding ("Could Grandpa meet George Washington in heaven? Will Grandpa's dog go, too?") Although many adults take comfort in the thought that a loved one is in heaven, to a child it can sound awfully far away.

Your child will appreciate concrete ways you can help him hold onto a *connection* with someone he's lost. Remind him of special times with the person—outings, overnights, shared hobbies or crafts, holiday gatherings and customs. (For suggested ways to help your child do this, see page 183.)

Even with all your support, your child may be demanding and clingy for a while. He may begin to eat in a more babyish way, hold onto a blanket or cuddly he'd set aside some time ago, or lose control easily. He may have trouble with his toileting habits. Be patient. Unskilled as he still is at expressing feelings verbally, he's showing his grief through his bodily functions. Even as long as a year later, he may have a harder time getting along with siblings. Set aside time to be alone with him no matter how preoccupied you are with arrangements and estate matters, and let him know that you understand how upset he is and are available to comfort him and answer his questions.

School-age children. By school age, children have usually become aware that death is real and permanent, and that it can happen to anyone, including themselves. Not surprisingly, this is a terrifying realization, and kids this age often ask many questions. "My son keeps asking me about death and dying," one mother in a workshop group told me. "Is there something wrong with him?" As we spoke it became clear to me that the child's questions were typical of those asked by many kids his age. The mother's worry, however, that he was "abnormal" or "weird" could deliver the message that the subject of death was one to be avoided, thus leaving him all alone with his fears. It's important to avoid "shutting down" a school-age child this way. When they express feelings and ask questions, they're expressing confidence and trust.

School-age kids who suffer a loss may have trouble talking about their grief directly, and instead have stomachaches, sleep problems, more arguments with siblings, or trouble in school. They're growing more independent, and proud of it, and when they feel the need for comforting they may believe they need to hide or control it. Boys, in particular, may believe that crying isn't something they're supposed to do, and often hesitate to start conversations that may end in tears. Some children, on the other hand, take on the outward appearance of sudden maturity; a girl may become the "little mother" after her mother's death, in an effort to "hold onto her" by identifying with her, instead of asking for the care and support she needs. They may get very attached to particular belongings they associate with the person who has died; one ten-year-old spoke little of her father after his death, for example, but wore his old college sweatshirt all the time.

For that reason, even if your child seems outwardly calm after a loss, don't assume he's "fine." Whether or not he can share his grief, and his memories, in ways that feel comfortable for him will profoundly affect his ability to form intimate relationships in the years to come. Without intruding, be sure he knows you're available if he wants to talk. He will not be able to mourn unless he knows you can handle it. "If you need some time to talk about Grandpa, let me know," you might say. Or simply, "How about you and I go for a walk together?" By offering him time and your company, with no interruption for errands, phone calls, or nagging, you create a safe space where he can talk when he's ready. Don't be surprised if his concerns reflect a return to the "magical thinking" of his preschool years; we *all* have trouble thinking rationally about death and dying. He may need to talk not only about the loss but also about other things on his mind. If a child was ashamed of a dying parent's appearance, he may feel guilty about that and wonder if his feelings caused the death. At the same time, he misses his family the way it used to be, with two parents who could balance out one another, and although he may enjoy having the surviving parent all to himself, he also worries that something could happen to that parent and leave him completely alone. Because he's aware that death is something that could happen to him, he may be afraid of the dark or worry about minor aches and pains. That feeling that there's something "wrong" with him is often reinforced socially; when a school-age child's parent dies, it's not unusual for other kids to tease or avoid him, making remarks like, "He's weird. His father died."

Check with your local hospice for a children's bereavement group that can provide support. If he doesn't have a chance to share his fears with you or others who care, his guilt and fear can lead to depression. If, after the first month, you are aware of problems in school—a drop in grades or an unwillingness to go—a withdrawal from friendships and activities your child usually enjoys, or any suggestion that your child wishes to "rejoin" the person he has lost by dying, it's wise to consult with a professional bereavement counselor or psychotherapist who can help you and your child deal with his grief. (See the Appendix on page 251 for referral sources.)

A child's response to the death of a grandparent depends a great deal on how often the two saw one another, and the kind of rapport they shared. If he has the opportunity to grieve with other family members, he is likely to recover fairly quickly. He may need to talk about problems in the relationship. And because he understands that the death of his grandparent means the loss of *your* parent, and wondering what that feels like, he will probably want to hear about your grief, not only your sense of loss but your memories of childhood and your appreciation of his or her life.

The school-age child's response to a divorce is similar to his reaction to a death in the family. His sense of belonging to an intact family circle is broken now, and he may worry that if one or both parents remarry he won't have any family to call his own. If he lives with one parent, he may idealize the other in an effort to avoid experiencing the loss. He's likely to fantasize that his parents will get back together. If you or your partner are upset and angry, it's not easy to be available to help him deal with his feelings, especially if he is testing your relationship with anger and blaming.

Adolescents. Your adolescent is especially vulnerable after a loss because he is in the midst of a major life transition. He thinks of himself as unique, eager for independence, and someone who will live forever. The death of a grandparent, which is often the first bereavement a child faces and which often occurs during this period, reminds him of his own mortality. If his relationship with his parents is fraught with conflict at this stage, he may have found the grandparent easier or safer to talk to, and he will miss him or her deeply. An adolescent is also intensely affected by deaths of public figures, people he thinks of as role models for his adult life. Although your adolescent may express his grief by complaining or attacking you, let him know that you appreciate how difficult it is for him to handle his feelings. Without criticizing, *let him know you care* about how he's doing. "You don't seem too cheerful since Grandpa died," you can tell him. "I'm worried about you. Is there anything you want to talk to me about?" An adolescent often needs other adults to talk to besides parents—a trusted teacher, a member of the clergy, a sports coach. Watch out for the warning signs of depression I've noted in school-age children, above, and trust your instincts if you think your child might benefit from professional help.

The story that follows, "The Mouse That Drowned," is a Czech tale that portrays the difference between healthy and pathological grief. When Little Mouse dies, no one in the barnyard can deal with his loss, until one person turns it all around by speaking from the heart. This isn't a story I'd tell or read to a child who has recently suffered a major loss (for suggestions, see the Appendix on page 249), but it's a good way to share at another time, as a way of opening up the subject of loss. It's fun to tell as a story "duet," with each of you playing a different character.

THE MOUSE THAT DROWNED

"Boo-hoo! Boo-hoo!" cried the sausage.

"Sausage, why are you crying?" asked the gate.

"What else can I do?" answered the sausage, sobbing. "Dear Little Mouse has just drowned."

"Drowned!" said the gate. "Well, then, I'm going to swing open so hard that I go right off my hinges." And the gate did.

When the fence saw that, it asked, "Gate, why have you swung off your hinges?"

"What else can I do?" answered the gate. "Dear Little Mouse has just drowned."

"Drowned!" cried the fence. "Well, then, I'm going to fall down." And the fence did.

Just then a bird that had been about to fly down and perch on the fence fluttered its wings and asked, "Fence, why did you fall down?"

"What else can I do?" answered the fence, sobbing. "Dear Little Mouse has just drowned. The sausage is crying, the gate has swung off its hinges, and I've just fallen down."

"Drowned!" cried the bird. "Well, then, I'm going to tie up one of my legs." And the bird tied up one leg with a piece of string. Then it flew into the forest and alighted on a tree.

"Bird," asked the tree, "why have you tied up your leg?"

"What else can I do?" answered the bird, sobbing. "Dear Little Mouse has just drowned. The sausage is crying, the gate has swung off its hinges, the fence has fallen down, and I've tied up my leg."

"Drowned!" cried the tree, letting its branches droop. "Then I'm going to fall down." And the tree did. Then a stag came along, amazed to see such a magnificent tree fallen to the ground.

"Tree," asked the stag, "why have you fallen?"

"What else can I do?" answered the tree, sobbing. "Dear Little Mouse has just drowned. The sausage is crying, the gate has swung off its hinges, the fence has fallen down, the bird has tied up its leg, and I've fallen down."

"Drowned!" cried the stag, bowing its head. "Then I'm going to shed my antlers." And he did, and then he ran through the forest and across the hills until he reached a spring.

"Stag," asked the spring, "why have you shed your antlers?"

"What else can I do?" answered the stag, sobbing. "Dear Little Mouse has just drowned. The sausage is crying, the gate has swung off its hinges, the fence has fallen down, the bird has tied up its leg, the tree has fallen down, and I've shed my antlers."

"Drowned!" cried the spring. "Then I'm going to go muddy." Just then a girl came along, carrying a water jug.

"Spring," she asked, "why have you gone muddy?"

"What else can I do?" answered the spring, sobbing. "Dear Little Mouse has just drowned. The sausage is crying, the gate has swung off its hinges, the fence has fallen down, the bird has tied up its leg, the tree has felled itself, the stag has shed his antlers, and I've gone muddy."

"Drowned!" cried the girl. "Then I'm going to throw this jug to the ground and break it into a million pieces." And she did, and she went home empty-handed.

"Daughter," asked the girl's mother. "Why have you come home without the water jug?"

"What else could I do?" answered the girl, sobbing. "Dear Little Mouse has just drowned. The sausage is crying, the gate has swung off its hinges, the fence has fallen down, the bird has tied up its leg, the tree has felled itself, the stag has shed his antlers, the spring has gone muddy, and I've broken the water jug into a million pieces."

"Drowned!" cried the girl's mother. "Then I'm going to pour a bag of salt into the bread dough." And she picked up the bag and started to pour. Just then her husband came in from the fields.

"Why are you pouring salt into the bread dough, wife?" he asked. "You're ruining it!"

"What else can I do?" answered the woman, sobbing. "Dear Little Mouse has just drowned. The sausage is crying, the gate has swung off its hinges, the fence has fallen down, the bird has tied up its leg, the tree has felled itself, the stag has shed his antlers, the spring has gone muddy, our daughter has broken the water jug into a million pieces, and I'm pouring salt into the bread dough."

"Drowned!" cried the husband. "How sad. We're really

going to miss our dear Little Mouse, aren't we? But making a mess of everything isn't going to bring him back. I'm going out to build a new henhouse." And out he went.

And when the henhouse was built, the woman mixed fresh bread dough, the daughter took another jug and went to the spring, the spring ran clear water, the stag sprouted new antlers, a new tree began to grow in the forest, the bird untied its leg and flew back to the fence, the fence stood back up, the gate swung back onto its hinges, and the sausage stopped crying.

But dear Little Mouse was not forgotten.

Kids ten and under enjoy this story for its singsong quality. It's a tale full of wisdom about the difference between healthy and unhealthy grief. Yet considering the subject, it falls surprisingly flat, don't you think? Although all the creatures in the barnyard and forest are reacting to the death of Little Mouse, it's hard to care very much about him. We don't end up knowing him at all, or grasping anything about his connection with the fence, the tree, the daughter, or anyone else. There's plenty of banging and falling and shedding and breaking in this tale, but what's missing is the expression of real *feeling*. With the exception of the sausage and the husband, the characters respond to the loss by acting in a variety of self-destructive ways, avoiding any emotional experience of the loss. Their actions seem more like reflexes than felt responses.

Then, just as the girl's mother is pouring salt into the bread dough, her husband comes in and turns the whole story around. He does this by grieving—in magically short and simple story style, true, but it's grieving all the same. First, he expresses his feelings and recognizes, unlike the sausage who cries alone, that others share them. "How sad," says the husband. "We're really going to miss our dear Little Mouse, aren't we?" Next, he accepts the reality of the loss: "Making a mess of everything won't bring him back." Finally, he goes out to build a new henhouse. Life goes on.

And suddenly the rest of the barnyard is transformed. One by one, instead of all that swinging and falling, the gate is back on its hinges, the fence stands up, the sausage stops crying, the stag sprouts new antlers, and so forth.

Most of us know what it means to react to loss like the creatures in the barnyard and forest. Sometimes we avoid our own grief by telling ourselves to "get over it." Often we try to fill up the empty space with work, television, food, alcohol, you name it. If we try to face it alone, we end up overwhelmed; like the sausage, a grieving person has a thin skin.

These are the ways of grieving that we pass on to our children, unless, like the husband in the story, we break the pattern. We do that not by "teaching healthy grief," but by offering the help and support they need to share their anger, sadness, guilt, longing, and other feelings. It's being presented to them in their loss, and if it affects us directly (as it so often does) by dealing with our own grief, that means the most.

Here are some of the most important things to remember in helping your child grieve:

- **Let him know that grief isn't just feeling sad.** It also means being angry or scared or having a hard time believing the person has died. Different people have different feelings at different times, depending on their particular personalties and on their relationship with the person who died. You or other family members may sometimes seem distracted, have a "short fuse," or be tearful or unusually quiet. Your child may have nightmares, difficulty sleeping, or trouble in school. Help your child understand that *talking* about feelings is a much more productive way to express them.
- **Invite him to participate in memorial observances to the degree he feels capable,** and let him know that you're available to hold his hand, and afterward to listen to him talk about the experience. Seeing the body at the wake helps a child take in the reality of the death and provides an opportunity to say good-bye.
- **Avoid trying to "make up for" a loss with a replacement.** If you give the impression that the loss can be made up for, then your child has no opportunity to experience it. She gets the message

that grieving is not allowed, or that you're worried it will over-whelm her. If your dog dies, he or she can't be replaced with a "new" one; the petting, playing, and growing your child has shared with this pet is a unique experience of childhood. Give your child the opportunity to treasure the memory and feel the loss.

- **Provide your child with a regular routine.** Keep in mind that a death and the events that follow drastically change a child's daily schedule. Help your child feel secure by not offering to let him stay home from school for an unnecessarily long time or stay up late or have more money to spend or more treats. These "extras" only distract him from his feelings, cover over the loss, and get in the way of his healthy grieving.

- **Help him hold onto his memories.** Make a scrapbook, photo album, or art project about the deceased's life, including special times he or she shared with your child and your family. Avoid ide-alizing the person; don't be afraid to talk about the struggles as well as the pleasures you shared. A child of middle school age or older might wish to collect money for a scholarship fund or memorial gift.

  Meeting with others who remember the deceased and may be able to share stories about him or her that a child would not have known—simple things, like a childhood fishing trip or how happy he was at the birth of a baby—can mean a great deal. My own father died after years of heart disease when I was in high school. At the time I was going through a minor ado-lescent rebellion, and he had been forced to cut back on his career because of his poor health. Communication between us was strained, to say the least. The day after he died, when someone from his office called and told me, "He talked about you all the time; he was so *proud* of you," it was just what I needed to hear.

- **Deal with your own feelings.** It's a hard balance to strike, but your child needs a parent who can reveal her responses without being overwhelming. If you are angry about a major loss—a death, divorce—keep in mind that no matter how justified your feelings are, your child needs help with *her* feelings. You will need to make an effort to set aside your anger and create a safe space where your child can be vulnerable, share her sadness with you, even remember good times in the past.

If you find your child's feelings too painful or upsetting to deal with, you may be responding to unresolved grief in your own past. This is especially true if you grew up in a household where family conversation focused on the *external facts* of particular situations, rather than on their *emotional impact*, where you often heard comments like "it's God's will" or "what's done is done." I hope the exercises in this chapter, and your conversations with your grief partner, will help you to deal with your unfinished mourning and to be kinder to yourself.

Family Time
"THE MOUSE THAT DROWNED"

Young children develop an understanding of loss with toys and people, not words. A ball goes under the sofa: "All gone!" Mommy puts her coat on, baby waves bye-bye. Some of the most time-honored childhood games—peekaboo, hide-and-seek—offer young kids opportunities to "work on" loss and death through play. In "Ring Around the Rosy," the refrain "Ashes, ashes, we all fall down!" is a clue to the game's origins during the plague in medieval Europe, when children saw illness and death all around them. Don't be surprised to overhear your preschooler use elements of this story in his fantasies. Here are some ideas on how to engage a young child in play with the story of Little Mouse.

Who else is in the barnyard and the forest? A two- or three-year-old who enjoys making animal sounds can imagine other creatures and their foolish responses to Little Mouse. What does the dog say when he hears about Little Mouse? "He turns over his water bowl," a three-year-old might answer. (Don't expect most two-year-olds to say more than "Bow wow" and, after some brainstorming from you, maybe "Dump bowl.") Offer some prompting: "What would the fish in the pond do? How about the flowers in the garden? What does the cow say?"

Now, without turning it into a lesson, help your preschooler learn the words for the feelings avoided in most of the story. Just talk about how the characters in the story respond, as though they were friends of yours. "They *miss* Little Mouse, don't they? They feel *sad*."

Talk about loss in your lives. If your *school-age child* seems eager for conversation, or whenever the time seems right, invite him to talk about something sad, or an experience of loss, in his own life. (Too often we give our kids the impression that their job is to make us happy by always telling us everything is "fine." As a result, we don't get to know what's on their minds, and they don't learn to articulate their experience.)

Maybe your child remembers a time he felt sad, or missed someone, when a friend moved away, for instance, or when a teacher moved to a different school. Don't turn this into a lesson in psychobabble. Instead, just let him know you're interested. Give him a chance to experience what it means to remember a feeling and talk about it with a responsive listener.

Ask if he or she would like to hear about a time *you* felt sad, and talk simply about an incident in your own life that connects with what your child has mentioned, without overwhelming him with your grief. If he's sad about switching to a new school, for example, you might let him know you have some idea what he's going through by telling about a time your family moved when you were a kid. Avoid discounting the loss with statements like, "And you know, after a month I'd forgotten all about my old neighborhood."

The Parent's Path
"THE MOUSE THAT DROWNED"

Plan your final meeting or meetings with your grief partner. There is no "standard" number of meetings that works for everyone. We all have different histories and different ways of dealing with loss. Pay attention to your own feelings. Don't short circuit your process or decide it's time to "put the past behind you." Meet with your grief partner until you *both* agree that you have come to terms with the relationships you are grieving. You'll find that by doing this work, arduous though it is, you will be better able to deal with transitions in your child's life that "trigger" your own old losses. At the same time you'll be more capable of helping him cope with grief when he needs your help.

It's essential in working on this exercise that grief partners help one another *balance* positive and negative memories. Idealizing the person who died only puts any problems in the relationship on your shoulders. Once you've worked on the exercises below in your journal, share them out loud with your grief partner. These are often painful and difficult to do and to talk about; it's important to feel comfortable with tears, and to offer a hug when it's needed.

Focus on what was left *complete* and *incomplete* in your experience of the person or event you are grieving. Write down your answers to these questions: What was positive in the relationship or experience? What did you gain from it? Try to be specific. You might include simple, everyday things like "She taught me to sew" or "He gave me his father's watch" or "She came and had lunch with me my first week on the job" or "He could really make me laugh."

What was left incomplete? What was unhappy about the relationship? Again, write down memories that are as specific as possible: "He was so quiet I often didn't know what was on his mind" or "He had a frightening temper" or "She borrowed my favorite dress when we were teenagers and got a stain on it, and we had a huge argument."

What do you wish you had said or done differently? Don't explain away things that happened or point out that now you know he or she really meant well or it's not that important.

What's important in coming to terms is *how you felt at the time;* what you would like to have said or done and never had the opportunity. Maybe there's an argument that was never resolved. Maybe you wish you had been more expressive of how much that person meant to you. Maybe you wanted to say "thank you" or "I love you," and the relationship was over too soon.

Take responsibility for your part in what was left incomplete without berating yourself. If you wish you had been more expressive or more helpful or more aware of your loved one's feelings or needs, accept responsibility for the fact that you weren't. This doesn't mean blaming yourself, or deciding you're a horrible person. Grief partners can be very helpful in pointing out to each other instances in which they are taking on undeserved blame or getting stuck in "if only I had" ways of thinking.

Instead, accept the reality of the relationship and your own participation in it. Often we get mired in particular patterns with those closest to us that are very difficult to recognize, let alone break. You and the deceased were both human beings with limitations. You may understand the relationship better now, but it's too late to change with that particular person. *Know that you both probably did the best you could at the time.*

Work toward reconciliation and letting go. You can either make a list or write a letter to the person who died, reflecting on the relationship and the times that were positive, negative, painful, happy.

Put into words what you would most want to say to the person if he or she were alive today. If there's something you want to apologize for, include that in the letter, and talk about how you've learned or grown since. Keep it brief and simple: "I'm sorry you and I talked so little about things that were important to us. I'm trying now in my life to open up more to people I'm close to. I can't change the way things were between us, but this is something I can do now."

If there are painful or negative things you remember, would you forgive the person if he or she were alive today? Keep in mind that the important question here is not whether you believe he or she was right or wrong, but whether you want to heal the rift in the relationship and hold onto an inner connection with the person who means something to you today. If you are willing to forgive him or her, write that in the letter, too: "I forgive you for the mean things you said to me." If you can't forgive the mean things, maybe you can forgive him or her for the emotional problems that led to them. Your partner may be able to help you with this part of the letter, when you're ready.

Now write down the things you wish you'd said. These are the emotionally connected statements you would make if you had the chance to talk to your loved one for just one last time: "Thank you for teaching me to say my prayers." "Thanks for teaching me to ride a bike." "I never told you how proud I was when I visited your office." "I always loved your smile."

Finally, now say good-bye, not to your loved one but to all that was incomplete in the relationship. Your time together in life is over, but now, with the hurt, confusion, and unresolved difficulties behind you, you can feel relief and hold the person you have lost in loving memory.

And having made this journey for yourself, you can better accompany your child as he deals with loss in his life.

Parents help kids deal not only with the losses they face, but with the urge to win, which is a part of so much childhood play. No wonder so many traditional tales are about races and contests! Let's see how stories can help you make competition an affirming experience for your child.

Nine

Promoting Healthy Competition and Fair Play

✦

When adults think of play, *games* are what we usually have in mind—tennis, golf, Monopoly, bridge. But for children, the capacity to participate in and enjoy competitive play is a relatively late development. Adults often find competition energizing, but just take a minute to put yourself in a child's soccer cleats. A two- or three-year-old has so little faith in her capacity to compete that she asks her parents to send the new baby back to the hospital. Yet as early as four or five, she's likely to be signed up for organized soccer, swim team, or Little League, and to feel the pressure from parents and coaches to score and win. Well-meaning parents, educators, and child-care authors, concerned about the effects of early team play on our kids, are advocating a shift to cooperative games and other noncompetitive pursuits. Many of these, like "ultimate football," which levels the playing field for small or slow kids, are worthwhile and enjoyable. Some—particularly those that rely on teaching slogans ("I am lovable and competent") or handing out trophies to every child who suits up—are recognized as bogus by even the youngest kids. "The Race Between Toad and Donkey," "The Competitive Tiger," and "The Most Precious Thing Under the Sun" will give you and your child some more meaningful ways to talk about competition.

Teaching a child to be a good competitor—to try her best, to be a team player, to be a gracious winner and a good loser—is important preparation for life in our individualistic society, where independence and resilience are highly valued. When parents, coaches, and kids are good sports, cooperation is *part* of competitive play; that's what teamwork is all about, right? With the proper support, your child can learn to successfully compete without sacrificing her self-esteem or her compassion for others. In the process, she can develop confidence, perseverance, and the sense of accomplishment that comes from working toward realistic goals. Most important, she'll have fun. In this chapter I'll focus on how to help kids in organized sports and games, but I hope you'll find the developmental guidelines, stories, activities, exercises, and advice useful in other areas, whether your child is competing in academics, music, theater, or everyday life with friends and siblings.

Competition and Development

Infants. Before we talk about how to teach your child to play fair, let's see how competitive play develops out of everyday experiences of childhood, starting as early as *infancy*. To do that we need to leave the playing field and imagine ourselves back in the nursery. The baby in her mother's lap is learning some important lessons about life that are laying the groundwork for her later ability to be a competitor. A baby who cries for food or cuddling, or who roots for the nipple and eagerly latches on, is gaining a sense of basic confidence: "Go for it!" Because an infant lacks a cognitive understanding of cause and effect, or even an awareness that the breast is part of Mother's body, we think she has a magical sense of herself as *creating* the fulfillment of her wish for food and sucking, as "making it happen"—somewhat like Aladdin with his lamp or Tiger Woods's uncanny way of sinking a golf ball. Melanie Klein, the British psychoanalyst whose understandings of infancy were usually expressed in colorful terms, called the baby who was seeking the breast "ruthless"—a word we might also use to describe a tough competitor like Microsoft's Bill Gates.

Toddlers. By the toddler years, your child is eager to explore the world around her with increasing dexterity—walking, running, manipulating household objects and toys. By providing her with childproof places to play and with a variety of materials—sand, cups, balls, soft blocks, building toys—you help her develop the coordination and perseverance to achieve her goals. (Right now these might be as simple as putting all the small objects inside all the big cups.) This is also a time when she is developing a sense of her own power. Now she can stand up beside you. She feels more separate and lets you know about it, but she's not always ready to go her own way; don't be surprised to find that sometimes she wants to be off on her own, and other times she'll ask for help with things you know she can easily manage herself.

Your toddler is very aware that you are much taller and more powerful than she, and when the two of you get into a power struggle she's not at all sure she can compete. Whether the conflict is over the way you cut her peanut butter sandwich or the time she goes to bed, she often reacts as though her whole life depended on winning. To her, it does. If you haven't worked through chapter 5 ("Raising a Motivated Child"), now is the time to go back and do it. On page 195 we'll take a closer look at why these battles start, and how to help transform your child's willfulness into the determination that will help her attain her goals.

Preschoolers. Between three and five your child is developing a somewhat magical sense of self-esteem. She imagines herself as a younger version of her same-sex parent who can do things the way Mommy does—cook dinner in her play kitchen, set up an office in her toy corner. And in her fantasies she is the ruler of an enchanted kingdom, where everything is made of silver and gold, and where she wears a jeweled crown and carries an ancient sword. For the most part she's grown from her two-year-old days, when she was devastated if everything didn't go exactly her way. That doesn't mean, however, that she's ready to play games by adult rules. When her sense of her own specialness is threatened, she's likely to "bend the rules" in her own favor or to dissolve in tears. For now, she needs to play games that encourage her to challenge herself and foster open-ended exploration. How many crayon colors can she use in a drawing? How many different ways—jumping, running, rolling, hopping—can she get from one side of the playground to the other?

One of the problems with a strong emphasis on academic learning at this stage is that it can easily dampen the creative potential that is the preschooler's greatest asset. Playing with blocks, she is a small discoverer who learns a great deal from what her eyes and hands teach her about spatial relationships and counting. Faced with a worksheet, she learns that there is a right and wrong answer to each question.

For now, in sports, game, and learning, your preschooler is eager to take *pleasure* in everything she's capable of doing. By affirming her joy and excitement in the world around her by offering opportunities to explore arts and crafts, music, and creative movement, you help her hold onto a lifelong sense of satisfaction in her activities. If you push her into competitive achievement too early, she is deprived of the joy of trying things for their own sake. When that happens, competitive "play" turns into work.

School-age children. By school age, your child may be eager to participate in organized contests, friendly academic rivalries, and team sports— soccer, baseball, swimming, spelling, geography bees. Yet particularly if she is in a highly competitive school or league, she still needs your support and help. She is ready to play what we think of as real games, but only if she feels that she can be "a contender," like Marlon Brando in *On the Waterfront*. Her primary motivation is not to win but to be a full participant in the game. Being part of the group reinforces her sense of competence. That's why at this point helping your child develop skills, from ballhandling to running to reading, is important to her self-esteem. If she's always on the sidelines because she hardly ever touches the ball in soccer or if she's "lost" in class because she rarely raises her hand, she will lose confidence in her ability to participate. For some kids, extra coaching or after-school tutoring can be a big help in making sure competition is a positive experience.

Now let's look at a Jamaican story about a very uneven race, and an underdog who does anything he can to win. It's not always easy for adults to understand competition from a child's point of view, but this tale offers a comical look at it from the perspective of a young child who feels a lot like Toad.

✧   ✧   ✧

THE RACE BETWEEN TOAD AND DONKEY

One day the king decided to have a race. He promised that the winner would get a big prize. Toad and Donkey decided to enter, and Toad bragged so much about how he was going to win that Donkey got angry.

The king announced that the race was going to be twenty miles long. "I don't see how anyone with legs as short as yours could keep up," said Donkey, but Toad said he knew he'd win anyway. Now Donkey got even more angry.

Just as the race was about to start, the king said he had a plan to keep track of all the runners. "Every time you pass one of the mileposts along the side of the road," he told them, "I want you to sing out at the top of your lungs."

As soon as he heard that, Toad told the king he needed a little extra time before he started running. Donkey knew Toad was a trickster, and he told the king to say no. But the king didn't pay any attention, and he said that the race wouldn't start until the next morning.

That night Toad called together his children—all twenty of them, who looked and sounded exactly alike—and took them for a walk along the road where the race was going to be run. "Now each one of you hide behind a milepost," he told them, "and when Donkey passes by, sing out at the top of your lungs."

The next morning came, and Donkey was sure he was going to win. The race started, but he just walked along nibbling on sweet-potato tops and grass. It took him more than an hour just to get to the first milepost, and when he got there he called out, "Ha! *I'm* faster than Toad." But what did he hear but Toad's first child sing out at the top of his lungs from his hiding place behind the milepost?

Was Donkey surprised! He'd been sure he was way ahead of Toad. Now he decided he'd better run the second mile a lot faster, and when he got to the next milepost he called out, "Ha! I'm faster than Toad," only to hear Toad's second child sing out at the top of his lungs. This time Donkey was *really* surprised, but he still figured he'd manage to catch up.

So Donkey ran even faster to the third milepost, and when he got there he called out, "Ha! I'm faster than Toad," only to hear Toad's third child sing out at the top of his lungs.

By this time Donkey was more angry than ever. He galloped at top speed to the fourth milepost and yelled, "Ha! I'm faster than Toad," but he heard Toad's fourth child sing out at the top of his lungs. Donkey galloped even faster to the fifth milepost, and even though he was very tired and out of breath he managed to gasp, "Ha! I'm faster than Toad," and he heard Toad's fifth child sing out as loud as he could.

Well, Donkey kept on bragging all the way through the whole race, and at every milepost he kept hearing the same loud singing he thought was Toad. After a while he felt so miserable he just gave up running. And Donkey hasn't run a race since.

Here's a race that makes no sense at all. Donkey seems to be the natural winner, and he doesn't mind bragging about it. Toad, by contrast, is the underdog—small, weak, short legged—just like a child. The whole idea of the race is nothing but a whim of the king's. The race is for the king's benefit, a set-up that Toad could never win. Toad's only way to stay in the running, as he sees it, is to lie and cheat.

Toad represents a particular genre of story hero you may have already met in the B'rer Rabbit stories or the Jamaican tales of Anansi. Toad is a trickster. The trickster doesn't concern himself with ideals like fair play or truth (how can he, with the odds always against him?) but will do just about anything to survive. In his study of archetypes in traditional tales Carl Jung called the trickster the first hero; like the two-year-old who sees every power struggle with a grown-up as a matter of life or death, he does anything he can to avoid being wiped out. Cultures around the world, especially those marked by oppression, have introduced the trickster to their children to send the powerful message that, even with the odds against them, they can survive.

If you've ever been faced with a young child who bursts into tears just because someone points out she's younger or smaller than a sibling, or who throws a tantrum when you tell her off-handedly, "You can't do that, you're too small," then you've met the Toad who needs to learn to be a trickster. Being small makes your child, like Toad, feel more vulnerable, less powerful, a born loser. That's why when you bump heads, she'll do anything she can to get her way. Losing feels like being wiped out. In her Darwinian universe, winning is a matter of survival. She's competing not against a worthy opponent but against an *enemy*. "Send the new baby back to the hospital," she suggests, convinced that you couldn't possibly love both her and a new sibling at the same time. (If your older kids' bickering reminds you of Toad and Donkey's power struggle, look for help with sibling rivalry in chapters 9 and 10.)

One of the biggest problems parents have coping with a child's power struggles is that many of us have never fully outgrown them ourselves. Notice that Donkey is bigger but not much better than Toad, bragging about himself every chance he gets. He's like the parent who gets drawn into power struggles with a child. Imagine how different the race would be if Donkey had offered little Toad a head start or a handicap. By learning to handle power struggles instead of getting "hooked," you can help your child feel stronger and more confident—and make life a lot more pleasant for the two of you.

Let's say you and your child get into a familiar battle. She's been watching television for hours and you've told her to turn off the set. "I want to watch TV," she insists, clutching the remote.

"You've already watched three shows," you reply. "It's time to play with your toys."

"I don't *want* to play. I want to watch my show!" she shouts, and without another word you stomp over to the set and click it off.

What's just happened? On the positive side, you've sent her off to play. But arbitrarily "laying down the law" this day leaves a young child feeling helpless and small, like Toad. Your little one is eager to explore the world around her, to test her new mobility, within clear limits. She needs to learn routines and solutions that take into account your needs and expectations as well as her wishes.

You can help by being clear and consistent. Just as a soccer game would turn into a riot without rules, your household is bound to turn into a series of confrontations unless you spell out your expectations. Instead of leaving her in front of the set until you decide it's time to shut it off, sit down together and talk about rules: one half-hour TV show a day or no TV after dinner or TV only on certain days of the week or a combination of these. Toddlers lack a concept of time and day, and they can't read the calendar, so you need to keep your rules concrete. If she seems capable, encourage her to be "in charge of" turning off the show when it's over. Help your child recognize that the limits you set are not imposed on her only "because I said so" or "because I'm the parent," but because of the demands of *reality*. Just as the electric sockets are dangerous places for fingers, too much TV is bad for children's brains and bodies.

When you can try to offer a choice between options, such as this show or that show, today or tomorrow. Invite her to see that you make choices in your life, too: You decide to go to bed early because you're tired, or you exercise instead of napping because it's healthy, or you buy the cheaper brand at the supermarket so you have money left in your wallet.

Most of all, especially as your child turns three or four and develops the capacity for fantasy play, make sure she has the opportunity to indulge her "trickster" self, to be powerful in the world of her imagination. Be sure that in addition to "real world" play with large and small toys, she has opportunities to become a princess or a fairy or a mother or whatever else her heart desires. In the world of story, tricksters are transformed, but it happens slowly; follow a trickster through a cycle of tales and you'll find he begins to be less like a wild animal, as he discovers the power of his own cleverness. His playfulness evolves, eventually, into a crazy · wisdom.

Older children. With a preadolescent or adolescent, power struggles are often harder to deal with, maybe because parents are doubly frightened of the consequences. Ask your child to do the simplest thing, and the answer is likely to be a rude no.

"Please pick up that napkin on the floor next to you," you say politely.

"I didn't drop it."

"It's right next to you," you reply. "Who else would have dropped it?"

"How should I know?"

"Pick it *up!*"

"I didn't drop it so I'm not picking it up. Besides, it's not bothering me. *You* pick it up if you think it's such a big deal."

If you find yourself getting stuck in exchanges like these, know that, like Toad's children yelling at the top of their lungs from behind the mileposts, your child is talking a good game, but she's less sure of herself than she feels. Try to avoid lengthy, legalistic debates, as well as critiques of your child's usual habits ("You seem to think you're a member of the Royal Family"). If the issue isn't really important, drop it. When it is, be brief and to the point: "Pick it up. *Now*. It's not optional."

Family Time
"THE RACE BETWEEN TOAD AND DONKEY"

You be the king. How would you and your child make the rules to set up a fairer race between Toad and Donkey? Maybe you'd let Toad start out ahead to make up for his short legs. Maybe Donkey could carry a heavy weight on his back to even the odds. Could they have turned the race into a yelling contest? Don't *correct* your child's suggestions; the idea is to get her thinking. One way kids grow to feel confident with competitive play, and to understand how and why rules work, is by making up their own games. (More on this below and on page 213.)

Make up a fair race between you and your child. Level the playing field. Try a race where the difference in your size, speed, or coordination doesn't matter. See who can spin a hula hoop the most times. Get out a broomstick and do the limbo. Try something silly, the kinds of contests kids are always having among themselves—staring, making faces, chest-pounding. See who can suck on a hard candy for the longest time without it dissolving. Invite your child to suggest a game or race.

Invent a board game. This is an activity for a school-age child. You need a half-size sheet of poster board, markers, dice or a numbered spinner (borrowed from another game), and small items to serve as game pieces (coins, small candies, buttons, or cardboard disks your child can decorate with marker and glitter). Help your child come up with:

- a *theme or setting* for the game (dinosaur life, fairyland, Camelot);
- the *object* of her game (what you have to do to win, e.g., reach the finish line, get ten points, take other players' pieces). With a younger child, a simple Candyland format works best, with the pieces moving around the board. Older kids enjoy quiz cards and puzzles, along the lines of Trivial Pursuit (sports statistics, verbal math problems, and riddles are popular);
- simple *rules* that keep the game moving forward, provide challenge, and make it fun. Don't forget the simple stuff kids often get caught up in. How do you decide who goes first? How do you win points or move forward? What's not allowed? Don't expect the game to turn into something as sophisticated as one you'd buy at the toy store; inventing it will probably be more satisfying than playing. If your child has trouble coming up with ideas, try the game-inventing activity on page 197.

The Parent's Path
"THE RACE BETWEEN TOAD AND DONKEY"

When was the last time you felt as small as Toad? Think back to a time when you felt really awkward or sure you just didn't measure up. Was it walking into a room full of strangers? trying on a bathing suit? making a presentation at a meeting when profits were down?

It's not always easy to identify with your child's Toadlike feelings of inadequacy, especially if you tend to be good at a lot of things. By adulthood, most of us have learned to recognize our strong points, and they tide us over the rough spots. Staying in touch with your own vulnerability helps you be more empathic toward your child's fragile self-confidence.

How do you react to power struggles with your child? Take inventory: Which battles do you find most challenging? Is there one issue in particular that "gets" you every time—homework, bedtime, clothes on the floor? What makes this one such a hot topic?

Now think about how you might make a change. Does a particular strategy seem to have worked in one situation? Could it be applied to others? One mother noticed that every time she asked her young adolescent son to do a household chore, they would argue:

"I'd ask him to take out the garbage. He'd complain. We'd end up arguing.

"I'd ask him to do the dishes. He'd complain. We'd end up arguing.

"One day a lightbulb went off in my head. I realized that his complaining was just a way of expressing his *feelings* about doing the chores. Instead of taking it personally, or worrying that he was refusing to do them, I tried empathizing.

" 'I hate the smell of the garbage, too,' and 'I hate looking at a sinkful of dishes, too,' I'd tell him. And what do you know? He'd just quietly go ahead and do it."

Just about everybody knows Aesop's tale about the hare and the tortoise, and its moral ("Slow and steady wins the race"). Here's a Chinese story that makes a similar point.

THE COMPETITIVE TIGER

One day a tiger was walking along, roaring, "I'm the most powerful creature in the jungle." Soon he came to a tree where a little bird was hopping from branch to branch, singing a little song. Tiger stopped and watched.

"Little bird, what are you so happy about?" he asked with a laugh. "Look how much bigger and stronger I am than you, and I don't go around hopping and singing."

"Tiger, I can't roar like you," answered the bird, "but even though you are big and strong, I'll bet you can't hop from branch to branch the way I do."

"Oh, yes, I can," roared Tiger. "Just watch me!" And he

leaped up onto the tree, only to come crashing down through its branches until he hit the ground with a loud thump.

The little bird laughed and laughed, hopping on the few branches left on the tree. "Who won the bet? Who won?" she chirped.

Tiger limped way, growling. He limped and growled all the way to a meadow, where he came upon a small animal that looked like nothing more than a ball of fur. Tiger stared at it, laughing, until he heard a high, squeaky voice say: "What are you laughing at?"

"At you, of course," answered Tiger. "You look ridiculous with no paws, or long legs, or eyes! What kind of animal are you, anyway?"

"I'm a mole," said the animal. "True, I don't have paws or long legs like you. But I wouldn't boast if I were you. See those people working in the field over there? You may be big and strong, but I'll bet you can't run past them faster than I can."

Mole and Tiger headed toward the people in the fields. As soon as they saw Mole they started chasing him, but he quickly scampered away.

Next it was Tiger's turn to leap into the field, but the minute the workers saw him they started beating him with clubs. It took all his strength to run for his life.

As Tiger licked his wounds, Mole lay down beside him and stretched out. "What are those twigs hanging from you?" asked Tiger.

"Those are my paws. They might look like twigs to you, but they work better than those big paws of yours," answered Mole. Tiger was just about to pounce on Mole, but Mole slipped into his hole. Tiger, who was too big to get in, was left sitting outside by himself.

Tiger limped away, growling angrily, until he reached a swamp. He lay down at the water's edge and took a drink. Just then a snail swam by. "Look how small and slow you are! And you have no mouth or legs!" said Tiger, laughing. "What good are you, anyway?"

"You may look big and fast, but I bet I can creep across this swamp quicker than you can leap across it," answered Snail.

Tiger laughed and laughed. "Let's try it," he said. "You start creeping, and when you're halfway across, I'll leap to the other side." Snail began to creep very slowly, and Tiger just sat there and laughed. When Snail finally got halfway across, Tiger took a high leap over the swamp. But Tiger was so heavy, and so tired from all his running, that he fell right into the water. He thrashed and struggled, but he only sank deeper and deeper. When Snail reached the other side, he turned around to see how Tiger was doing, but Tiger was nowhere in sight. All Snail could see were a few bubbles rising to the top of the swampy water.

A young child's games. Tiger might be bigger and stronger, but with cleverness and perseverance the little bird and Mole and Snail can triumph over him. Clichéd though that may sound to adults ears, it's just the reassurance your child needs when trying new games, sports, and other competitive endeavors, especially if she is under seven. As the developmental pioneer Jean Piaget pointed out in his fascinating study of the way Swiss children learned to play marbles, children under the age of seven or eight tend to make up their own games (like Mole who races Tiger across a field full of workers) and think of winning in terms of their own point of view, rather than try to compete in a standardized game against peers. (After all, if Mole does try to win fair and square, he only runs up against the reality of bigger and stronger Tigers.)

"The child plays for himself," wrote Piaget in *The Moral Judgment of the Child*. "His interest does not in any way consist in competing with his companions and in binding himself by common rules so as to see who will get the better of the others. His aims are different." Your young child plays in order to feel like part of the group, and to test her own abilities, but she doesn't yet grasp the abstract idea of impartial rules. That's why "It's not fair" means exactly the same thing as "I didn't win" to a young child. Making sure she always plays by the rules, which means, inevitably, that she always loses, doesn't teach her to respect you or to play fair. It teaches her that she is powerless, that against the Tigers of this world, she hasn't got a chance.

The best way to teach your child to be a healthy competitor is to start out by building her confidence in her own abilities. Learning to lose is something that takes time. She first needs to learn to *play*. That's why I don't mind repeating myself here: Let her start out with some extra points, or change the rules, to create a level playing field. Preschoolers often enjoy making up their own games, and parents are often mystified by the lack or frequent changing of the rules. Don't worry that she's going to be a poor sport or a cheater because she likes to do it her way for now. With time and patience, she will develop the confidence and maturity to participate in standard games and sports and to play by the rules.

Your preschooler brings her magical thinking to these games: "You have to hold the magic wand to cross the bridge without falling into the moat." That's an important step in the development of her self-confidence; it helps her feel powerful, like the young Arthur with the sword Excalibur. If her tricks strike you as silly, keep in mind that few of us ever fully outgrow magical thinking in competitive situations. Maybe you've worn a "lucky" suit or tie to a job interview. And remember those gold sneakers Michael Johnson wore in the 1996 Olympics?

Developing self-confidence and enjoyment of the game. As your child reaches kindergarten and early school age, she may enjoy informal opportunities to try some sports and games in noncompetitive ways—playing catch with you, hitting a tennis ball (in any direction), learning to boot a soccer ball. For now, keep the focus on fun. Think of your "tasks" during this period as introducing your child to the pleasures of organized play and as helping her feel confident about her ability to participate.

Many children are signed up for competitive leagues as early as kindergarten, but they're not usually ready. Parents often observe that they spend their time on the soccer field watching the birds go by. If you can keep your sense of humor about that, your child may enjoy the sense of belonging being on a team can provide, but if you're frustrated, it's wise to wait until she's a few years older.

Given the high cost of college, many parents are eager to discover that their child could one day win a soccer, hockey, or baseball scholarship, but there's no evidence that rushing your child into early training will turn her into a star; for the most part, now is the time to encourage her to try a wide variety of games and sports and find out what she enjoys. Likewise, even if you think your child is not especially well coordinated, don't assume she will probably be on her high school chess team and give up on sports altogether. Focusing too soon on high performance in one area can limit her opportunities to explore a range of activities, and to take pleasure in the game itself. (On pages 208–12 you'll find guidelines to help make participation in organized sports and games fun and beneficial for your school-age child.)

Family Time
"THE COMPETITIVE TIGER"

Visit the zoo or aquarium. Invite your child over three years of age to look carefully at different animals and see all the ways they're equipped to survive. Notice special features—size, shape, feet, feathers, fur, feeding habits—that enable animals to escape enemies or survive in a harsh climate. *Preschoolers* are interested in the camel's hump, the giraffe's long neck, and the butterfly's pollen tube, for example. Talk about what might happen if the animals you're seeing decided to have a race. What if you moved the race to a different habitat—the ocean, a tropical rainforest, the desert, the Arctic? *Older kids* are often interested in details of animal anatomy and habitats; encourage your child to read the signs and guidebooks and teach you. Appreciating nature's diversity and the often astonishing adaptations of even the smallest living creatures to their environments is a vivid illustration for your child that size, strength, and speed aren't all that matter.

Do something pointless. You've probably seen parents at the sidelines who shout at their kids, the coaches, and the ref as though life depended on a kid's soccer or baseball game. If you love to play competitive games, it's not always easy to relate to your child in ways that don't involve winning or losing. One way to get in touch with the way young kids play is to try some aimless diversions—doing a craft, drawing a design, meditating, going for a walk, birdwatching. Don't wait for a rainy day; set aside time this weekend. Better yet, sit down on the floor with your child and let her lead you in a fantasy game.

The Parent's Path
"THE COMPETITIVE TIGER"

How do you like to play? What recreational activities do you really enjoy? On the weekend or on vacation, how do you have fun? In your journal, write down all the different ways you enjoy yourself, including sports, games, relaxation, and cultural interests. (Include things you actually do as well as those you wish you had more time for.)

Now take a look at your list. Do your recreational activities tend to fall into specific categories? Notice whether you favor those that are:

- primarily *noncompetitive* (going for a walk, gardening, cooking, reading);
- *fantasy* or *imaginative* fun (theater, dance, art, murder mystery weekends);
- competing *against yourself* or the environment (jogging, running, hiking, exercising, kayaking, biking, travel);
- *individual competitions* (chess, tennis, one-on-one basketball, racquetball, squash);
- *team competition* (softball, soccer, volleyball, bridge).

What does your list tell you? Do you tend to dislike or avoid certain forms of play? Why? Or do you work so hard that you don't make time for play?

These are important questions, because they can tip you off to ways you may limit your child. If, for example, you tend not to enjoy competing against yourself or the environment and prefer team sports, you may share with your child an enthusiasm for Little League but neglect individual activities such as canoeing.

Is this really such a bad thing? Let's face it: We all share with our kids the things we enjoy most. We teach them to try the things we know how to do, and one day they go on to try new things for themselves. If your child doesn't share your enthusiasm, though, or needs encouragement to try things you don't favor, it's important to recognize and honor that. I once knew a man who'd played professional football. His son was a small, fine-boned boy with a sensitive disposition and no desire to play football. Yet instead of encouraging his son to take up tennis or golf or sailing, or appreciating his love of nature, this father saw him for what he was *not*; he would never be a football player, and therefore in his father's eyes he was a disappointment and a born loser.

The Spanish story that follows is an illustration of mature competition and the way it can lead to growth. Striving to win a young woman's heart leads three rival princes to the ends of the earth, where they make discoveries that turn out to be a big help at home.

✧ ✧ ✧

THE MOST PRECIOUS THING UNDER THE SUN

Once in a far-off land there lived a king whose wife died, leaving him with three handsome sons. In the next kingdom lived a queen whose husband had died, and she had a lovely daughter. The king and queen decided to marry. They all lived happily together at the king's palace.

But one day the king's sons realized that they had all fallen in love with their beautiful stepsister. The three princes went to see their father. "Choose one of us to be her husband," they asked him.

"How can I choose?" he answered. "One of you must win her hand. Go out into the world and look for the most precious thing under the sun. The one who brings it back to me will win the princess."

And so the three sons set out on their journeys. The first prince rode and rode until he came to a large city, where there were many merchants. He searched all the shops, looking for something precious, until in one he found a flying carpet.

"Sit on this carpet, and press your finger on the secret

spot," said the merchant, "and the carpet will fly into the air and take you wherever you want to go." The prince gave the man a thousand pieces of gold, sat down on the carpet, pressed the secret spot, and flew home to the palace.

Meanwhile, the second son had arrived at a town, where he met a man who showed him an amazing telescope.

"Look into this telescope," the man told him, "and you'll see whatever you want to see." When the prince looked into the telescope, he thought of his older brother. Sure enough, at that very moment he saw him heading home on the flying carpet. The second prince paid the man a thousand gold sovereigns and left for home with the amazing telescope.

By this time the third brother had arrived at a village where an old man stood in the marketplace calling, "Apples for sale! Magic apples for sale!"

"What's magic about your apples?" asked the third prince.

"Hole one close to your face and sniff it," said the old man, "and you'll be cured of any sickness in the world." The prince paid the old man a thousand pieces of gold and headed home, carrying the apples in his pouch.

On his way home the second brother, the one with the amazing telescope, caught up with the first, who was passing by on his flying carpet. The two of them looked into the telescope together and saw the youngest brother walking home with his apples. They sat down on the first brother's carpet, pressed the secret spot, and flew to meet their brother.

The three brothers were all eager to see the princess. "I'm going to look in my telescope," said the second brother. But when he looked in, he saw her lying on her deathbed, pale and sickly.

"I'll get us home quickly," said the first brother, and off they soared on the flying carpet.

When they arrived at the palace, the youngest brother opened his pouch. "I'm going to give her one of my magic apples!" he cried, and he ran to the princess's room and stuck one right under her nose, just as she was drawing her last breath. The princess sniffed the apple, and in an instant her cheeks were glowing, her eyes were shining, and she sat up straight.

Now the three brothers decided it was time to go and see the king. Each one wanted to convince him that he was the one who had found the most precious thing under the sun. "I should win the princess," said the oldest, "because I'm the one who brought us home on my flying carpet in time to save her."

"No, I should win her, because without my amazing telescope we wouldn't have known she was about to die," said the second.

"I should win her," said the youngest. "After all, my magic apple cured her."

The king frowned and rubbed his beard and murmured, "Hmmmm." Finally he said, "I think that the telescope is the most precious thing, and so the second prince should win the princess."

But the princess did not agree. "It was the magic apple that saved me," she said. "And the youngest brother has always been my favorite, anyway. He's the one I'm going to marry." And so she did. But perhaps it was just as well that she had not told anyone who her favorite was earlier, because then the three princes would not have traveled around the world, or found their precious things, and we would not have had this story.

Does your children's battling—for the biggest piece of pie, the aisle seat at the movies, the last word on Monopoly rules—make this story sound like a scene from a gentler age?

The three brothers are good sports. They work together. They appreciate one another's achievements. They share their discoveries. They are motivated by love.

Maybe one reason their race is run so fairly is that they live in a very gracious kingdom. Notice how the king doesn't decide his sons' fates for them; he sets up a contest that spurs them toward growth and exploration. Powerful as he is, he values their freedom. As for the princess, in the end she bases her choice on both the merit of the man and her own feelings. When mercy and justice go together, competition is tempered by love.

In mature competition, your aim is not to destroy your opponent but to do your best against him. (In the developmentally earliest form of contest, the kind waged by Toad and other tricksters, *survival* at all costs is the aim.) When our kids engage in healthy competition, it becomes a means to growth and achievement, as well as an opportunity to respect the talents and accomplishments of others.

Does that still sound idealistic? Keep in mind that it develops gradually. Just as at the end of this tale each brother explains to the king why the object he has found is precious, your child needs plenty of chances to talk with you about the rules of each game, and to practice trying to use them in his own favor—in other words, to argue—before he learns to play fair. That's why he makes such a big deal when the ball looked out of bounds to him, or when he thinks it's really his turn and someone else goes. Debating the rules teaches him to understand and accept them, and even to take pride in following them. Meanwhile, he needs a chance to try his best to win. Notice how, in this story, the teller points out that we wouldn't have had a chance to enjoy the story—and the princes wouldn't have had their adventures—if the contest had been decided at the start. Competition only spurs growth and achievement when the players have a chance to really prove themselves.

Let's see how those fairy-tale lessons apply to the way your child experiences organized sports and games.

Keeping competitive situations healthy for your child. With more than twenty million American children involved in organized athletics, we need to pay attention to what they're learning. Handled appropriately, competitive situations can teach a child to win and lose gracefully and to play her best. Often parents are motivated to get their kids to participate for other reasons. They may want to raise a child who is a "star" to make up for what they themselves haven't achieved. They may worry that a child will feel like a "loser" unless she's a winner. (That's only true if you communicate that that's how *you* think.) Parents worry about doing the right thing: Am I doing as good a job as the next parent, whose child gets high scores in sports or academics? If my child is sitting on the bench for half the game, what am *I* doing wrong? (To explore your own experiences with competition, be sure to do the exercises on pages 214–16.) To make matters worse, the widespread violence in TV sports—where players are paid to get into fights—as well as the anorexic girls who carry off the medals in Olympic gymnastics, can easily communicate the message that being a winner is more important than being a human being.

Keep in mind that coaches, teachers, and even role models come and go, but there are no substitutes for parents. For the most part, let the coach work on your child's playing skills. You attend to her soul. Your relationship can provide the cushion your child can fall back on when the going gets tough. She needs to know you want her to do her best, have fun, and enjoy the game. Praise efforts at teamwork, not just winning scores. In a team situation, talk to her about good plays you appreciate on both sides. Is the sport fun for her? Is she tired? Does she need time with friends? Is it hard to balance practices with schoolwork?

When you talk about the game afterward, don't focus on whether your child won or lost. Was it fun? What did she do in the game—pass the ball to another player, block a goal? What part of the game did she enjoy most? Compliment your child on what she does well and on any particular talent or strength you notice—speed or agility, a strong arm, a willingness to practice hard.

Check for signs that your child really enjoys a sport. Does she spontaneously play without your nagging—tossing around a ball, doing stretches? Does she look forward to next week's game? Does she volunteer information about how practice went or tell you about a big play she's excited about? Has she made friends on the team?

Support the timid or uncoordinated child. I'm always amazed at the number of parents I see who get upset with a child who misses the ball or hangs back from play. Naturally it's frustrating to see a small soccer player kick the ball as hard as she can into her own goal, but kids need our patience if they're to develop confidence. A child who's reluctant to play, or anxious about her abilities, needs *support*, not scolding.

Keep the focus on fun and good health. Offer pointers, but keep in mind that when you give advice, you're letting her know you expect her to do better. Wait until she asks. By keeping communication about the game open and nonthreatening, you'll give your child the space to let you know what she needs and wants from you.

Know that kids develop at different rates and go through clumsy periods; even if she's not doing well now, don't label her "unathletic" or "uncoordinated" for life. Help her recognize her strengths; she may be slow but graceful, or a little uncoordinated but strong. Instead of limiting her to the sports her friends are involved with, offer her opportunities to try things that may better suit her abilities.

On the other hand, if she seems discouraged or holds back from participating because she lacks skills, she needs your support. Being the worst player on the team week after week is no fun. Set aside time to teach your child to kick, dribble, pitch, or bat at home, or sign her up for a clinic.

Help your child learn to lose. Ideally, being part of a team helps a child with the experience of losing. She's not alone with the defeat, and together the team can figure out how to do things differently next time. But your help is important, too. When your child does lose, let her know you realize how hard it is. Avoid telling her she's a crybaby for being disappointed. Avoid knocking the other team or accusing the ref of unfairness. Your child can only learn to accept losing if *you* can. Tell her you're proud of the way she played, and that what matters to you is that she's learning and growing.

Share stories of your own defeats and hard times. No matter how klutzy you are, know that a child under ten thinks of you as a Michael Jordan, of sorts. After all, look how much farther you can throw, and how much harder you can kick, than she can. Knowing you've been through disappointments and learned from them helps her know that she can weather these, too.

Keep in mind that sometimes even the best players get discouraging messages. One seven-year-old soccer player was talented enough to be selected for his league's traveling team, but as the youngest member of the team he spent a lot of time on the bench. To make matters worse, his team often lost to other select squads. He began to get the idea he wasn't good at the sport. Many coaches are beginning to question whether select or traveling teams are good for young kids; because children develop at different rates, ranking them at early ages doesn't necessarily make sense, and they all benefit from opportunities for frequent, low-pressure play.

Know your child's competitive environment. In a survey of children ages ten to eighteen taken by the University of Michigan's Youth Sports Institute, youngsters said winning wasn't very important to them. When asked why they participated in sports, "to win" was not among the Top Ten reasons for girls and ranked only seventh for boys. When asked how they would change their favorite organized youth sport, "less emphasis on winning" made the Top Ten list for both boys and girls. A majority of young athletes polled said they'd rather play for a losing team than sit on the bench for a winning team.

Guess how parents and coaches responded to the same question. More than half rated winning "very important" to preteen athletes' success in sports. One coach told me about a father who tried to pull his daughter out of a soccer game because their team was trailing 7 to 3. "We've got a lot to do this afternoon; no time to waste on a losing team," he said, motioning her off the field as the coaches and ref watched in amazement. (The girl was apparently a better sport than her father; she refused to leave her teammates and stayed for the whole game.)

Pay attention to what your child tells you, and trust your own judgment. "My son is a happy kid who swims fast," explained a mother whose eight-year-old was in the state finals. That probably has a lot to do with the positive attitudes of coach, the other swimmers, and the parents involved. A coach is much more than a skill builder; he or she is someone your child can admire—or be afraid of. He may give the most playing time to his "stars," or reward kids who work hard and show up regularly for practice. Although most leagues provide some training in child development, many coaches are unaware of children's needs. They may be coaching because they loved playing the game in college, or because they want a winning team, rather than out of a dedication to bringing kids along in a particular sport. Be wary of a coach who lets kids play if they're injured or who allows kids to hurt other players in order to "take them out." Coaches and players should not use violent or insulting language. Pay attention to whether your child seems to trust the coach, and whether she's learning from him or her.

Are you comfortable with the other parents involved with your child's team? At a basketball game between six- and seven-year-olds in San Antonio, parents and coaches who were angry at a referee's calls stormed the court, and the police had to be called to protect him.

Consider possible links between gender and competitive styles. A great deal of research still needs to be done on how kids learn about competition. It's interesting to note that Piaget found that girls were more flexible about rules than boys. But he concluded that girls were therefore backward creatures with a "far less developed" legal sense than their male counterparts.

In her landmark work on gender differences, *In a Different Voice*, Carol Gilligan points out that girls may in fact be less confrontational than boys and more skillful at collaboration and compromise. She notes that traditional girls' games like jump rope and hopscotch are turn-taking games, where competition is indirect, since one person's success does not necessarily eliminate another from the running, and arguments are less likely to occur. She cites one study that found that when a quarrel broke out among girls, they often ended the game rather than argue about the rules. The same study found that girls tended to be concerned with relationships and cooperation, playing in smaller, more intimate groups and having one "best friend." Boys, on the other hand, seemed to be more forthright about competition, and therefore to learn independence and organizational skills.

Whether or not these gender patterns resonate with your own personal observations, it's worth paying attention to the balance between these two poles in your child's life. *Helping children learn to compete can build confidence, but only when they have opportunities for noncompetitive activities.* Be sure your child has time for learning a craft or hobby with you or another trusted adult, going for a nature walk with a parent or friend, writing in a journal, expressing herself through art or music.

Listen to your child. She'll tell you how she wants to help. Otherwise, sometimes even with the best of intentions, you may miss the mark. One mother told me that having grown up in a highly competitive environment herself, she was determined not to put her son in the pressure-filled situations that had once made her feel so miserable. With great reluctance she signed him up for Little League, which he insisted on joining because all his friends were doing it. "I watched the first game and I was disgusted at all the parents who were screaming at their kids to run and get the ball and hit a home run. Then when the game was over, my son came off the field with tears in his eyes," she recalled. " 'Mommy, all the other parents were yelling and screaming. Why didn't you shout for *me?'* he said. Boy, was I shocked."

Family Time
"THE MOST PRECIOUS THING UNDER THE SUN"

Be a prince. Here's a "what-if" game to play with a child over three who enjoys fantasy: If you were to go in search of the most precious thing in the world, what would it be? Let your imagination take over. Choose an object from another country, from your own backyard, or from a fantasy land. If you like, get out your crayons or markers and draw it.

A younger child might imagine a magical toy or a golden treasure chest or a beautiful doll. A school-age kid might suggest an herb that cures cancer or a virtual-reality computer program that lets you play in the Super Bowl.

"Racing" with the three princes gets you more engaged with the story, and is a nonthreatening way to see how competition can encourage you to reach for new possibilities.

Now pretend you're the king or the princess. A child who is ready to talk about rules, usually early school age, will enjoy this activity. What do you like about each gift the princes find? Which gift do you think is the most precious? Is it hard to choose?

Now change the story a bit. If you were the king, would you make any rules about the objects the princes were supposed to look for? Assume you said they were only supposed to help sick people or to help people travel in mysterious ways. Who would win?

Don't correct your child's answers; just focus on inviting her to think about these questions and talk over the possibilities. Most of the games kids play—Candyland, soccer, hearts—already have the rules in place. In giving your child a chance to make up her own rules, you're giving your child a chance to develop her judgment capacities and understand how games work.

Turn the story into a game. Here's a project to do with your school-age child, who can participate in devising the game, discussing the rules, and designing and decorating the board and pieces. Once you've made the game, you'll need to develop and refine the rules as you go along. Although I've offered suggestions here on how to make up a board game, keep in mind that active kids may prefer to invent something that includes opportunities to run or jump—like the popular Twister. In that case, your whole living room or backyard becomes the "board" or "world" where the princes' contest takes place.

Each player is a prince (or traveling princess). Players advance around the board to reach the finish line and marry the princess (or a prince). Now invent your own variations. Use dice or a spinner. There might be "telescope cards" that show you disasters and send the players backward a certain number of spaces. Maybe you'll have "flying carpet spaces" that skip players ahead on the board. You might include "princess spaces" or cards that give special instructions from the princess. Or, just as in the story the princes arrive home by helping one another, your game might include ways players can cooperate to help one another advance around the board.

If your child finds this theme too constricting, go back to the game-inventing activity on page 197.

The Parent's Path
"THE MOST PRECIOUS THING UNDER THE SUN"

Write up your own "competition scorecard." Sit down in a quiet room with your notebook, and set aside half an hour. Go back to your biggest childhood competitions—on the playing field, in the classroom, with brothers or sisters. Picture yourself in a gymsuit and sneakers or at your family's dining room table around a Monopoly board or at your school desk facing a blackboard. What were competitive situations like for you when you were a child? The following questions are designed to jog your memory; if you don't connect with a particular question, go on to the next one. (This is not a test.)

Who were the kids you usually competed against?

Were they friendly rivalries, or do you remember a lot of bad feelings?

Did you have a helpful coach or support from your team or encouragement from your parents? Or were you often facing pressure alone?

Do you remember ever having cheated, or fouled, to score points or win?

Was there a "big game" or an important exam on which it was important to do really well? How did you feel before the big day? What kind of help did you get from parents, teachers, or coaches? What really helped?

How important was competition in your family? Did you and your siblings spend many hours at competitive sports and games? Were other activities—conversation, long walks, craft projects—encouraged? Did kids tend to turn everyday situations into a race—"First one to get to the front door first wins" or "Whoever finished dinner first wins"?

Were you encouraged to try things you weren't good at, just because you enjoyed them, or did you get the message they were a waste of time? "My brother was supposed to be the family athlete, and I was the 'brain,' " said one woman, now a college professor. "He'd get a baseball glove for Christmas, and I'd get a science kit. I never really got involved in a sport until my twenties, when I started doing tai chi while I was writing my dissertation. I'll *never* label my own kids that way."

Were there certain areas—math, basketball, jumping rope—you felt particularly competent in and others you didn't? Were you valued for what you were good at, or did your parents want you to be different? "I loved having bike races with all the other kids in the neighborhood," said one woman. "But my mother always complained that I wasn't neat and clean and dolled up every day like the girl down the street."

Maybe you remember something about the attitudes of your coaches or teachers. Do you remember being praised or encouraged for your *efforts* or only for high performance? Do you remember any favorite sayings they used to repeat—"It's not whether you win or lose" or "Do your best" or "How come you only got an A-minus instead of an A"?

After your initial half-hour writing time, set aside your notebook. Over the coming weeks and months, you may find yourself recalling more about your childhood experiences and wishing to go back to your notebook and add to what you've written.

How have these childhood experiences affected your attitude toward competition today? Look over your notes and see what connections you make. Are you in a highly competitive field today, or do you shy away from intense competition?

Are there ways your early experiences of competition helped you discover your strengths or added to your confidence?

What did the adults in your life do that really helped?

One of the best lessons I ever had in taking a realistic attitude toward competition came when my high school marching band faced a halftime performance at a football game whose own award-winning band had played at the Rose Bowl. How could our straggling group of rayon-suited marchers with squawking clarinets and belching brass ever look anything but ridiculous against this precision unit? "Okay, kids," our director announced the morning of the game. "Today at halftime, we're going to surprise everybody. No formation. Just run out on the field, pick any spot you want, and stand there and play." Standing there blaring my alto sax into the cool autumn air, I learned a little bit about the idea that winning isn't everything.

Now think about the negative side of things. Were your own early experiences of competition damaging in particular ways, scaring you off things you weren't good at or bringing bitter feelings into your friendships or sibling relationships? Did you learn to be so competitive that it's hard to be vulnerable?

Come back to your life as a parent today. What did you learn about competition when you were growing up that you'd like to pass onto your child?

Now consider how you might like your child's experiences to be *different* from your own. Would you like your child to feel less pressure or more support, have more fun or opportunities for more creativity? Looking back over this chapter, find three ideas or activities that can help make that happen in your household.

We've seen how traditional tales can provide a shared vocabulary for talking about wants, fear, aggression, loss, and competition. Often we tend to dismiss storybook *love* as unrealistic, as something entirely unlike the caring commitment we seek to nurture in our children. In the next chapter you'll find tales that offer much more than happy-ever-after endings.

Ten

Love and Compassion

✧

Schools and community organizations across the country are offering classes in sensitivity training, conflict-resolution techniques, and empathy in an effort to remediate what may be the most pressing problem of all among our young people: why Johnny can't care. By now you won't be surprised to hear me say that the capacity for love and compassion grows out of something much more deeply rooted in a child's psyche than any formal program can reach. Real teaching about love needs to be more powerful than skill building. Helping a child progress toward a mature loving relationship, in which both parties are *strong* enough to be whole individuals and *caring* enough to connect, demands that we engage with our whole selves. It happens as we and our children experience the tenderness of babyhood, the defiance of the toddler years, the playfulness of the preschooler, and even the anger of the adolescent. "Two Childhood Friends," "The Husband and Wife Who Switched Jobs," and "Pushing Up the Sky" portray some of the different elements of love in ways that touch the heart.

I guess one of the biggest challenges most of us face in teaching kids about love is that we ourselves are rarely as loving or compassionate as we'd like to be. Really caring about others, and engaging in intimate loving, is in many respects the crowning achievement of emotional development. We struggle with them all through life. Real love isn't just niceness or simple kindness or even nonviolence. To be loving isn't to be a smiling do-gooder. Loving draws on our strengths and vulnerability, tests our needs for closeness and separateness. Who knows these things better than we parents, who discover through the years that we are forging a love that needs to be both more selfless and more demanding than we ever imagined possible?

In this chapter we explore how we can prepare our children to grow toward a capacity for mature love and caring, to appreciate love not as a fleeting urge or wish but as a conscious choice, a commitment, even a struggle. Here you'll find stories, information, activities, and exercises to help you enhance the development of your child's capacities to *empathize*, to *respect differences*, and to feel *compassion*. We'll see how these everyday "lessons" lay the foundation for healthy childhood friendships and meaningful teachings about love and sexuality.

The development of empathy. The word itself comes from the Greek *empatheia*, a term for "feeling into," or having the ability to perceive another person's subjective experience. There's considerable evidence to show that empathy is something human beings naturally develop out of very early feelings of connection with others. During infancy, it's almost as though feelings were contagious. When a baby hears another child crying, he becomes distressed. As children grow, when their own feelings are responded to and mirrored appropriately, they hold onto that capacity to share in the experience of another.

The first kind of love human beings know is an almost magical oneness with those closest to us. An infant learns that when he cries, someone comes and offers milk or a diaper change or a hug. When he feels like flexing his legs, someone laughs and helps by letting him push against her lap. When he's excited or happy, someone responds to his joy with a smile and twinkling eyes. Long before he can speak or understand words, a child is learning what love means. By attending to the common "language" of touch, glances, daily rituals, and babbling that happens between caregivers and baby, you teach your child to trust, to feel at home in the universe. He is developing a sense that others offer kindness, acceptance, and even friendliness. He is learning what it means to receive a reasonably attuned response. He is learning that he is loved. As he comes to recognize the smiles and eyes and smells of the important people in his life, he learns to trust that they respond to him, that he is loved just because he *is*.

For the time being, you may find that learning to "read" a baby's cues is often puzzling. Trust your instincts. By playing back his feelings in another way, like responding to his babbling with playful words of your own or to his squirming with a gentle tickle or bounce, you let him know you're responding to his communication. Sometimes you'll miss his signals and he'll let you know how frustrated he feels. On those occasions, maybe all you can do is offer comfort. In time he'll come to express himself more clearly. For now your willingness to be attentive and to try to respond naturally are what really count.

In these early months, as you learn your baby's special ways of communicating with you, you are teaching him that he can depend on you to understand and respond to him. With all his gurgling and crying and waving and squirming and cuddling, he's using the only ways he knows to tell you something about the way he feels. When he seeks eye contact and you look back at him or when he turns away and you let his gaze go or when he wants to cuddle and you hold him close, you let him know that others can share his feelings. That connection is his earliest human bond. He is developing the capacity to communicate through glances, body language, and touch. Later on, he will draw on this knowledge to recognize the nonverbal social cues that help him be part of the crowd on the playground, and as an adult it will prepare him to speak the often wordless language of intimacy.

At any age the main way your child learns to love is to feel loved. To be able to see things from another person's perspective, to feel empathy, is essential to any real love relationship. Before we look at the way empathy grows after infancy, let's hear an African tale whose humor is reminiscent of Laurel and Hardy.

✧   ✧   ✧

TWO CHILDHOOD FRIENDS

Once there were two friends who had known each other all their lives and never had a single argument. They built their homes right next door to one another, and there was nothing between them but a dirt path.

Now in the town there was a troublemaker who decided to start an argument between the two friends. He made himself a coat that had one red side and one blue side. One day as the two friends were working in their fields, he came walking along down the path that ran between their houses. Each of the friends looked up as he went by, and then they went back to work.

"Did you see that man who went by?" asked the first friend.

"Yes, I did," answered the second.

"Did you see that bright coat he was wearing?" asked the first.

"I sure did!" answered the second.

"What a nice red it was," said the first.

"Red! What do you mean?" asked the second friend. "I saw it with my own eyes. It was blue."

"No, my friend, it was red," said the first.

"It was blue, and I'm not going to say another word about it," shouted the second.

"If you think it was blue then you're an idiot!" yelled the first.

"An idiot? You're calling me an idiot? You and I have been friends all our lives, and now you're calling me an idiot? Well, that settles it. That's the end of our friendship."

The two friends kept on bickering until finally their wives shouted at them to be quiet. Then they both went back to their houses and sat in front of their doors, scowling and refusing to say a word. But before long the troublemaker came back, still wearing his red-and-blue coat. When the two friends saw the trick he'd played on them, they were sorry they'd had an argument, and they warned the troublemaker never to walk past their houses again.

Here's a story about two people who can't empathize at all with one another, and how it nearly costs them the friendship. At the beginning of the story, we meet the two friends, who have never had an argument and who live right next door to one another. They seem to have the kind of symbiotic closeness I've talked about earlier, the sense of oneness that bonds babies and their loving caregivers. They think alike, but that's not empathy. When the two friends discover that they have experienced something in entirely different ways, how do they react? By name-calling. (As time goes by and your child gets to the defiance of the toddler period, maybe you'll notice that the two of you begin to sound like the two friends having a fight.) By the end of the story both farmers realize what has gone wrong; each one can now see the situation from his friend's perspective. That's empathy. Now, they can make peace; from now on they won't let the troublemaker visit again.

Toddlers. When a young child makes the discovery that his point of view is often different than those of the other people he loves—they don't want to let him play with the VCR, or he can't go to bed whenever he wants to—he reacts in a way that's not at all surprising. He gets furious. He sees them as "bad" or "mean." (At better times, they're "good" or "nice." What's important is that to toddlers it's all black-and-white, with no room for ambiguity or different points of view.) If your child is a toddler, he's likely to want things "his way" more often than you ever thought humanly possible. Sadly, this is a period when empathy is all too frequently nearly snuffed out, as a child's insistence on his own autonomy leads parents to impose harsh discipline and control. When that happens, the child is obedient, but his feeling self—his soul—is "split off," suppressed, and along with it his capacity to respond from the heart to the feelings of others. If a child is harshly disciplined, if he is repeatedly told he is "bad" or treated abusively, or if he fails to sense that he is acknowledged or understood, but only that he is being disciplined, he loses touch with his own feelings and, in the process, with the capacity to connect with the feelings of others.

This certainly isn't an easy period for parents, though. When your child seems like a little monster, remind yourself that the foundation you've laid during infancy—the tenderness and attunement that blessed your relationship then—hasn't disappeared. For now it's just covered up by your child's growing awareness of himself as an individual.

One mother was dismayed at her two-and-a-half-year-old's insistence on wearing mismatched clothing. "To me it looked mismatched, anyway," she recalled. "I told myself I needed to let this one go, that it was my problem if I had a need for a daughter who looked like a perfect little doll. Then one day she told me, 'Stripes and dots! Pretty!' and I realized that she had very carefully chosen to wear everything she liked best, all at the same time." By accepting her daughter's idea of style, this mother helped the little girl know that in their relationship, she could choose things for herself.

When a toddler wants his own way, often, when his health and well-being, or your sanity, are at stake, you do need to be firm. But if you avoid making a big deal about things that aren't really important, you let him know you understand how he feels. Then he doesn't lose touch with his feeling self, or feel forced to split it off, like the two friends in the story, who get so angry they break off their relationship.

Surprisingly, even at this challenging stage, kids show early signs of a kind of awareness related to empathy. In one study a toddler tried to soothe a playmate who was crying at her mother's departure from the room by bringing the child over to his *own* mother. The toddler may not have understood that the playmate might not feel the same way about his mother as he does, but he was showing a concern about her feelings.

Preschoolers. By age three or four, your child has developed into a very appealing little person. You may be surprised by his remarkably improved coordination, his capacity to learn colors, letters, and numbers, and his suddenly agreeable nature. It's tempting to try to channel all that potential of his by getting him involved in early academic learning. Keep in mind, though, that this is a precious time for your child to gain a fuller sense of himself and to learn some important things about getting along with others. He may be capable of recognizing words on a page or learning from educational computer programs. If these take up too much of his day, however, he misses out on playtime with other children and with open-ended materials that can teach him irreplaceable lessons about himself as a person and his capacity to love.

With clay, paints, fabric scraps, blocks, and even the simplest of household supplies, he learns to explore his own creativity, to imagine himself in different worlds. With your encouragement, he can develop a sense of his own abilities, of what makes him special. That "healthy narcissism," or self-esteem—what our forebears called "generosity of spirit"—will open his heart to an appreciation of the uniqueness of others around him. Playing in a group with dress-up clothes, hats, crowns, small figures, building materials, and other toys, he learns that he and others can share and cooperate, that everyone brings something different, special, and fun to the project.

Sibling relationships offer some of life's most important lessons in coping with differences. Research in families with an older sibling and new baby shows that when mothers offer older siblings a chance to see the world from a new baby's point of view, by explaining what the baby likes to eat, why she's crying, what colors she likes, and so on, the siblings tend to get along better as they grow. As kids get older, keep in mind that their different ages and interests tend to send them off in different directions. You'll need to deliberately set aside family time so that family members can "catch up" with one another. No matter how busy everyone is, encourage them to support one another at dramatic and musical performances and sporting events.

School-age children. By school age, your child is likely to be more involved with people outside his circle of family and friends. At school and in the community be sure he has opportunities to meet people from different backgrounds. Now is a time to encourage him to appreciate and understand different cultures and traditions—holiday rituals, special foods, crafts, music. If they're new to you, too, make this a shared exploration. Check the newspapers for festivals and celebrations you may be able to attend. Ask a friend to invite you to a holiday meal or ceremony.

Conversations with school-age children often reveal a surprising tendency to stereotype. Keep in mind that as they meet new people and face new situations, the broad generalizations they favor are one way they organize their world so that it makes sense to them. If a child sees a peer whose skin is a different color from his own behaving a certain way, he (like many adults) is likely to decide that everyone with skin that color acts that way. Because being part of the group is so important to kids at this stage, a child who is different may suffer painful teasing unless adults intervene.

Help your child empathize by reminding him to look beneath the surface to recognize how much he has in common with people who look different from himself. It's important for parents and teachers to be clear and firm: no stereotyping, no racial or ethnic slurs, and no gender-biased or homophobic put-downs. But if your child does have a negative experience with someone from a particular group, that doesn't mean ignoring or denying his observations. When he's upset, he needs *your* empathy.

Start out by acknowledging that he's hurt or angry. Once you've made it clear that you are sensitive to his feelings, point out that when he stereotypes he's not respecting the feelings of others.

Adolescents. Listening to your adolescent talk, you might begin to believe that his altruistic personal values and ideals reflect an enormously developed capacity for empathy. He speaks passionately about his caring for others, particularly those less fortunate than himself. His everyday self-absorption presents a startling contrast, doesn't it? It's hard to think of a period of life when a person has a more narrow idea about what it means to be acceptable. While he occupies himself with trying to get the "right" clothes, listen to the "right" music, and hang out with the "right" crowd—and deciding anyone who's different is a loser—he seems to use his newly developing social consciousness as a yardstick by which to measure the hypocrisy of the adults in his life.

Be patient. With time and life experience, he'll mellow. For now, when his noble ideals strike you as ridiculous, keep in mind that his flattering view of himself as a great humanitarian is an important step toward the growth of a kind of love that could be called universal. He is extending his sense of personal connection beyond his family and friends to include strangers, people in need, and victims of injustice.

Family Time
"TWO CHILDHOOD FRIENDS"

Try a "perception" experiment. This is a fun, nonthreatening way to try seeing things from the points of view of other members of your family. Take a walk with your child (preschool or older). Go to the park, a nature sanctuary, or just around your kitchen or backyard. When you get back, ask your child to write five things he saw on the walk. (A child too young to write words can make simple drawings.) Without showing it to him, make a list of your own.

Now compare notes by explaining your lists or drawings to one another. How are your recollections different? What caught your attention about the things you've remembered? Try to recall details—colors, sizes, shapes, smells, sounds. In my own family I'm often noticing new blooms on the perennials in a neighbor's garden, while my kids are hearing the music on the ice cream man's truck.

Do a family history project. Here's an activity for school-age kids and adolescents to share with parents. Set aside half an hour for everybody in the family to write down the events they consider important over the past school year. (A younger child may appreciate help from, or a chance to dictate to, a parent or older sibling.)

Together, share your different accounts. Notice the things some include and others leave out. Listen for contradictions. Glue your notes onto a sheet of posterboard, or save them in a binder. You've assembled a multifaceted family history.

The Parent's Path
"TWO CHILDHOOD FRIENDS"

How were differences handled in your family when you were growing up? This is a helpful question for partners to explore separately and then compare notes on afterward. What happened when conflicts arose? Were they stifled? Did they go out of control? Or were they tolerated and talked through?

Were differences in talents, temperament, interests, and opinions among siblings, or between parents, honored? Or was everybody expected to conform to a particular model of what it meant to be "good" or "part of the family"? Did you feel that your own opinions and feelings were appreciated and respected?

Now, if you like, share your answers to these questions with your partner. How are the two of you carrying forward or changing your particular family tradition in raising your own children?

How well do you and your partner listen to one another? What happens when you disagree? Is there room for differences of opinion in your relationship, or does one or both of you consistently try to "prove" the other one wrong? It's not easy to make room for two contrasting points of view in one household, but your capacity to work this out may well be your child's most memorable lessons in how love can triumph over disagreement.

Would you like to change the way the two of you handle differences? If so, how?

Here's one way to begin to change the pattern. Next time you're tempted to try to get the last word, don't. Instead, tell your partner you've heard what he's said. Try rephrasing his statement in your own words, then checking with him: "Is that what you mean?"

Once it's clear that he feels understood, you can introduce your contrasting point of view. "I hear what you're saying, but I see this issue another way." State your opinion as simply and calmly as you can. Ask him to rephrase it back to you until you feel understood, too.

Don't expect overnight results. Transformation takes time, but you'll be surprised to find out how effective one person's efforts can be in sidestepping power struggles.

Respecting Differences

Infants. Keep in mind that right along with a baby's feeling of oneness with his mother, there is an awareness that she is a different creature, and that this awareness is also part of learning to love. Much of the most recent research on infants is focusing on their early awareness of themselves as separate from their mothers. It's not at all easy to talk about babies' "experience" or "thinking," because those words imply a capacity for reflection that infants don't yet possess. Yet there is increasing evidence that even in the first months of life, babies have some sense that their mothers are separate beings. A baby doesn't really understand his mother as a whole person, of course, as though she were a woman in a painting by Mary Cassatt. But her milky smell, the fragrance of her hair and skin, the softness of her breasts: the baby actively seeks opportunities to encounter these experiences of mothering. He nuzzles her blouse or neck, and she recognizes that it is time to cuddle or feed him. When there is a good "fit" between mother and baby, it may look and even feel so intense and blissful that it is as though they are thinking the same way, but in reality they are *responding* to each other in the most intimate possible ways.

This awareness of his own separateness is an essential aspect of the growth of empathy. Unless a child learns to really know that he is a separate person from those around him, what he may think of as "empathy" is really just assuming that everyone has the same feelings he does. Maybe you've had the experience of sharing a problem with an acquaintance who elbows you and blurts, "I know *just* how you feel. I felt the same way when it happened to me." She didn't really, did she?

Toddlers and preschoolers. The lessons in love that come as a shock to parents during the toddler years are so important. Your child is learning that she can get angry and disagree with you, that she can be her own person. At times your relationship hardly feels loving at all. But don't be fooled. In all his testing of you—the hide-and-seek games, the obstinacy, the tantrums, the clinginess that takes you by surprise—he is coming to discover whether he can be himself with you and, in the future, with others whom he recognizes as separate. He is learning to tolerate difference.

By preschool age the process is somewhat less painful. In fantasy play, your three- or four-year-old is imagining himself as wonderful and powerful enough to create entire kingdoms and universes, big enough to be a firefighter or parent or gourmet chef in the world of grown-ups. He is developing his perspective-taking ability. Like King Arthur, who according to some legends was transformed by Merlin into all the different creatures of the forest so that he could grow in wisdom and love, your imaginative preschooler is learning to see life through the eyes of all the different people he can pretend to be. He is learning to really empathize, to appreciate that others have feelings different from his own, and to connect with them. Unlike the toddler, whose concern leads him to offer a favorite pull-toy to a crying baby or a lollipop to a tired parent, the preschooler is learning to walk a mile in other people's moccasins.

At this age your child is likely to be identifying more strongly now with his same-sex parent. He may be imagining himself as "Mommy's little man" who loves her just the way Daddy does. His affection, his eagerness to draw you into his play, these are ways he is seeking to learn whether someone he loves can share his dreams.

He is interested in other kids now, eager to win your approval, and that, along with his growing capacity to imagine the world from others' points of view, makes this an important time for him to learn to get along with playmates. When he does something inappropriate, instead of just telling him "that was bad," or labeling him "naughty," keep in mind that he is more likely to develop an awareness of his "social responsibilities" if you call attention to the *effects* of his behavior on other people. Ask questions that help him focus on the feelings of others: "How do you think Susie feels now that you've knocked down her block building?" or "How do you think Tommy feels when you shout at him to go home?"

Treat conflicts among playmates as teachable moments. That's not the same as rushing in to intervene; many parents make it a rule not to do so unless there's danger of a child getting hurt. Often children resolve conflicts for themselves in ways that may not necessarily make sense or sound completely fair to adults, but seem perfectly reasonable to them and keep the peace. Why interfere?

If a child is getting hurt or property is being damaged, on the other hand, you need to step in. If the situation seems manageable, enter as a negotiator: "I see you both want to play with the same toy. What can we do?" The children may generate their own solutions—taking turns, bringing out another toy, play together—or you may need to suggest a few options yourself. If all else fails, it's time to end the play date: "Next time we get together maybe you'll be more cooperative."

School-age children. By school age your child spends most of the day in the classroom, away from parents' and caregivers' watchful eyes, and he may begin to talk less about his concerns. (For suggestions on how to keep communication open, turn back to pages 24–28.) When he does share a problem he's having with school or friends, he may tend to make sweeping statements: "I *hate* Andrew!" or "White people are mean!" Now is the time to *teach him the difference between personal experience and stereotyping.* Maybe *one* white girl said something mean to him, and he feels really hurt; that doesn't mean *all* white people are unkind. He may know one African American boy who didn't do his share of a group project, but that doesn't mean *all* African Americans aren't serious about their studies.

By the time they reach adolescence, kids are a bewildering mix of tolerance and intolerance. They may proclaim a belief in universal love, yet cling rigidly to styles of dress, music, and slang that mark them as members of a particular clique, and exclude or ridicule anyone who is different. It's not easy to see the logical consistency between what your child says and does at this age, but keep in mind that his insistence on defining his own style from head to toe is an important part of the formation of his *identity*, and this is essential if he is to participate in mature loving relationships as an adult.

In the following Norwegian tale, a self-centered husband learns to see things from his wife's point of view, and in the process to appreciate her more for who she is.

The Husband and Wife Who Switched Jobs

Once there was a couple who divided all their chores. The man did all the work outdoors in the fields, and the woman took care of the house. Every night the man came in and complained that his wife never did anything right: The meals didn't taste good, the rooms weren't clean, and the baby was crying. One day his wife, who was a very clever woman, came up with a plan.

"Tomorrow, why don't we switch chores, so you can have a rest?" she suggested sweetly. "I'll go out and work in the fields, and you can take care of the house." The husband quickly said he would.

Next morning, the wife walked out to the hayfield, carrying a scythe. The baby was still asleep, so the husband decided to get started on household chores. He went into the kitchen and filled the butter churn with fresh cream, then churned for a while until he got thirsty. Then he went down to the cellar to fill his mug with ale from the barrel. As soon as he turned on the tap, though, he heard a crash from the kitchen. Up he ran as fast as he could, only to find that the pig had wandered in from the barnyard and knocked over the butter churn. Butter and cream were streaming all over the kitchen floor. And right in the middle of all the mess lay the pig, grunting and squalling so loudly that it woke up the baby. The man got so angry that he kicked the pig just as hard as he could, and the pig flew right out the kitchen door.

Just then the man remembered that he'd forgotten to close the tap on the barrel of ale. Back downstairs he ran, but it was too late. The whole cellar was flooded with ale.

He went back up to the kitchen to churn more butter while the baby played on the floor next to him. Soon he remembered that he had forgotten to feed the cow. "If I walk her all the way out to the meadow now, I won't have time to churn the butter," he said to himself. "I'll put her up on the roof and let her eat the grass on the thatch." But before he did, he decided to go to the well to get the cow some water. To make sure the baby didn't knock over the butter churn, he carried the churn along on his back. But when he got to the well and stooped down to draw up the bucket, all the cream ran out of the churn and into the well water.

By now it was almost time to eat, and the man decided to forget about making butter and start cooking. But now he was worried that if he put the cow on the roof by herself while he cooked, she would fall off. So he climbed up with her, tied a rope around her neck, and slipped the other end down the chimney. Then he went down to the kitchen and tied the end of the rope around his own leg. As the man stood at the stove stirring the hot porridge, the cow fell off the roof and pulled him up the chimney by the rope.

That's where he was stuck when his wife arrived home for dinner. She took one look at the cow dangling from the roof, picked up her scythe, and cut the rope. Down dropped her husband from the chimney into the porridge pot, and when the wife came into the kitchen that was where she found him, standing on his head.

Here's a story that comically portrays the difficulty of tolerating someone very different. As the tale begins, the wife does all the housework, the husband tends the fields, and never the twain shall meet. (This couple might have learned something from reading *You Just Don't Understand* or *Men Are from Mars, Women Are from Venus*.) The man judges his wife's work as easy; after all, isn't a house a lot smaller than a hayfield?

The wife, on the other hand, has never learned to express her own feelings or stand up for herself. As the story progresses, she comes up with a manipulative way to lash out at her husband, to teach him a lesson, and manages to leave him upside down in a porridge pot. It's almost as though when she gets home and finds him standing on his head, she's finally satisfied. *Now* he's got what he deserves. That's the kind of destructive, vindictive anger that characterizes the thinking of a toddler or anyone else who is threatened by difference.

What's lacking is an appreciation of the other's plight. There isn't open sharing or real understanding in this story. It's all vindictiveness and punishment. In some versions of this tale the wife sweetly offers to continue the job trade tomorrow, which the terrified husband refuses to do.

How does this translate into your life with your child? Keep in mind that methods of discipline designed to humiliate a child and "teach him a lesson" or to deprive him so that he will do what you want may produce good behavior *temporarily*. But it does little to help him feel appreciated as an individual. Let's say he tries to carry a cup into the living room and spills it. There are at least three ways you can handle this. You can scold him: "Bad boy! No juice here." Now you've set a clear limit, but you've shamed him in the process. Clumsy though he is, he was probably proud to be carrying around his own juice cup.

Or you can say nothing and mop up the juice yourself. By doing that, you're not setting a limit that helps him grow aware of the consequences of his own actions on other people. And you'll probably find yourself cleaning up a lot of juice.

The third alternative is to affirm your child's wish to do things for himself while pointing out the consequences of how he's gone about it: "It's hard to carry a juice cup. Now the living room floor is sticky and not nice to walk on. Can you help Mommy clean it up? And no more juice in the living room, please."

Adolescents. This is the kind of scene that repeats itself during adolescence: It's Friday night. You're exhausted and looking forward to a quiet evening at home. "I'm meeting Sarah at the movies tonight," thirteen-year-old Dana cheerfully announces, adding, "She's already bought the tickets." Guess who's driving Dana to the movie theater?

It's tempting to answer like this: "You are *not* going to the movies! How dare you make plans without asking me! I never heard anything so thoughtless and inconsiderate in my life!" If this scenario is a familiar one, of course, that might be perfectly appropriate. But otherwise, except for solving the immediate problem (you get the quiet evening you were looking forward to), putting your foot down this way is not much more than the kind of "lesson" the farmer's wife taught her husband. It doesn't increase Dana's capacity to empathize with you as a human being who feels tired. It doesn't teach her much about cooperation or communication. In fact, it probably only convinces her that her parents are unreasonable people who don't understand her. Since your adolescent is often likely to believe that even when you *are* being reasonable, why add to the problem?

Instead, use this opportunity to *empathize* with and *educate* your child: "I know you and Sarah are good friends and that you like having the independence to make plans for yourself. I'm really tired tonight, and I don't feel like driving anywhere. I was hoping to put my feet up and watch a mindless TV show. I'll drive you just this once, but next time, before you make a plan with a friend, I expect you to check with me and make sure we aren't already committed to doing something else and that I don't mind driving. If you don't, I'll have to say no, even if she's bought the tickets." By offering an explanation that helps your child recognize that you have needs, too, you help her develop an empathic understanding of your own wishes and needs. That doesn't mean she won't be angry or resentful, of course, or wonder aloud why you're making such a big deal. But over time, these are the frontline lessons in empathy that really stick.

Family Time
"THE HUSBAND AND WIFE WHO SWITCHED JOBS"

Finish the story. With your child (preschool or older), role-play a conversation between the husband and wife about the day's events. How did it feel to do the partner's job? Do they feel any differently about each other now? How would each of them like to assign the chores for tomorrow? Don't worry about coming up with right or wrong answers. This is an open-ended activity that helps you and your child engage with the story by giving you a chance to imagine the way the characters in the story might be feeling.

Trade places. Set aside half an hour for a "family role switch," when everybody does everybody else's jobs. This is a family sensitivity training exercise. Parents become kids, kids become parents, brothers are sisters, and sisters are brothers. This is the most fun when you're doing something together—eating dinner, playing a board game, tidying up the living room. When time's up, sit down and compare notes. Share your experiences about playing a new role: How did the switch feel? Did you have a hard time pretending? What was the most fun about "being" somebody else? What did you like least? What did you learn from the role-play?

Now talk about how it felt to see someone else play your role. Did anything surprise you? Did they notice things about you that you weren't aware of? Was there anything you wish you hadn't seen? Did they seem more aware of your feelings than you expected?

The Parent's Path
"THE HUSBAND AND WIFE WHO SWITCHED JOBS"

Imagine being your child's age today. It's not always easy to see things from a child's point of view, and, after all, times have changed since you were a kid. Set aside twenty minutes and a quiet place where you can let yourself get lost in thought. Find a comfortable place to sit, in a straight-backed chair or on the floor. Close your eyes. Breathe deeply into your abdomen and let your body relax. Feel your arms and legs go limp, your fingers and toes dangle. Inhale and exhale slowly a few times.

Now picture yourself as your child, waking up in the morning. Hear the clock radio alarm go off or feel Mom give you a good-morning kiss. Have breakfast, get dressed in your favorite clothes, climb onto the school bus, see your friends and teachers.

As you "move" from one scene to another, try to imagine the sounds, smells, and textures all around you. Pay particular attention to your feelings—excitement, fear, joy, envy, pride. Go all the way through the day until it's time to go to bed. As you put your head on the pillow and pull up the blanket around you, slowly open your eyes and let yourself come back to the present moment.

What have you learned from this experience? Were any of your feelings unexpected? If you had a hard time imagining a certain part or parts of the day—lunch in the school cafeteria, math class, the substance-abuse prevention program—find an opportunity to tell your child you're interested in learning more about it, and ask him if he'd like to describe it, or some of it, for you. Remember, the goal isn't to pump him for information, but to open up communication insofar as he's willing and interested.

What do you wish your partner understood better about *your* day? Do you face challenges, struggles, and good news in the course of your work, errands, and other activities that you find hard to share with your partner? Think about the fears that may hold you back from talking about these. Are you afraid he or she won't "get it" or would be critical? Do you yourself believe it's not really worth talking about? Conversations between you and your partner are among your child's most important lessons in how to handle differences and share feelings.

It may not be easy, but perhaps you can find the courage to try. If you often feel as though your partner isn't as attentive or appreciative as you'd like, try to clearly focus on the kind of response you seek and express it clearly: "I don't need advice, just a hug," or "Let's celebrate!" or "I just need to blow off some steam and know you're listening." Make this a two-way exercise; ask your partner what you can do to be a more loving listener.

Cooperation, caring, and commitment. Here's a story that holds out the hope that with patience and attention, we human beings, no matter how different, can learn to communicate, find common goals, and meet them. This Native American creation story begins with the creatures of the earth recognizing that they are in a predicament. It is adapted from a longer tale told by the Snohomish people in the Pacific Northwest.

✧ ✧ ✧

PUSHING UP THE SKY

When the Creator made the world, he made many different groups of people and gave them all different languages to speak. They couldn't talk to one another, but they did agree about one thing. They didn't like one thing the Creator had done: He'd put the sky so low that the tall people were bumping their heads up against it.

One day all the wise men and women from all the different tribes got together and decided they should lift up the sky. They talked and talked about how to do it, until finally they understood one another well enough to make a plan. All the creatures of the earth should get together, they said, and try to push up the sky. If all the people and animals and birds could push at the same time, they said, the sky would move up.

"But we all speak different languages," one of the wise men reminded the others. "How will we know when to push?"'

The wise ones talked and talked until at last they agreed on how to signal to one another. When it was the right time to push, they decided that someone should shout, "Ya-ho." That was the word that meant "everybody lift together" in all the different Indian languages.

The wise ones told the plan to all the people and all the animals and all the birds. The people cut down giant fir trees to use as poles that could push up the sky.

Soon the big day came. The people all raised their poles so that the tips were just barely touching the sky. Then the wise ones shouted, "Ya-ho!" Everybody pushed, and the sky moved up a little bit. They shouted again, everybody pushed again, and the sky moved up a little bit more. The wise ones kept on shouting "Ya-ho!" and everybody kept pushing together, pushing and pushing until the sky moved up just as high as it is now.

Ever since that day nobody—no matter how tall—has bumped his head against the sky. And today when people are using all their strength to get hard work done together, we still shout, "Ya-ho!"

✦   ✦   ✦

In this story the world is full of people who can't communicate with one another, and the sky is so low there isn't enough room for them to stand tall. If you've ever had the feeling that there just isn't enough room for you and your toddler, or you and your adolescent, in the same household, then this story probably strikes a familiar chord. How do the wise ones deal with this state of affairs? They struggle to find ways to communicate, and they work together to solve their problem. In the course of daily life with your child, these are some of the most emotional lessons a parent can impart. I guess that's why I've chosen this story here, instead of a romantic-sounding fairy tale about a prince and princess living happily ever after.

At home, basic courtesy is one of the most time-honored ways human beings have found to do that. When parents and children say "Please" and "Thank you" and "Excuse me" to one another, you set the tone in your household for mutual respect.

When your child has a social problem outside the home, sitting down together and brainstorming solutions can be a tremendous growth opportunity. One mother told me about the day her son came home complaining his science teacher "hated his guts."

"Robert's a bright kid, but I know sometimes he can be a real pain in class," she said. "Sometimes he asks so many questions he drives the teacher nuts. He can also clown around. I'm easily tempted to tell him he needs to learn how to sit down and shut up or he's bound to get on the teacher's bad side. But I know from experience that if I tell him that, he just gets mad and we get nowhere. So this time I just listened. I asked him how he knew the teacher hated him, and how he felt about it. He griped and complained and moaned and groaned, and when he was all through I said, 'Sounds rough. Maybe we can think of some ways to change things.' "

Robert and his mother talked about how he could change his behavior in order to stop irritating the teacher and to channel his interest and enthusiasm in positive ways. "By the end of the year," she said, "the teacher sent me a note telling me he was a delight to have in class."

Adolescents. As children grow toward the teen years, parents and educators devote considerable energy worrying about sex education, and especially the question: How do you explain sexual functions and contraception accurately without encouraging premature sexual activity? There's no evidence that teaching children about sex is a direct cause of their participation. The important question is one that's almost never voiced: How do we educate children about what *love* really is? Addressing that goes a long way toward resolving most parents' concerns about talking about sex.

Unfortunately, kids' ideas about love as gleaned from the media tend to equate it with physical attractiveness or sexual activity. In the media, love equals sexual attraction, and a romantic relationship is often portrayed as one that meets *all* of a person's intimacy needs. With today's kids potentially exposed to overstimulating images in the media (much of it misleading and exploitative) at increasingly early ages, it's important for parents to exercise discretion in what they are allowed to watch. A church youth leader who asked her preadolescent group for a definition of the word *love* got this response: "Love is what you feel toward a person who's good-looking and nice and fun to be with." Did loving mean *giving* anything? asked the leader. The kids looked blank.

When kids bring up questions about sex and love, they need both accurate information and sustaining values. The process starts as early as preschool. Start by *listening*. Invite your child to explore his own questions with you. "I'll be glad to tell you if I find out what your ideas are first." That way you learn both how he's feeling and what misinformation he may have heard.

I'll say it again: The most important lessons you teach your child about sex are unspoken ones; long before he can even ask a question, through years of feeding, bathing, hugs, and kisses, you help him learn to cherish the connection between love and touch. Keep in mind that a child's healthy understanding of sex grows out of the way you share affection with your partner, and with him. By letting him know, even in your earliest explanations about where babies come from, that sexual activity is a pleasurable expression of love, you help him understand it in the context of relationship.

When an adolescent asks what love feels like, he doesn't usually have in mind a philosophical answer. This may well be a way of telling you that a particular relationship is starting to mean a great deal to him, and that it may be becoming sexual. Stay calm. He's come to you because he trusts you; don't close off communication now. Encourage him to explore the question with you: What does he think love would feel like? What does the word *love* mean to him? What has he learned about love from friends, from movies, from books? Point out how much he's learned about love growing up in your family. Love includes trust and acceptance; it grows over time; it's not something to be taken lightly. If you're comfortable with it and he seems receptive, you may wish to share some of your own experiences. That doesn't mean divulging the details of your sexual history, but briefly talking about what love in its broadest sense has meant in your own life; what you appreciate about your partner, family, and friends, and maybe something you've learned about it over the years. (The Parent's Path on page 239 will get you started.)

Keep in mind that if you're doing your job right, no response to a question your child asks about sex or love will be the last word. Each answer you give is one more step in an ongoing dialogue that's bound to grow richer—and more challenging—through the years.

Family Time
"PUSHING UP THE SKY"

Invent a new way to communicate. Because most of us spend our time with people who are speaking the same language, we tend to assume that we understand one another. Actually, particular words and phrases often mean different things to different people, but we're not always aware that we need to cross that communication gap. This activity gives you and your child a playful chance to explore what it means to invent fresh ways to connect and to really try to understand another person.

Imagine being in a council with the wise ones, with no two people speaking the same tongue. You need two or more people. Decide on a goal or problem you want to solve. Depending on your child's age and interests, it might be agreeing on what to have for dinner or which bulbs to plant in the garden or how to build a spaceship with blocks. Now, without speaking in English words, sit down and try to communicate about it. Struggle along in a foreign language. Make up your own words, gestures, musical tones, or signing. Remember, no two of you are supposed to speak the same way.

Once you've reached your goal—or given up—talk about the experience. How did it feel not to share a common language? How did you manage to connect?

Set up an admiration society. Once a month, sit down together and, one by one, name something unique and special about each member of the family—musical talent, naturally curly hair, problem-solving skills, patience with pet training. Young kids will be willing to clap and cheer for themselves and everybody else.

As kids grow toward adolescence, invite them to expand the society beyond your household. Ask them to collect pictures of friends, role models, and people who make contributions in the community, government, sports, and the arts. The point is to highlight the ways in which people are different and how you can appreciate one another as well as the diverse community outside your home.

Make a list of the "Ya-ho!" chores around your household. Sit down together and make a list of all the tasks that need to get done regularly—making lunch, dishwashing, cleaning, carwashing, room cleaning, laundry. Now check off the tasks that could get done more quickly if people worked together. Are different family members willing to pitch in? Taking into account people's different schedules and skills, try to come up with a plan to work together.

The Parent's Path
"PUSHING UP THE SKY"

Reflect on the ways you communicate love without using words. Gestures, tokens, glances, touch—these are some of the unspoken ways we express appreciation and tenderness. Particularly during periods of tension, such as a child's adolescence, simple touch can help keep the warmth alive in a relationship.

Think about your relationships with your partner and children. Do you long to be more expressive, or do you wish your loved ones were more demonstrative? What's missing? Do you long to be more affectionate? Some couples find it helpful to set aside a specific time for closeness away from work, chores, television, and talking about the kids. If that sounds too "staged" to you, then deliberately introducing more touch and physical closeness into your day—a hug at the kitchen sink, a quick kiss as you pass each other in the hall, a back rub during a TV show—might suit your style.

Are you so busy that you've "lost touch" with your kids? Even though school-age kids and adolescents aren't as cuddly as little ones, they still appreciate closeness. An arm around your preteen during a conversation, a hand on his shoulder, a stroke of his face—these are ways to respect his status as a "big kid" and still nurture the bond between you. Don't try this in front of his friends. On the other hand, don't be too surprised to find yourself getting hugged back now and then.

Which relationships have meant the most to you in your life? What is important to you about them? You'll probably think of one or both of your parents, maybe a grandparent or teacher, a dear friend. Choose one of these relationships and use your journal space to consider some of these questions:

- What do you especially value about this particular connection?
- What was painful or challenging?
- How do you imagine that the other person might describe the relationship?
- How has knowing him or her made a difference in who you are today?

Now look over your answers. What have you learned from this relationship that you'd like to pass on to your child? What would you like to do differently?

How is the relationship alive in your family life today? How does your memory of the relationship help you better understand your connection with your child?

One man who was surprised at his "cool" adolescent's eagerness to caddy for him on the golf course was suddenly brought back to the times he'd caddied for his own late father, and how special it had felt to be alone with his dad and helping him. The recollection brought him closer to his son, and to the father he hadn't seen in years.

The human capacity for love and compassion—and every facet of emotional wisdom—can grow all through life. Sometimes it's hard to imagine that an ordinary mortal, one who hasn't got it all worked out—who holds the phone away from her ear when a particular acquaintance is on the line maybe, or gets cranky at the end of the day—can be a creative, nurturing parent. I don't see it that way. Who doesn't have limitations? Our children learn something even from hearing the stories of how we deal with our shortcomings. Parents don't need to be the Buddha, or Jesus, to offer our children sustaining wisdom. We just need to share ourselves.

Appendix

✦

Making the Jump from Reading to Telling Stories

When you begin, it's scary to put the book aside and rely on your memory. When I first started "winging it," I was always worried I'd run out of words. Right there in the middle of a sentence, I imagined, I'd stop dead without the faintest idea how to get to the ending. What I quickly discovered was that the trick to remembering is to *make the story my own*. Instead of struggling to memorize a tale as though I were studying for a test, I learn it "by heart."

One great confidence booster is to learn, word for word, the first and last sentences of a story. But for the most part, don't get caught up in the words. As you tell a story, try to *picture* the action in your mind, as though you were watching a movie. Then the story will come naturally to life in your own words. Your child, especially if he is under five, is hearing the story in pictures. Tuning in to his way of thinking helps you keep the telling colorful and lively. Once you've read a particular story in these pages, try to think of it as a series of dramatic *scenes*, not words.

Make a story map. Some people find this a helpful way to remember a tale. You pare a story down to its bare bones, naming one turn in the plot after another. If you were mapping "The Three Little Pigs," your story map might look something like this:

mother pig so poor she sends pigs out into world to seek fortunes ➜
first pig builds straw house ➜
wolf knocks at door, pig says no, wolf blows house in ➜

second pig builds stick house →
wolf knocks at door, second pig says no, wolf blows house in →
third pig builds brick house →
wolf comes along and pig says no →
wolf huffs and puffs, goes down chimney, boils to death. →

Keep in mind that the story map isn't a "crib sheet" to help you tell a tale. It's *the process of making the map* for yourself that helps you take in the story. Try mapping a story you've enjoyed in this book. Once you've pictured the story in your mind's eye, you'll discover that the tale has jumped off the page and into your soul. You're a storyteller.

Learn to keep it lively. Practice this with the story you've chosen in the previous exercise. You've got the gist of it. Now, to bring more expressiveness to the telling, imagine yourself in the main character's shoes. What is he or she happy about? afraid of? determined to accomplish? Try to see the world through the characters' eyes by spending some time "in their company." Have a fantasy conversation with a character. Make up dialogue between different characters.

Does a character in a story remind you of anyone you know or have read about in the papers—an eccentric neighbor, a politician? Baba Yaga in "Vasalisa the Wise" reminds me of Mrs. Finbar, an elementary school teacher I had who automatically marked every school composition an *F* if it contained a single incomplete or run-on sentence. I can still see the big mole that stuck out of her chin. Whenever I tell the story of Vasalisa's encounter with Baba Yaga, I picture Mrs. Finbar in my mind's eye, and I have no problem at all conjuring up a mean and scary witch for my listeners.

Naturally, you won't include most of your fantasies directly in your telling. These informal exercises are ways to prepare yourself, to help the characters come alive for *you*. Don't burden your listeners with long-winded descriptions of the characters' thoughts or inner dilemmas. In the world of story, people reveal themselves through their deeds.

Use tricks and techniques you notice when you hear other storytellers, or in everyday speech. To involve listeners in the action, speed up your words and raise your voice. To create suspense, try a slow whisper. A well-timed pause heightens the intensity of a tale. But don't try too hard. Unless you're a natural-born ham, be sparing with the funny voices.

Being too deliberate and studied about it gets in the way of the intimacy that storytelling can foster, and it's the intimacy that's most important. Your child needs a deep connection with a real person, not a character actor. Don't force drama that you don't feel. Open up to the tale. Let yourself go. As you respond to the story, you will naturally convey your feelings to your listener.

Organize a story-sharing group. Although this might conjure up an image of a circle of women in a remote mountaintop community telling tales while stitching a patchwork quilt, story groups are on the rise throughout the country. A story-sharing group can be profoundly nurturing. For many of the parents I work with—particularly those who yearn for conversation that engages them more deeply than the diaper-brand comparisons and developmental-milestone competitions they often say they encounter in playgroup settings—sharing stories with other moms and dads has been very rewarding. It can be lively and interesting, but the goal isn't intellectual uplift, like a book group. Likewise, members can give one another advice and support, but the aim isn't mutual analysis, like group therapy.

A group like this is meaningful because it offers an opportunity to gather with others and create "a space apart" where you can let a story touch your hearts. There is something of the sacred about it. Once you have had the experience of really connecting with a tale and hearing how others do, you have so much more to share with your child.

To start your group, invite a number of friends, or advertise on bulletin boards to parents in your community. (Four to ten members works best.) Try to set aside a regular meeting date—once a week once a month. Find a quiet, comfortable space to meet, either in one home or on a rotating basis.

Try to be patient and let your group find a structure that suits the members. You might want to start with an open half hour to catch up on one another's news, then hear a story. At least one person can come prepared to tell a story; use notes or a story map (see page 243) if you need to. Have fun with it.

The teller can invite the group to participate in the "performance" by making animal noises, joining in refrains, and playing the role of a particular character. Although you'll soon develop a facility for remembering the tales you hear, members will appreciate a written copy to bring home and share with their own kids.

Once the story has been told, members of the group can respond to it as they wish, either by sharing a feeling, a personal experience, or another story. The Parent's Path questions in this book can be used to help members of the group connect the tales with their own lives.

You may wish to share family stories in your group. Bring in a family picture, pass it around, and tell a story about the picture (try using the story starters on page 70). Some groups like to include music, ending the meeting with a favorite recording brought in by a particular member.

Each of the stories in this book has been told and retold in a storytelling group that meets regularly in my home office. Together the women in the group have laughed and cried over the tales and what they connect us with in our own lives. We've grown close to the stories and to one another, and we've come away with nurture for ourselves and our children.

Books and Websites to Share with Your Family

Nurturing Intimacy in Your Household

What does it mean to be a family? How do our relationships grow and change with the passing years? How can we enrich our family time together? These books offer a variety of answers.

Debra Frasier, *On the Day You Were Born* (New York: Harcourt, 1995).

Phoebe Gilman, *Something from Nothing* (New York: Scholastic, 1989).

Eda LeShan, *When Grownups Drive You Crazy* (New York: Macmillan, 1988).

Debora Shaw Lewis and Greg Lewis, *When You Were a Baby* (Atlanta: Peachtree, 1995).

Reeve Lindberg, illustrated by Susan Jeffers, *The Midnight Farm* (New York: Dutton, 1987).

Lois Lowry, *The Giver* (New York: Laurel Leaf, 1996).

Lucille Recht Penner, illustrated by Jody Wheeler, *The Tea Party Book* (New York: Random House, 1993).

Alice and Martin Provensen, *The Year at Maple Hill Farm* (New York: Aladdin, 1989).

M. J. Ryan, *A Grateful Heart: Daily Blessings for the Evening Meal from Buddha to the Beatles* (Berkeley, Calif.: Conari, 1994).

Anne Shelby, illustrated by Wendy Anderson Halperin, *Homeplace* (New York: Orchard, 1995).

Margery Williams, *The Velveteen Rabbit* (New York: Doubleday, 1991).

Creating Family Stories

Most picture books—including any fine art or photography book, a young child's wordless storybook, or even a coffee-table book, and *certainly* your family photo albums—can provide the "raw materials" for shared story-telling. As you and your child look at the pictures, you can take turns telling stories or true-to-life anecdotes, or make up a tale together. Here are some titles that are especially appealing and useful.

Allen Ahlberb, illustrated by Colin McNaughton, *Tell Us a Story* (Cambridge, Mass.: Candlewick, 1996).

Peter Asbjornsen, *Norwegian Folk Tales* (New York: Pantheon, 1982).

Bob Greene and D. G. Fulford, *To Our Children's Children: Preserving Family Histories for Generations to Come* (New York: Doubleday, 1993).

Lucy Micklethwait, *A Child's Book of Art* (London and New York: Dorling Kindersley, 1993).

David Weitzman, *My Backyard History Book* (Boston: Little, Brown, 1975).

Wonderful Collections of Traditional Stories

When you and your child are ready to move beyond the tales included in these pages, here are some books you'll enjoy.

Barbara Berger, *Animalia* (San Francisco: Celestial Arts, 1987).

Henry Blassie, editor, *Irish Folktales* (New York: Pantheon, 1997).

Roberto Brunelli, *The Macmillan Book of 366 Bible Stories* (New York: Aladdin, 1988).

The Children's Bible (New York: Golden, 1965).

Sara and Stephen Corrin, editors, *Stories for Under-Fives: Stories for Six-Year-Olds; Stories for Seven-Year-Olds; Stories for Eight-Year-Olds* (London: Faber & Faber, 1989).

D'Aulaire's Book of Greek Myths (New York: Doubleday, 1962).

Virginia Hamilton, *The People Could Fly: American Black Folktales* (New York: Random Library, 1987).

Madhur Jaffrey, *Seasons of Splendour* (New York: Viking, 1992).

Madeleine L'Engle, *Ladder of Angels* (New York: HarperCollins, 1980).

Gretchen Will Mayo, *Earthmaker's Tales* (New York: Walker, 1991).

Ethel Johnston Phelps, *The Maid of the North: Feminist Folk Tales from Around the World* (New York: Holt, 1987).

Ethel Johnston Phelps, illustrated by Pamela Baldwin Ford, *Tatterhood and Other Tales* (New York: Feminist Press, 1989).

William F. Russell, *Classics to Read Aloud to Your Children* (1992) and *More Classics to Read Aloud to Your Children* (1994) and *Classic Myths to Read Aloud* (New York: Crown).

Lore Segal and Leonard Baskin, *The Book of Adam to Moses* (New York: Schocken, 1989).

Ineke Verschuren, *The Christmas Story Book* (Beltsville, Md.: Gryphon, 1988).

Jane Yolen, *Favorite Folktales from Around the World* (New York: Pantheon, 1986).

Motivational Books with Determined Protagonists

Karen Cushman, *Catherine, Called Birdy* (New York: Harper Trophy, 1995).

Susan Fletcher, *Dragon's Milk* (New York: Aladdin, 1997).

Monica Furlong, *Wise Child* (New York: Random House, 1989).

Anne E. Neuberger, *The Girl-Son* (Minneapolis, Minn.: Carolrhoda Books, 1997).

Robert D. San Souci, illustrated by Jamichael Henterly, *Young Guinevere* (New York: Doubleday, 1996).

T. H. White, *The Sword in the Stone* (New York: Dell, 1988).

Kate Douglas Wiggin, *Rebecca of Sunnybrook Farm* (New York: Bantam, 1990).

Facing Fear, Developing Courage

T. A. Barron, *Heartlight* (New York: Philomel, 1990) and *The Ancient One* (New York: Tor, 1994) and *The Merlin Effect* (New York: Tor, 1996).

Frances Mary Hendry, *Quest for a Maid* (New York: Sunburst, 1992).

Theresa Tomlinson, *The Forestwife* (New York: Random House, 1997).

Learning to Cope with Loss

By including these books as part of your child's regular reading, you will help her come to recognize and accept loss as part of life. If your child is *currently* experiencing a bereavement, the Grollman book below is highly recommended. I've offered age guidelines here, because although some of the books on this list may be on your child's *reading* level, they may not be within your child's *emotional* grasp. To be sure your child has the support she needs, I encourage you not to send your child off to her room with any of these books, but to let her know you're willing to read together or just listen to her impressions of what she's read.

Natalie Babbit, *Tuck Everlasting* (New York: Farrar Straus & Giroux, 1986)—for middle readers.

Barbara Cooney, *Miss Rumphius* (New York: Viking, 1985)—appropriate for young children.

Verley Flournoy, illustrated by Jerry Pinkney, *The Patchwork Quilt* (New York: Dutton, 1985)—appropriate for young children.

Earl Grollman, *Talking About Death: A Dialogue Between Parent and Child* (Boston: Beacon, 1991).

Bill Martin Jr. and John Archambault, illustrated by Ted Rand, *Knots on a Counting Rope* (New York: Holt, 1987)—appropriate for young children.

Katherine Paterson, *Bridge to Terabithia* (New York: Harper Trophy, 1987)—for middle readers.

Judith Viorst, illustrated by Eric Blegvad, *The Tenth Good Thing About Barney* (New York: Aladdin, 1976).

E. B. White, *Charlotte's Web* (New York: HarperCollins, 1952)—for ages six and up.

Charlotte Zolotow, *I Like to Be Little* (New York: Harper Trophy, 1990)—appropriate for young children.

Anger and Aggression

Many children's books are too "nice" to deal with these subjects effectively. Here are some conversation-provoking titles.

Chris Crutcher, *Ironman* (New York: LaurelLeaf, 1996)—for middle school and up.

Maurice Sendak, *Where the Wild Things Are* (New York: Harper Trophy, 1988).

Judith Viorst, *Alexander and the Terrible, Horrible, No Good, Very Bad Day* (New York: Aladdin, 1987).

T. H. White, *The Sword in the Stone* (New York: Dell, 1988)—suitable for reading to age nine and up.

Love

I'm not too attached to preconceived notions of "age-appropriateness." You might be surprised for how long your child loves *The Runaway Bunny* and *The Velveteen Rabbit*.

Margaret Wise Brown, *The Runaway Bunny* (New York: Harper Trophy, 1977).

Jane Cowen-Fletcher, *Baby Angels* (Cambridge, Mass.: Candlewick, 1996).

Robie Harris, illustrated by Michael Emberley, *It's Perfectly Normal: Changing Bodies, Growing Up, Sex and Sexual Health* (Cambridge, Mass.: Candlewick, 1996).

Ethan Hubbard, *Straight to the Heart: Children of the World* (White River Junction, Vt.: Chelsea Green, 1992).

Shirley Hughes, *Giving* (Cambridge, Mass.: Candlewick, 1995).

Buddy Kaye, Fred Wise, and Sidney Lippman, illustrated by Martha Alexander, *A You're Adorable* (Cambridge, Mass.: Candlewick, 1996).

Lois Lowry, *Number the Stars* (New York: Dell, 1990).

Laura Krauss Melmed, *I Love You as Much . . .* (New York: Lothrop Lee & Shepard, 1993).

Internet Links for Family Storytelling and Support

"Meeting" and "sharing" on the Web are no substitutes for real-life intimacy. Nonetheless, the grief home pages below can offer invaluable support and opportunities to share experiences. And at the storytelling Websites you'll find beautifully illustrated tales, some with audio; sit down at the computer with your child and enjoy them together.

America Online's Storytelling Home Page   users.aol.com/storypage/jmaroon.htm

Annual Digital Storytelling Festival   www.dstory.com

Crisis, Grief, Healing: Tom Golden's Home Page   www.dgsys.com/~tgolden/1grief.html

Elderbarry's Raven Tales (Inuit)   www.seanet.com

Family Planet online magazine   family.starwave.com

Family Resource Online   www.familyresource.org

Online Children's Stories   www.ucalgary.ca/~dkbrown/stories.html

Parent Soup online magazine   www.parentsoup.com

The Realist Wonder Society (stories and fables)   www.wondersociety.com

Storytelling links   www.ccc.nottingham.ac.uk/~enyjwe/links. html

Story Web   www.webspace.com/~storyweb/welcome.htm

Tales of Wonder   www.ece.ucdavis.edu/~darsie/tales.html

TLC Group "Grief Briefs"   www.metronet.com/~tlc/grfbrfs.htm

USENET Grief Newsgroup   alt.support.grief

USENET Storytelling Newsgroup   alt.arts.storytelling

Telephone Sources

National Association for the Advancement of Psychoanalysis (for referral to
  certified psychoanalysts): 212-741-0515.
The National Storytelling Association: 615-753-2171.